SHTF Survival Boot Camp:

SHTF Survival Boot Camp:

*A Course for Urban and Wilderness Survival During
Violent, Off-Grid, and Worst-Case Scenarios*

SELCO BEGOVIC AND TOBY COWERN

SHTF Survival Boot Camp: Copyright © by Selco Begovic and Toby Cowern. All Rights Reserved.

Contents

	Cover	vii
	Acknowledgements	viii
	Welcome from Selco	ix
	Foreword	xi
1.	Chapter 1: Introduction, First Steps, and Psychology of Survival	1
2.	Chapter 2: Urban Survival	38
3.	Chapter 3: Wilderness Survival	130
4.	Chapter 4: Violence	238
5.	Chapter 5: First Aid & Hygiene	270
6.	Chapter 6: Preparedness	351
	About the Authors	389
	ALSO BY	391
	An Amazing Offer	392

We would like to thank Jay for starting us on our journey and providing the support and confidence in the beginning. ~Selco and Toby

Welcome from Selco

Welcome to the Survival Boot Camp. In this course, I share the most essential survival lessons with you. The things I would teach someone if I could only have one week to teach them about survival.

This course's goal is that you understand survival better and maybe can also think more like I do. Not because I'm so smart, but my way of thinking is practical and helped me in many difficult situations during war and when working in emergency services and facing smaller and bigger disasters every day.

Regarding writing style, I wrote the whole course but first, Jay and then Laurie, our editor, fixed up my English for most parts. That is simply to make it enjoyable to read and clear for everyone. We left passages with personal stories and insights more or less unedited.

The course focuses on the most important parts of survival. I picked what I believe are the most important lessons for each area: the things that will most significantly impact your survival and matter most. No fluff, just solid information, and my take on almost every area of survival. I received thousands of emails with questions during the last four years since starting the first course, and this course provides answers to most of them.

In this first chapter, you get to know the basic mindset of a survivalist. You also learn how to assess your situation and better deal with emergency situations, so they feel less overwhelming.

If the mind breaks, the body soon follows. People with an iron will to survive have accomplished extraordinary things. Getting to know yourself, your weaknesses, and your strengths and building an unbreakable resolve to keep going and fighting even if the odds you make it look slim is one of the first things and one of the most important things to practice.

You focus on the options and do not get caught up in your worries. You see many more options than people around you because you learned about survival and know what is possible. You also have plans for different scenarios. Even if you find yourself in a new emergency, you can properly assess emergency situations and know what to do next. You also learn how to function under high stress and get yourself quickly back in a state to make the best possible decisions and act.

Let's get started.

Foreword

The year 2020 has rendered in-person education unachievable in many situations. Going off to take a survival course in Europe is nearly impossible, especially with an American passport. As of the time I'm writing this foreword, September 2020, entry into most of the European Union is banned for Americans.

This doesn't lessen the need for this type of course. In fact, learning about SHTF survival is more important than ever. The dangers are more imminent than ever.

So, Selco has opted to bring the course to us.

In this book, you can learn the survival skills that kept Selco alive during the wars in the Balkans in a city under siege. Selco fought to survive in his urban setting against marauding gangs, he evaded sniper fire from the mountains above the city, and he scrambled for the limited resources available.

He shares the secrets that allowed him to survive in the course for which this is a textbook. You can learn about urban survival, wilderness survival, what to do before the SHTF, and how to prepare for all of it. Learn the skills he staked his life on. It may not be long before we're doing the same thing.

I'm honored to call Selco a friend, and I can say quite honestly that the things I learned when I was able to travel to Croatia and Bosnia and study with him have changed the way that I look at survival. It affected the way I prepared during the early stages of the pandemic lockdown and it completely changed how we hardened my daughter's apartment when civil unrest was only blocks away during the summer.

While most of us won't be getting to Bosnia anytime soon to learn from Selco directly, this guide is the next-best thing to an in-person experience.

Daisy Luther
Sept. 10, 2020

1. Chapter 1: Introduction, First Steps, and Psychology of Survival

Chapter 1: Introduction, First Steps, and Psychology of Survival

Note: Even if you already understand why survival matters, it is important that you learn to motivate others to start thinking about survival. If you want to increase your chances of survival dramatically in a post collapse world or other survival scenario you need a group of people around you who you can trust and in the best case who also know at least basic survival skills. Part of preparing for bad scenarios is building your group around you and it all begins by helping them realize that learning about survival matters.

The idea of a natural or manmade disaster may seem like something that will never happen, something that only happens in the movies. However, a look at the past couple of decades proves this idea wrong. There have been hurricanes and other natural disasters, riots, and terrorist attacks. And the aftermath of a disaster can be just as bad as or worse than the disaster itself: people don't need much of an excuse to loot, steal, and even kill.

And it isn't just an event at home that can incite chaos. We depend on other countries for staples such as fuel, and if something happens to interfere with how we get the basics, it will drastically change our way of life.

You can't anticipate what will happen or when. You can't anticipate how people around you will react if something bad happens. You can't anticipate what your government will do after a disaster—or even if they will be in a position to do anything at all.

The only thing you have control of is how prepared you are. When you have a plan, take the time to think ahead, and take care of some basic preparations you greatly increase your chances of surviving a crisis.

Other people might think survivalists are crazy or are overreacting, but these are the people that aren't even prepared for the little surprises in their everyday life, and they are also the people that think someone else will save them when the worst happens.

Here is why learning about survival matters and how you can help others to understand this.

- If you learn about survival, you can take care of yourself to not have to rely on others or the system to take care of you. That is not only great for you but also for the surrounding people, because if something happens, you won't be one of those demanding help from others. Those who are unprepared will be able to get more support for themselves because resources don't have to help you.

- We humans have been "survivalists" for most of the time we have existed. With industrialization, urbanization, and the huge growth of cities in the last 100 years, most people have forgotten how to provide the basics for themselves and their family. It is actually more natural for humans to know how to live with nature than it is for them to totally depend on the system. So, in the end, the "weird" people might be those who don't know about survival.
- When you learn about survival, you learn about life. It is a great way to get more in touch with nature, spend more time outdoors, and learn to think outside of the box. You learn how to use everyday items, such as duct tape, rope, and trash bags, creatively. You also train yourself to make tough decisions when faced with challenges quickly.
- If you go out and practice survival, you also get to know your mental and physical limits. That can shape your character and is great for people of all ages. It can make you a more humble man who understands his limitations but is, at the same time, more confident because he also knows his strengths.
- Being a survivalist impresses people. Survivalists can tie a rope, find their way through difficult terrain, and patch people up and give them first aid after an accident. The skills you learn are practical, and when you use them to help people out, they are impressed and grateful. People love to be around someone who has practical skills that can come in handy or provide them with more security.

You don't have to be a survival expert to make some basic plans and stock up on some necessary supplies. You can't control what happens, but you can control how you react to it, and how prepared you are for it – and that can make all the difference. And that is why learning about survival matters.

What is Survival all about?

When you hear about a survivalist, you might imagine a jungle fighter or an adept woodsman. Survivalists can look like all sorts of people, but they have some things in common.

While we focus on surviving disasters in this course, the lessons you learn can be used in all areas of life. You don't need a hurricane, earthquake, or war to be faced with problems such as not having enough food for yourself or your family or having to spend a night outside in bad conditions with little to no protection.

Learning about survival means being less dependent on others, the system, the government, and the comforts of modern society that we have gotten used to. In the end you also gain a new sense of freedom because you know you are more capable of getting through hard times than the average Joe. You learn how to find creative solutions, get things done even if you are under stress, and become confident in your abilities to get by with little or nothing.

SELCO ON HOW HE LEARNED ABOUT SURVIVAL

I was forced to learn about survival during my time in the war. Being locked down in the city for a year with violence from the army that surrounded the city and violence from gangs fighting for resources was a crash course in survival. Surviving the atrocities of war taught me lots of things, most importantly it taught me about acceptance of things you cannot change and correct way of approaching problems. Whatever problems come up.

Real survivalist is not the man who takes big problems and laughs about them and deals with them like they are small problems. Real survivalist is a man who accepts bad things as bad things but continues to live and face them.

Real survivalist is a man who already has learned about ways of dealing with all sorts of problems or thinks flexible enough to find ways to deal with them.

Living in today's world, I clearly understand that there are bad things all around me, but I am still able to enjoy life. And I know what I can do. I am prepared.

We grow up learning to trust people and feeling safe and secure. Things around us seem to be under some kind of control, but the reality is that life and nature are very random. When you see lion babies getting killed by a big male lion because they are not his offspring, it might feel wrong, but it is the way things go.

Most of us will face moments or even longer periods of time when life catches up with us and things don't go the way we thought they were supposed to go. Remember that nature isn't fair or unfair, it is just what it is. Looking at the direction our modern society is heading, we might find ourselves in a new and much more hostile environment very soon.

What matters is that you are still able to act and make the right decisions in critical moments, instead of being dependent on others for help.

SELCO ON HOW HE REALIZED THE WORLD AROUND HIM CHANGED

When I saw for first-time people getting killed on the street, and only reason for killing them was because guys wanted to kill someone I felt a change in me. Feeling when you are thrown from the normal way of things in some new reality. And for some time I waited for someone to end all that, for the situation to come back to normal.

Luckily for me, I did not wait too long, I just accepted the new reality, adapted and in the end survived. Just because things are nice around us now, it does not mean it will be always nice. Change happens fast and leaves you in shock if you do not recover from that shock very quickly that change can leave you or your loved one's dead.

Survivalism vs Prepping

Survival is what you really want to learn, being prepared is just a backup that is good to have.

We, humans, have been survivalists for thousands of years and learning to live with nothing should be your top priority (instead of obsessing if you have the right amount of blueberry muffins for a whole year).

Some people who call themselves survivalists are only preppers and seem to believe that having weapons and full storage they plan to defend is all it takes. This is better than having no skills and no preps, but when things get chaotic more often than not your plans will change and this might include abandoning most or all of your preps. What's left is just you and what you know and can do.

We encourage you to not make the mistake many preppers do and think you can buy safety. It takes time and practice to learn today what our ancestors have been learning and practising their whole life. Survival and preparedness go hand in hand, but you will always have your skills and knowledge, and making the right decision at the right moment matters more than anything else.

SELCO ON SURVIVALISM AND PREPPING

Survivalists and prepper are on the same page, but there are some big differences in my opinion. Survivalism is more like a state of mind, it is (or it is supposed to be) to fully understand of what you need to BE in order to survive, while preppers are somehow more about what man is supposed to HAVE in order to survive. While this is not something like a general rule and if everything works out some preppers might have more chances to survive than unprepared survivalists, the problem is in the way of thinking and approaching everything.

Where preppers have lots of coffee stored, survivalists know with what plant he will substitute coffee, or he will not need it at all. Think about two completely different things: To BE or to HAVE. Man who IS something will carry that forever, while man who HAVE something (material) will eventually lose it, spend it, run out of it etc. and then they will be in a mess.

Of course when it comes to SHTF, point is to have what you need and to know what you do. But your main goal should be to BE survivalist (to have knowledge, skills etc.).

People these days start with buying things and not learning skills. It is the quick fix society where you spend money on machine or device that makes your life easier and then without those things they are again helpless. If you do not want to trade being dependent on the system for being dependent on your generator, learn survival first or at the same time as you start buying equipment. My time in war where I had nothing showed me this. You will carry your knowledge and skills always with you. Everything else is good but extra.

Omnia mea mecum porto. *(All I have I carry with me.)*

```
                    Survival
                 Part of survival skills

      First Aid          Preparedness
              Wilderness Skills
      Voilence    Resilience      Psychology
            Evasion      Bushcraft
                 Hunting   Tactical Skills    Fishing
      Improvisation
                    Foraging        Scavenging
              Food Conservation   Tracking
                    Self Defense    Hygiene
```

SELCO ON WHY SURVIVAL SKILLS REALLY MATTER

My grandfather told me long time ago that when you lose everything material, only then you will realize how rich (skilled) you really are.

Truth is that living modern and "normal" life mostly prevents you from developing useful survival skills, real skills. Society works on making things easier. Somebody else hunts or raises your food, cooks it and transport it to you. Your only job is to open your mouth. When man find himself without that circle of helping around him he realizes that he is a cripple actually, compared to what natural humans know, he is unable to live on its own.

Living in society is like still living in parents house. Mom does the washing and cooking. To be a prepper means that you have lots of good thing stored for SHTF. But people forget that SHTF does not wait for best case scenario. So you can expect that your storage will be looted, burned, wasted or simply SHTF scenario will catch you and you are many miles away from your storage. And then you are left alone with your skills.

Do not transfer all mistakes from modern way of living to your way of preparing for SHTF. Raise your skills for dirty, cold, dangerous, unknown environment. Having a full storage needs planning and some money but that are not the skills that keep you alive when you are out on your own.

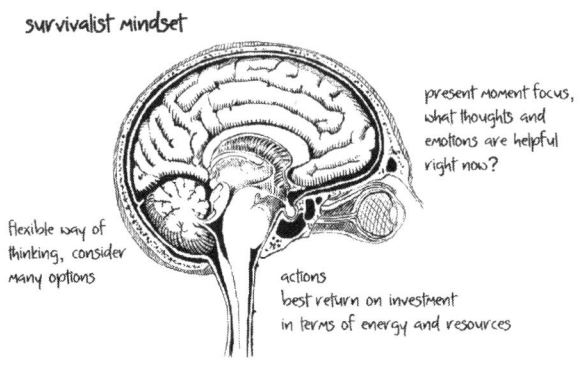

Have a plan but expect that it will fall apart. Things change, especially in survival scenarios because so many other factors influence what happens. You need to make a plan and have a goal you work towards to stay motivated. However, you should be mentally prepared to abandon your plan and make a new one at any time.

You have to be very resourceful with your energy. Wasting energy on a plan that does not make sense anymore because external factors have changed might make the difference between surviving or not.

When things do not go your way it is easy to get frustrated and lose hope. The best thig you can do against this is to not expect anything.

Humans suffer because they compare their current state with their desired state and dislike the difference.

If you expect help will arrive within three days and it does not you suffer from the difference between what is and what you expected. You have to accept your situation and realize that you can't expect anything.

Focus on the task at hand and do not waste your time and energy to build up expectations or think about all the "what ifs." You won't gain anything by having expectations. Unmet expectations will just diminish your will to survive.

When you have nothing to do, think about your loved ones. Think about seeing them again or anything else that motivates you, but keep any predictions about the future vague to avoid disappointment. That is hope and hope is what keeps your will to survive alive. Once your will to survive is gone your body will follow soon after.

Be hopeful and confident and try to see situations from the perspective of a realistic optimist.

As a realistic optimist you believe you will succeed but also know that it will not be easy. Thoughts and emotions that do not help you have no place in a survival situation. Be smart about how you use your mind and mental resources just like any other resources you have.

SELCO ON NOT LOSING HIS WILL TO SURVIVE

When things started to go from very bad to very very bad, and then worse and worse I expected somehow that it is going to end, because it is not fair for people to suffer, women, kids, innocent folks.

I expected on both levels, deeply inside on some kind of spiritual or religious level that so much suffering cannot last for too long, and also on different level that someone from somewhere outside would come and say something like "OK now it is enough, stop this". But nothing happened, and nobody came, at least for some time. You are on your own.

After you realize that you are alone and throw away your big expectations then you can be "cool". In that moment I learned to stop worrying about bigger picture, to find joy in single real cigarette and just be happy to live another day.

True survivalists are people who can deal with change, even drastic change, and have the knowledge and skills to overcome whatever gets thrown their way. They thrive when facing adversity. They don't give up and do whatever it takes to survive.

The Most Important Skill Every Survivalist Has to Master

Resilience: Dealing with fear and stress

The crippling effects of fear are well known, but please keep in mind that having fear isn't wrong. In fact, the purpose of fear is to promote survival. In the course of human evolution, the people who feared the right things survived to pass on their genes. If it had been possible for the people with no fear to survive, we would all be naturally fearless by now.

It is important to first understand why humans often aren't able to react quickly and in a rational way when they are faced with a crisis. In the early twentieth century, Harvard physiologist Walter Cannon described the "fight or flight" response for the first time. In this response, when you perceive something as a threat, your body mobilizes you to either fight or flee. This reaction is almost out of our control and takes place in a very old part of our brain, sometimes referred to as the "reptile brain."

Your nervous system releases chemicals called catecholamines that shut down the blood flow to your digestive system and at the same time increases blood flow to your heart and skeletal muscles. Blood flow to your smallest blood vessels, the capillaries, also decreases, so that if you are wounded you will bleed less. A lot of things happen in your body to get you ready to fight or flee.

Multiple brain regions are also affected by these chemicals and help you to better concentrate on whatever you perceive as a threat. Part of your brain, the amygdala, is also working better than before and that's why threatening or traumatic events become stored in your memory and are hard to forget.

Overall, that doesn't sound too bad, right? The problem is that in this state many of your higher cognitive skills do not work so well. You have more power, but less control over yourself because you act instinctively instead of thinking clearly about what does and does not make sense.

There is little we can do to influence this first response. Martial artists modify their "flinch response," that automatic response people have to a certain stimulus, such as someone throwing a punch at them. They do this by exposing themselves to this stimulus over and over again and training themselves to react how they want to, for example, raising their arms to block. This way their new response is automatic.

This does not work for many other scenarios because every crisis is different. So, while you can't modify the fight-or-flight response as much as you might like, you can learn to recover quickly and quickly access your knowledge and rational thinking abilities, which might end up saving your life.

Initial reaction to a fight-or-flight situation
- Increased blood pressure, heart rate, blood sugars, and fats in order to supply the body with extra energy
- Growing pale or flushing, or alternating between both
- Inhibition of stomach and upper-intestinal action to the point where digestion slows down or stops
- General effect on the sphincters of the body
- Blood vessels throughout much of our body constrict so that blood can be sent to the muscles
- Inhibition of the lacrimal gland (responsible for tear production) and salivation

- Dilation of pupils (mydriasis) to help increase clarity
- Relaxation of bladder
- Inhibition of erection
- Auditory exclusion (loss of hearing)
- Tunnel vision (loss of peripheral vision)
- Disinhibition of spinal reflexes
- Shaking
- The blood clotting function of the body speeds up in order to prevent excessive blood loss in the event of an injury sustained during the response
- Increased muscle tension in order to provide the body with extra speed and strength
- Increased perspiration to prevent over-heating due to the increased metabolic rate

SELCO ON DEALING WITH HIGH-STRESS SITUATIONS

When it comes to stressful and shocking situations, I reacted at the beginning like everyone else – with shock and panic. I have seen in the first few shootings and shellings that most of the victims would not even get killed or wounded just if they control themselves for a few seconds and gave themselves time to understand what is happening. So I saw the guy who was shot in back and killed just because he panicked and started to run leaving the cover. More than once I have seen people getting killed in shelling just because first instinct they had was to run without any real plan what to do and when to run.

You have to do something, but something that makes sense. So clearly I learned that it makes more sense to be "small" (lay down, use the nearest cover and assess the situation) before starting to run in a random direction.

I even catch myself doing that today sometimes 20 years after walking the crowded street and imagining what nearest and best cover would be if that man 50 meters from me suddenly would uncover AK47 and started to shoot...

In short, the best way to control your stress response in a critical situation would be to take cover and assess the situation and figure out what to do. It is not easy and I remember in beginning I could not separate my heart beating sounds in ears from outside noises but it can be done. Panic makes you do things without any reason and then you get killed. Point is that you cannot really control adrenaline shock, but you can learn how to deal with it better...

How can we deal better with our fight or flight reaction?

You can't really turn off your fight or flight response and you would not really want to, anyway. But you can learn to better control it.

You can learn how to deal with your fear better and use it in a way to help you instead of crippling you. You have some options to overwrite your instinctive reactions because your brain cannot distinguish between real and perceived danger.

The more you learn about survival and actively think about the dangers you could face the more you get used to them and the more confident you feel about dealing with them. Over time, what you once perceived as danger becomes more like a challenge because you know what to do. As a result, the initial intensity of your fight or flight response is easier to control.

Let's have a look at the factors that can determine if you feel you are up to the challenge:
- How threatening you consider a certain event to be
- How well you feel you can cope with this new event

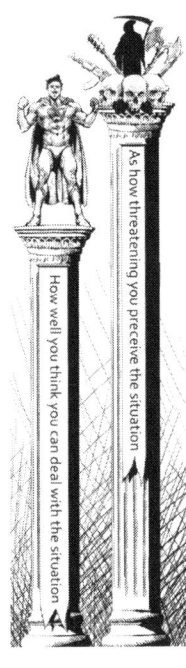

How threatening you feel an event is may be directly related to your knowledge and your ability to apply this knowledge–your skills that can help you solve the problem. This can be helped by your preparations, which are your tools and resources you have at your disposal.

How well you can cope with things that are new and not under your control is related to how well you can accept the situation and its consequences. For example, how you think about death and dying can be a factor in how you cope with a life-threatening event.

To help you to act and make the best decisions possible this course will cover what you need to know (knowledge), how to use this knowledge (skills), and what tools and resources can make this easier for you (preps).

You gather the knowledge you need by watching videos and reading books. You hone your skills by doing practical exercises and you build up your own preps by getting the right tools and resources to make survival easier.

The Big Picture

The fight-or-flight response is just the first stage of what is known as the stress response. Knowing the different stages of a typical stress response will help you to get through it faster.

Remember the acronym **F.E.A.R.** to get you ready for action.

•   **F**ight or Flight Phase: "DAMN! I'm screwed!" You are overwhelmed by what just happened.

•   **E**motional Release Phase: "Oh no! Why did this happen? I hate this. I'm gonna die…" You experience a wave of all sorts of emotions such as helplessness, confusion, shock, anxiety, disbelief, and anger.

- **A**cceptance Phase: "Alright this is my situation, I hate it but I have to deal with it." You try to look at your situation realistically and accept it.
- **R**eturn to Action Phase: "What can I do to fix this? Let's do this!" You plan the next steps. You take action and try to overcome whatever gets in your way.

If you are aware of these different phases, you can run through them faster and while you do this, you activate the higher levels of your brain that help you to think more clearly and take control of the situation.

Accept which phase you are in and then proceed to the next one. You can even say things out loud if you are alone or comfortable doing this in front of others. This helps you to calm your internal storm and prevents you from getting stuck in one phase.

Remember: **If you are in a chaotic and stressful situation, the first thing you want to get under control is yourself.**

SELCO ON COPING WITH LONG-TERM STRESS

It is impossible to take some things with humor, and to stay positive too, but with some other things you gonna see that it is much easier to cope if you approach them with humor. We made lots of jokes about being dirty and smelly; it is not like we liked that state, but it was much easier when we made fun about that.

More ways to stand up against the storm
- Physical activity actively recycles excessive amounts of stress hormones, but keep in mind that in most survival situations you will want to limit the amount of energy you spend because it is hard to replenish. If you are in a group and someone seems too stressed out, finding some physical work for this person can be a good idea.
- Remember stressful events in the past and try to find what specifically caused the most stress for you. Question if getting

stressed about those triggers provided any benefit for your situation. Challenge your thoughts.
- Stay busy to avoid fear kicking in and keep in mind it can spread like a virus.
- Structure your days to have a sense of control and order. Daily rituals can help you stay sane and give you a feeling of normality.
- Try to stay positive and take things with humor.
- If you cannot stay positive, allow yourself to feel however you feel, but keep in mind that you need to act, so talk yourself through the stages with F.E.A.R.
- Do not label yourself or your reactions as crazy. Accept them.
- Fear of the unknown is one of the most common and crippling kinds of fear. The best way to fight fear is to know what to do. Keep learning about survival.
- Keep in mind that people have been in extreme situations like yours before and have survived.
- Do not try to numb your feelings with drugs.
- If you are with a group, talk to others and do not isolate yourself. Talking about things helps and can help you to deal better with traumatic events.
- Help others if you can, because it will make you feel better too.

SELCO ON HOW TO KEEP YOUR SANITY

Survival is not boring in a way that every day is the same and that you will be bored. Every day is a fight for something and you are definitely not going to be bored. But there is a chance of getting yourself in the loop of thinking that survival is not worth it, or you even lose touch with reality simply because you are under constant threat for your life and suffer from a huge feeling of uncertainty.

Good way of keeping everything together is to realize that life is simply still going on. However strange this may sound with many people dying around you. You just need to try to act like a normal human and keep going.

You still need to try to keep normal contact with your family, have a conversation with them, daily rituals... It will keep you going on, it can make a difference of you staying alive and sane or turning to an animal without any touch to reality anymore.

In my time we tried very hard to keep the ritual of daily coffee drinking, and it was not because of coffee addiction. I know that for sure because we drank coffee substitute for months, and it was nothing like real coffee. It was about keeping something that makes us feel normal and still human.

Keep this in mind when you and your group face extreme uncertainty or you have to face one of the more ugly sides of nature, death.

Summary

You do not learn to become a fearless warrior. Do not get arrogant when you learn to handle fear better than others. Ego has no place in survival. You only learn this to get back to your regular mode of operation quickly, and that's it. People do not survive because they are brave, they survive because they make the right decisions and act (or they are simply lucky).

We said this before and we say it again... practice matters! If you practice your skills and apply your knowledge you become more confident in your abilities and as a result more confident dealing with problems and threats. Simply being aware of the different stages of a stress response and talking yourself through can get you quickly back to action as well.

Getting a Better Understanding of Your Current Situation

To make the best possible decisions, you need the best possible information. Make sure you gather all important information about your area, groups and people around you and other factors that might be worth knowing about before any disaster strikes.

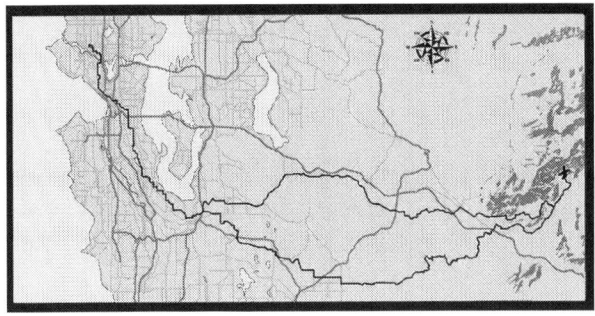

Situational awareness, basically knowing what's going on around you, is crucial on many levels for survival. Having the right background information to make sense of situations is something you can gather right now and that will help you to make better decisions later on. ? **Your area:**

Use Google Maps or other maps such as topographic maps to find important strategic locations in your area. What places might be looted first? What places offer defensive advantages? Who has resources in your area? What paths out of the city make sense? Go for walks to get familiar with your area if you aren't already. Print the maps and keep several copies of the map at hand. If you are in a survival situation and have to send single people or small groups of people out you can give those maps along. See our Local Disaster and Threat Assessment Checklists below for more details. ? **People around you:**

Start to profile people you are most likely with during survival scenarios. Write down their skills, strengths and weaknesses. Think about ways to help them develop more useful skills. Make sure several people in your group have the same skills just in case someone is unable to help. ? **Groups in the neighborhood:**

Learn about who forms opinions or has influence on a street level in your area. Tight knit groups will stick together in survival scenarios. Know who to speak to and maybe even better, get to know them and form relationships. ? **Possible threats:**

Research what kind of natural disasters have affected your area in the past and might strike again. Monitor the local media. Get an emergency radio scanner and follow local reporters on twitter or other social media they use to provide moment to moment news updates. ? **Environmental data:**

Research what temperatures you can expect at night throughout the year. Know the approximate time when sun rises and sun sets. Learn about common wind directions in your area and how they change throughout the year.

Once you have become aware of these factors, check them on a regular basis. Review and reassess your situation every few months or weeks and note if anything has changed. If you think about disasters always consider possible secondary effects. Those are the direct or indirect consequences of a disaster.

Disaster / Threats

Manmade Disasters
- Economic Collapse
- Peak Oil
- War (conventional / nuclear / civil)
- Pandemic
- Terrorism (explosive / chemical / biological / nuclear attacks)
- Totalitarian State
- Genocide
- Cyber Attacks

Natural Disasters
- Earthquake
- Wildfire
- Blizzard
- Drought
- Flooding

- Volcanic Eruption
- Tsunami
- Severe Thunderstorm (with hail)
- Hurricane
- Landslide
- Extreme Heat
- Comet / Meteor Strike
- Global Climate Change
- Tornado
- Solar Flare / Coronal Mass Ejection / EMP
- Pandemic

Local Threats / Problems
- Disease
- Sinkhole
- Gang fight
- Job loss
- Disease
- Disability
- Road Accident

Secondary Effects
- Civil Unrest / Violence
- Looting
- General Lawlessness
- Water Outage
- Power Outage
- Food Shortage
- Fuel Supply Interruption
- Communication Blackout
- Evacuation
- Quarantine

Important structures to mark on maps

Resources
- Medicine

- Medical Service Provider

- Pharmacies
- Hospitals

* Food

  - Supermarkets
  - Convenience Stores
  - Farms
  - Shopping Mall
  - Restaurants
  - Distribution centers
  - Factories

* Water

  - Municipal Water and Storage Tanks
  - Wells
  - Springs

* Human

  - Neighbor A has a lot of X
  - Neighbor B who is experienced in X / works as X
  - Organization C or Club C who do X

* Misc.

  - Factories nearby (note the products they manufacture)
  - Hardware stores
  - Gas Stations
  - Weapon Stores
  - Police and Military stations
  - Parks, forests, and other green areas for wood and plants

Hotspots
- Threats

- Gang hangouts
- Problematic neighbors / housing estates
- Bad neighbors

- Strategic

- Elevations, good lookout / scouting positions
- Choke points (e.g. bridges or tunnels)
- Hardened structures such as jails, banks or security related businesses
- Subway stations, underground tunnels (if accessible sewer entrances)
- Influential neighbors
- Allies or friends
- Meeting points

SELCO ON WHAT INFORMATION REALLY MATTERS

Good suggestion from my own experience is that if you have little time you only care about information that have impact on YOU and your immediate surroundings (your family, group and similar) and to forget about anything else.

Spend time on other information to better understand big picture before disaster strikes if you want to, but especially in survival situation you have more important things to do. Too much information that does not immediately concern you can give you false hope or false fear and both can be dangerous.

Channels of Information

As long as regular life goes on and you can stay informed about events that might affect your safety, it makes sense you do. The best possible information is unfiltered information.

Local human sources

Stay connected with local people who know about your area. The barber who takes care of most people in your town might only know some gossip but even that is valuable. The best people to learn from what's going on are people working in emergency services, law enforcement and politicians. Contacts in the criminal scene can be very valuable as well but of course being friends with these types of people can often lead to more problems than it is worth it.

Everyone has to decide for themselves how far they want to go when it comes to making strategical valuable friends. In general just paying attention to what's going on a local level and who people listen to makes a lot of sense.

News stations

Every news station or network has an agenda. This agenda may be based on who owns them, who writes for them, what country they are in, or who gives them the most money. Do your own research to get the best possible information. That means getting news from many different sources instead of just one.

We humans tend to suffer from confirmation bias and that means we try to find information that confirms our ideas and beliefs, instead of listening to information that might prove us wrong. We want to be right and hear about things that fit into our world view, but this is dangerous and can lead to an incorrect assessment of current events.

The Internet

The Internet is a powerful tool and can provide you with some of the best real time information available from the comfort of your home. ? Whenever you come across something you are interested in, read about it on websites of different international and national news agencies, such as NPR, Reuters, Fox, AP, BBC, AlJazeera and others so that you get a more balanced view of what's going on. ? Stay up to date by subscribing to Google news alerts. You can also get alerts if Google finds certain words on websites by using the following search string for example if you look for news related to flooding: *flood site: yourlocalnewspaper.com*

- Form your own opinion based on the facts you gather by doing your own research. Do not believe in opinion pieces, they are usually written in a very one sided way by someone who wants to convince you to share his opinion. If you read opinion pieces read several with different points of view. Remember that the most accurate information and understanding of a situation enables you to make the best decisions. This starts on a global level, and goes down to a very very local level when you have to decide which road you take while escaping an area.

• Use social networks to listen to people who have first-hand experiences of what is going on. Look for opinion leaders and follow them. If several parties are involved in protests for example, make sure you follow all of them.

If you do not have access to the Internet (anymore) try other news sources.

• Get a small portable TV to keep in your car.

• Get a hand crank AM / FM radio. The AM frequency matters because due to changes in the earth's atmosphere in the evening and at night you can receive broadcast signals even from far away (so you can receive information even if your local radio towers are down).

- Get a radio that supports SW frequencies and you can even listen to radio stations from all over the world.
- If you are in the US get a radio that supports NOAA frequencies, which are the frequencies on which local weather and other hazard news are broadcasted. ? Get a scanner and add some local frequencies to it to listen to police and emergency radio communication (www.radioreference.com). If you have money, invest it in a scanner that can also intercept digital transmissions. We suggest the Uniden Homepatrol scanner.
- Listening to radios with headphones is usually more energy efficient.

What to do once you have no access to current information anymore

SELCO ON LIVING WITHOUT RELIABLE INFORMATION

To find yourself in situation that you do not know what is going on is very scary, and you cannot do too much about it. Actually point is that you do not even try to do something (on larger scale, like understanding the bigger picture or similar) because you cannot do that anyway, and you are probably wasting valuable time and resources.

In real life that means that (during my SHTF situation) I wasted valuable time waiting and trying to find correct information about what is going on (shooting on the street, violence, chaos etc) in terms that I was trying to find out WTF is going on. Other folks use that time and obtain resources (chaos in malls and similar). While I was waiting for information from "reliable" source (radio, TV, government etc.) Some folks used available information (seeing that people are getting killed, absence of law...) and took some real action (leave city, or took resources).

Lesson here is that you do not have to try to make sense of things or understand things at all costs. If you cannot get good information work with information you have and do other more important things instead.

When SHTF be sure that you KNOW what kind of information have REAL value. SHTF means that rules are changed so information that are make sense in "normal" life may be completely unimportant.

Rumor was main source of information during my SHTF time. Of course there was whole bunch of misinformation and lies, but if you carefully "hold ear on the ground" you could use even the lies, because lies often were planted for certain reasons. For example rumor that "income" of tobacco in area will be cut for more than half (for any reason) mean that price will go up, and could be planted by the guys who had a lot in storage maybe.

Just like any other information you need to be able to choose what (and how) you gonna use it and separate the good from whole bunch of lies and half lies and unimportant news.

For example in first days I knew people who get killed because they wanted to go to their jobs, they did not realize that SHTF they thought "oh it is temporary mess, something like rioting after football games, and my job is something that is important"

They think in old terms "job, school, law, society..." instead of in new terms" security, food, water, steel plates on windows"

They do not understand that important info is "is that street 100m from me secure to go through" unimportant info is "what is going on with state today"? if you understand.

You have to start thinking on a much "smaller scale"- you, family, security, food, etc. Good example would be me today, I am worrying about what to do, where to find job, earn money, I am checking for word on the street about jobs, or anything similar in town.

But one day when I "smartly" conclude that rules have changed my new worries will be where closest shop or market or mall is if you understand me, and where I can expect gangs to go, what street is secure on my way to my bug out location and similar...

Point is that change between these two "ways of thinking" can be sharp, I mean it can be quick, and if you still think in old way and everything is changed you are screwed. That is important to understand.

Having an information blackout can be really scary, especially since we got so used to always be connected and have information on demand. Your next best choice to understand the situation and make the right decisions are people you can trust. To stay in touch with them you need to become aware of all different ways to keep communicating with them even or especially when all hell breaks loose.

That's why creating an emergency communications plan matters. If you don't think this is important just imagine not being able to determine if your family is safe after a crisis. This is what happens to most people who are not prepared.

Cell phone towers that are overloaded after a disaster, widespread power outages after natural disasters or even governments that black out their own country are all part of our reality today.

Here are some questions you should ask yourself before creating your emergency communications plan.

- Who are you responsible for? Who do you want to contact?

- What is your typical lifestyle? Do you travel a lot? Use the subway to commute every day?
- How far away are the people you want to communicate with?
- How often and over what period of time do you have to communicate with people?

Answers to these questions help you to realistically assess your communications needs. More about creating your communication plan in the next topic.

Creating Your Emergency Communication Plan

SELCO ON THE IMPORTANCE OF HAVING ALTERNATIVE COMMUNICATION CHANNELS

You absolutely need to think about some alternative ways of communicating when SHTF. Cell phones, radios, CB and other means are great but you need to consider that they all gonna fail, so besides them include other ways of communicating in your preparing.

For example, have places where messages can be left, and in what days. And of course, have "backup" places if "first choice" places would be compromised in any way.

In real life that would be for example: in case of SHTF you will check for messages from a member of your group (or family) every Sunday evening, under the rock in old can, next to your favourite cafe. Or have some code word when you are entering your home so you can let other folks aware that you are forced to do something or similar. Think about all possible scenarios and think for solutions for them.

Remember that S. will hit the fan probably when you are not expecting it, and consider that.

Choose very carefully persons that know some confidential information about you your family and home. For example, you do not

need to tell your neighbour about your secret stash just because he is a nice man (decent).

When wrong people know info about you in SHTF time that can be very dangerous, so if you are thinking on way "as more people I include in schedules, info planning etc. that is better" you are probably wrong.

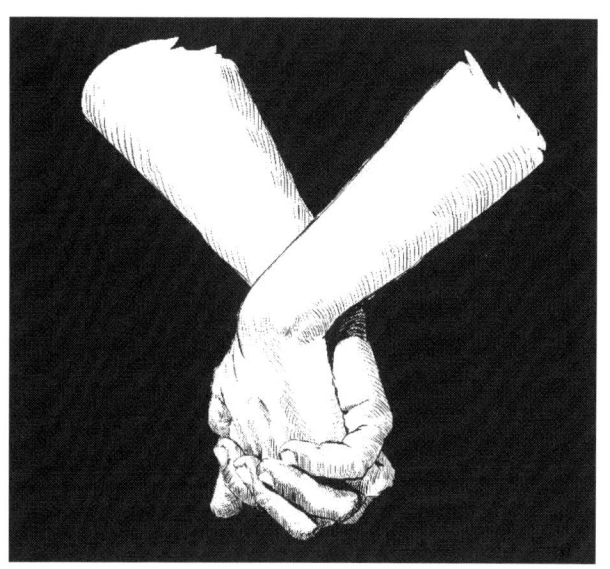

How to create your emergency communications plan

- Create a calling schedule for emergency situation. That way, if someone has a low cell phone battery they know to turn on their phone right after sunset or every full hour. If person A still did not get a call five minutes past the hour from person B, person A calls person B. Try calling twice, followed by a 5-minute break.
- Write important phone numbers down or memorize them in case you lose your mobile phone.
- Have a backup plan. If person A and person B can't get a hold of

each other to agree to leave a message on voice mail or with person C.
- Make sure the people that matter to you know what steps you are likely to take next. Will you immediately look for transportation back home or are you more likely to wait for a disaster out?
- Write your plan down, along with all relevant information such as numbers, people involved, and rules of contacting each other.
- Talk about sources of information people around you are most likely to use during an emergency situation and include this information in your communications plan.
- Incorporate other devices and means of communicating in your plan.

Notes: This example emergency plan gives you an idea of what you should think of.

Choose meeting points that they are far away from each other to most likely still be viable in terms of a localized disaster but easy to get to by just walking. For example choose to point A in between both workplaces and point B slightly more towards the outskirts of the city.

Talk about different scenarios you are preparing for. Align meeting spots along with your bug out route and incorporate your bug out location into the plan as well.

Adding more people to the group makes things more difficult of course. Try to delegate responsibilities in larger groups (e.g. who picks up the kids, who check on friends and family...). Keep in mind a communication plan, just like all your preparations can just give you better chances and cannot guarantee that everything will work out.

A simpler plan everyone understands is much better than an elaborate plan with many conditions that only half of the people understand and get right in high-stress situations. Practice these plans or include places that you often visit with your family so they are easy to remember for everyone.

Consider adding a few ideas of the emergency communication plan to your and your family's everyday life. For example, switching off mobile phones when they have only 15% power left and switching them on for a few minutes at set intervals to be at least available at certain times. Besides being helpful in emergency situations, many things you learn in this course are simply good habits to have that make life easier.

The big benefit of an emergency communication plan is that everybody has a guide and system to follow so the chances to meet and reconnect are much higher than without it.

Alternative Ways of Communicating

Alternative Two-Way Communication

Inform yourself about what kinds of radios you are allowed to operate without special licenses in your country. Of course, during an emergency situation or if you want to be found you should utilize any form of communication that helps.

- Get some FRS/GMRS radios. These are cheap ways to communicate over short distances (cut off half of what manufacturers claim and another half of that if you use it in an urban area). An added benefit: More than 50 million of these two-way radios have been sold in the US and you might be able to communicate with other people in your area who also use them in case of an emergency. (They also might come in handy to gather intelligence if you use them to listen to others talking.) Suggested brands: Midland (something like the Midland XT511), Motorola, and Uniden.
- Get CB radios if you live close to a highway to communicate with truckers passing by.
- Get EXRS radios to communicate privately. Their range is similar to FRS/GMRS radios but they use a frequency switching technique to make the transmissions impossible to intercept with consumer-grade equipment (you can't buy equipment to intercept the transmissions at the moment). This

can become very useful if you have gang activity in your area or simply don't want your neighbour to listen in on you.
- Satellite phones are expensive but might be worth it depending on your situation. First select a network provider such as Inmarsat, Thuraya, Globalstar, or Iridium and check what areas their satellites cover. Iridium covers the whole planet while Thuraya covers only certain continents. Then, decide on a phone and plan. Now there are also some prepaid plans available but their credit usually has to be used within a certain timeframe.
- Amateur radio (ham radio) is one of the most effective ways to communicate during emergencies, and you can use it to relay your messages over long distances (with the help of repeaters, antennas that amplify your signal). To send broadcasts you have to get a license in most countries. Listening to amateur radio is often allowed without a license. You can also transmit text messages along with GPS coordinates and much more. We recommend you get a handheld ham radio you can carry, from either Icom, Kenwood, or Yaesu. Get a waterproof radio capable of putting out 5 watts and invest in a good whip antenna (because most factory antennas that come with these devices aren't that good). You can get a stationary radio for your home later on.

Alternative One-Way Communication Devices

A modern personal locator beacon transmits on 406 MHz. This frequency is monitored by search and rescue satellites that will relay your distress signal, which allows rescuers to locate you. One problem with PLBs is that you can only send and not receive with them. Another is that accidentally hitting the emergency button can quickly become expensive when everything is set in motion to find you.

The SPOT Personal Tracker is a popular personal locator beacon that works with a subscription service and has a few more options, such as the ability to send non-emergency messages. PLBs can be cheap alternatives to satellite phones when going on outdoor adventures.

General Radio Advice

- Broadcast from the highest elevation possible.
- Keep in mind that the strongest radio signal radiates out from the length of the antenna, not the tip, so pointing the antenna towards something does not help.
- Most radio broadcasts start at full or half hours, so if you want to reach people, try to transmit at these times.
- If you have to relay important information come up with a code that you can use to talk with others.
- Get enough backup power sources to power your communication devices!
- Make sure you are familiar with your communication devices and how well they operate in different conditions.
- Join local amateur radio or emergency communication clubs.
- Test your communication plan with everyone involved.
- If you communicate to be rescued, be especially active in the first 24 hours because that is the time when most search parties will head out.

Signaling

SELCO ON SIGNALING

Signaling in the city was used but not on the way that makes sense maybe in some other places or situations. Signaling with open fires or lights in a densely populated area when the law is gone usually means trouble.

In the beginning, signaling with blanket on windows (covering light) was used but pretty soon it turned out that was too dangerous because of snipers.

I used using small lamps and lights for signaling that friends are coming, but most of the time signaling was in terms of letting someone know that something was wrong by using signs, leaving some item at a certain spot for example. It needs to be as simple as possible.

More about signaling and how we used it when moving through the city and in attacks and home defense in next chapter.

Signaling becomes important in situations in which you want to be found or if you want to relay a simple message.

Keep in mind the best way to be found is to let other people know where you are going (it is best if you do this in writing). But once you are out there, you can take steps to make it easier for people to find you.

- Always carry a small high-powered flashlight with you, which can be seen from at least 8-10 miles away.
- If you move through a lot of dense forest or jungle terrain, take some smoke flares that create thick colored smoke with you. It is easier for the human eye to spot movement so make sure you move any source of light or visual signal to make it easier for others to spot. Instead of turning lights on and off quickly just use your hand to cover them to save energy.
- Set controlled fires to lone standing trees or bushes.
- Use smoke from fires to catch people's attention. Use green leaves, young twigs, or rubber to create thicker smoke.
- Use reflective clothing, space blankets, or mirrors as signaling devices.
- Spread out clothes or other items to form signs on the ground such as SOS or HELP that can be spotted from the air.
- Everything in groups of three is considered a distress signal in the US (in the UK and European Alps things in groups of six are a distress signal). For example, three whistle blows or light flashes in quick succession, three fires, or piles of rock in a triangle.
- Wave your clothing or use sticks to create flags you can wave so you are easier to spot.
- Wave outstretched arms slowly up and down to signal distress.
- If you receive a distress signal, try sending a confirmation if you can.
- Consider learning Morse code to transmit messages. The

internationally known distress signal for SOS is: short, short, short ,long, long, long, short, short, short.
- Gunshots or loud noises at 1-minute intervals are also considered distress signals.
- The word "Mayday" spoken into radio is another distress signal.

Creating your EDC (Everyday Carry)

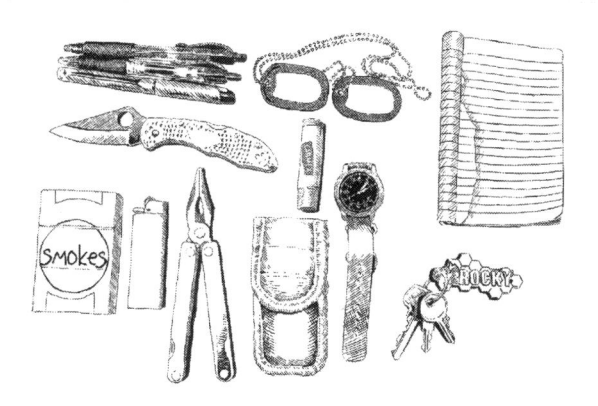

Every day carry or in short, EDC refers to all the things you carry with you every day. For most people, these are tools, gadgets and equipment to overcome the little problems in life such as cutting something, having some light and maybe some means of self-defense.

SELCO ABOUT HIS EDC

Here is my current EDC I carry in a bag with me:

- *Pistol with two magazines*
- *Pocket knife*

- *Flashlight (torch)*
- *Cellphone*
- *Keys*
- *Lighter*
- *Some hard candy*

Additional carry (sometimes):

- *Penlight (example)*
- *Emt shears (example)*
- *Rescue blanket (example)*

I have a few smaller bags that usually go with different types of clothing and I use when going to different places. Sport bag, shoulder bag, waist bag and sometimes I do not have a bag at all- I carry things in pockets (and weapon on my waist or holster). It depends where do I go, what kind of weather is outside and similar.

The weapon usually needs to be accessible, fast, so in every bag, it goes on top. If it is dark outside, then my flashlight is also on top, or accessible in a pocket.

All things for EDC are on same places, always on some shelf next to the door of my apartment. So I take stuff that I need when I leave. Routine is that I always take some things such as (weapon, wallet, keys) and sometimes other/extra stuff (rescue blankets and so on).

I also always carry a small pack of hard candy, it helps me when I am hungry, but that is just something psychological for me and gets rid of the feeling for some time.

We recommend you start with a very small EDC (knife, flashlight and fire starting kit) and add to it step by step. There is no point in buying a lot of tools that you end up leaving at home.

A small Swiss army knife for your key chain could be the first thing you get. These small knives are great little presents too if you want to warm up people step by step to the idea of preparedness and having the right tools to overcome little everyday problems.

Example of a budget EDC

- A bic mini lighter (get some more, lighters are always good to have and in case of SHTF to trade).
- A small capsule with tinder such as cotton pads with vaseline.
- A lightweight and sturdy Mora knife.
- A small flashlight.
- A leatherman micra.

Having a good knife, tools to make fire and some light are the essentials. From then on you can get creative.

- Folding scissors.
- A waterproof notebook.
- A good pair of tweezers
- A sturdy ballpoint pen that can be used for self-defense or as a glass breaker.

There are many specific mini tools that can make your life easier, such as the Leatherman Rime or the Burktek Pocketwrench.

There are also companies that specialize in EDC tools such as True Utility.

To make carrying your edc tools easier, you can add them to a flexible key ring for example.

Some people carry small guns such as the Walther PPS or lock picking sets which are helpful for urban survival scenarios if you know how to use them. Adding a paracord bracelet and compass are good ideas too.

Creating and improving your EDC is your first step in learning to get prepared. In the next chapter, we will talk about bug out bags and towards the end of the course, we will get into stocking up on food and supplies to get you and your family going for a year or more.

Creating your EDC is not only fun but it gets you into the right mindset of being prepared and having the right tools to overcome problems in everyday life. It is also great for kids to get them into the preparedness mindset.

2. Chapter 2: Urban Survival

Urban survival is especially important these days. Most of us live or spend a lot of time in urban environments and depend on the systems there to feed us, take us from point A to point B, and protect us from harm.

The whole system is fragile, and if disasters such as a hurricane, a terrorist attack, or a complete collapse happen, the urban system easily gets out of balance and leaves not only you but thousands of people helpless and desperate. Cities can't sustain themselves without power, and people were doing their jobs to make things happen. In disaster scenarios, this stops, and the system breaks down. You learn about survival, so you are not helpless, but the real danger comes from the humans around you. Humans are the most dangerous animal on this planet, and once they get hungry, scared, and desperate, most show their very primitive and violent side.

Even if the system (or parts of it) is still working, social order is a psychological construct. Once some people realize they can do whatever they want, all limits are gone. Criminals will feel like a kid in a candy shop and like they are allowed to take whatever they want.

Don't count on any outside help. Someone might come to help you, but learning about survival means learning to take care of things on your own, or even better with a group of people who can take care of things on their own.

The first decision you have to make is to stay where you are (bug in) or leave to try to find a safer place (bug-out).

To Bug Out or Bug In

To stay or to go?

If your plane has crashed and you are one of the few survivors, make sure that you get out of any possible fire or explosion radius before doing anything else. If you try to be a hero and help others but get blown up with them, it is just one more life wasted. Helping your loved ones might be the right choice for you, but think about your personal safety first.

Once you are confident you are safe, it is better to stay put in most cases when you are lost somewhere or have had an accident. People might know where you were heading **(in the best case scenario, you told someone your detailed plans, this is normal for solo hikers)**, or in the case of accidents, a car or plane crash site is much easier to locate than a single person. Of course, if you know the way back to civilization and feel confident you have the energy to get there on your own, by all means, go **(but leave some hints as to which direction you went)**.

Keep in mind that stress, injuries, and conditions like hypothermia affect your brain and your ability to make judgments. Take some time to think about what makes sense and what does not.

Here are the questions you should ask yourself:

- **Duration:** How long is this survival situation most likely going to last?
- **Dangers:** What are the biggest threats that I might have to face if I stay or leave?
- **Departure:** Do I know a place that is safer and how to get there?
- **Delay:** Do I have the resources to stay where I am?

We cannot give you the ultimate guide to every situation because way too many factors are involved, and each needs careful evaluation before you make your decision. What we recommend, though, is to think realistically and not get caught up in doing nothing but hoping for the best.

SELCO ON HOW HE MISSED HIS CHANCE TO BUG OUT

It was the time of great confusion, and now when I look back, it looked stupid how I did not understand that sh!t gonna hit the fan so hard, but now it is easy to say that.

In those times, people simply did not believe that something so bad could happen, some did not believe in that simply because it is hard to believe in something that you never experienced, and also most of the media was promoting the "nothing gonna happen" idea. So people simply wanted to believe. It is also hard to let everything go.

Some people did go, people who had information (correct information), and people who simply had the right mindset at the right time. Better to travel one time too often than being stuck in a city surrounded by enemies.

Signs were there, but people simply did not want to believe or did not recognize signs. The most important thing is to get out of harm's way. What makes sense depends on the kind of survival situation you are in.

Bug Out Location (BOL)

Unless you are extremely skilled at outdoor living, the idea of grabbing a few supplies and heading for the hills to live off the land in a long-term collapse is bound to fail. That's where bug-out locations come in.

A bug out location is a safe place that you can retreat to in case of a major disaster or collapse of the system.

It is a place that has supplies and everything you need to weather the storm, sustain yourself, and stay safe. Since most of us don't have the money to build an elaborate underground shelter that is hidden from sight and big enough and properly equipped to sustain your life and that of your loved ones for several years, we have to make do with something else.

If you are serious about survival and being prepared for whatever might happen, **getting a BOL should be part of your plans.**

Most people immediately think about a cute little cabin in the woods, but be realistic. Can you hunt, fish, and forage enough to keep living there once you run out of food supplies? It might be the safest place to be, but have a backup in case you discover that you cannot live there. A small remote village where neighbors have tight bonds and accept you (maybe because you grew up there or you helped them in some way) is most likely a better solution than the remote cabin.

Of course, if you don't have any connection to the locals and just show up, things might be very different

SELCO ON HIS BOL

My BOL place is simply a community (village) of the people who are mostly blood connected (relatives). It is a rural community where people are used to hard life and life connected to nature. We have (and still develop) needed skills, so all fields are covered (medical, farming, mechanical...)

My experience is that strongly connected groups (family, close friends-group) in rural settings have a good chance to do good when SHTF.

Things like water (creeks), fuel (wood), and wild animals are also near our BOL.

Important Factors to Consider When Choosing a Bug Out Location

- It should be in a place with few other people nearby or only people nearby you can trust and rely on.
- It should have plenty of water and good land to farm or be surrounded by other sources of food that can sustain you for a long period of time (fishing, trapping, or hunting, for example).
- It should be out of the way of the natural disaster zones in your area.

- It should be easy to get to within 2–3 days by foot, but far enough to keep away any crowds of people who are fleeing the city.
- It should be quite a bit away from any major traffic routes because that is how most people will try to get   out of the city.

Other Factors That Would Be Nice to Have

- A diverse economy with different professions that could sustain the area during a complete breakdown of society or at least speed up the recovery.
- Many people are still working in hands-on jobs which can fix things, such as carpenters, plumbers, mechanics, electricians, etc.
- Farms and other life-sustaining businesses, such as medical centers or doctors, in the area.
- If you live in a rural area, more than a full tank away from any major urban areas, have great ties with your neighbors, and maybe even have family members that live in a small town nearby, then you already live in a great bug out location. Congratulations.

Strength in Numbers

If there is one concept that is flawed in all of the mainstream ideas about survival, it is the idea of the lone wolf roughing it and surviving alone in the woods. We, humans, are social animals, and that helped us to survive in the past, and if the system has collapsed will enable us to survive again.

Survival alone is very, very hard. Survival in a group is much better, and once your group gets to a certain size of maybe 15-20 people and the diverse skill sets of members cover all that you need, life can actually start to become almost normal again.

So keep in mind, to survive and thrive, you want people around you that you can rely on. Wherever you plan on bugging out to, plan to connect with the people in the area and make some friends.

Your family or close friends that you trust is your inner circle, but having good connections to neighbors can help you to add another layer of security. You might want to call it the "outer circle."

Bugging Out

If a disaster affects your area or the area around you, we recommend you bug out right away.

One of the biggest controversies in the survival community is should you bug in or bug out, and there are countless arguments for both options. Your decision should be based on what makes sense and not what is more convenient.

Do not hesitate and get out while you can, at the first sign of trouble. In the worst-case scenario, you have made the trip to your BOL (or friends or family located outside of the urban area) for no reason. In the best-case scenario, this trip has saved your life.

SELCO ON BUGGING OUT

You need to get out of the urban area. When SHTF knowing the right moment for getting out from a dangerous environment (urban SHTF is a very dangerous environment) requires some basic knowledge in recognizing signs of SHTF and some knowledge of basic human behavior.

Between the first signs of violence and the complete absence of any restraints in violence, there is a gap. Depending on the specific situation, that gap can be shorter or longer, but you need to use it and leave the area.

In the true SHTF situation, after that gap is gone, people realize that there is no usual punishment (law, police, public...), and then everything is becoming harder.

Cities can easily become death traps once law and order are gone. Lots of survival-themed movies and books show us empty and deserted cities after SHTF, but the reality is quite different. **People stay where they are because most people simply have no other place to go.**

Once the masses try to escape the city and get stuck in traffic jams or stopped by armed gangs at checkpoints, most people think twice before going anywhere. If no armed gangs stop the traffic flow, the government might coordinate an evacuation that can also result in hours, if not days, being stuck at a place. In the case of hurricane Katrina, people who were "evacuated" had to wait for days for further help (not only at the Superdome stadium downtown).

As a result, in most SHTF scenarios, you will have too many people in a small urban area with too few resources.

This can escalate to people fighting for resources, gangs controlling the resources, and a lot of desperate violence by people who did not prepare for this kind of situation.

The common saying "we are just three meals away from cannibalism" isn't too far off. The looting, raping, and murdering after the typhoon Haiyan hit the Philippines in November 2013 is another example of this. People in western countries do not know how it feels to be truly hungry and how that can cause people to take extreme measures after just a few days to get food.

If you are living in an urban area, that alone is reason enough to have a bug out plan.

If you are alone and want to stay where you are, so be it. You might even remain unnoticed, but if you are with family or a group of people, get out.

Never be lazy when it comes to avoiding risk. Be the first at the door. Be the "coward" when others still want to stay. Better safe than sorry is true.

Party Time for the Bad Guys

Keep in mind that while regular people worry about a lack of law and order and chaos, other people have waited for this moment their whole life. Some people feel they finally have the freedom to do whatever they like and get on "power trips" when they see how easily they can control people who fear them.

Groups like gangs do not even have to get overly organized. They have strength in numbers and weapons. Instead of fighting for areas for dealing drugs, they simply fight over areas to completely control.

Besides these criminal elements, there are people who are usually good, but they realize that in this fight for survival, only the tough survive, and they quickly start robbing and killing because it seems like the only way to live (which is correct in many situations).

One of the reasons we prepare for survival scenarios is that this ensures we do not have to take desperate measures and can ride out the storm while still sticking to most of our principles and taking fewer risks.

Besides violence, the spreading of diseases is another major disadvantage you most likely have to face if you stay in a densely populated area.

When thinking about bugging in or bugging out, simply consider where you will be exposed to the most risk. Most likely, you will come to the conclusion that you will not want to be in or near a city.

In any case, there is no definitive answer to this, as every situation is different. Always have a plan. The idea of bugging out is not running for the hills in a bout of panic.

Things to Consider before Bugging Out

If you choose to bug out, you probably have good reasons for that. But bugging out without any preparation, plans, or thinking about your situation means you are running wildly into the unknown, and that can easily end up in a deadly situation.

A few things need to be considered when you are bugging out:

- Why are you bugging out?
- When are you bugging out?
- How are you bugging out?

Even in the most deadly situations, when you do not have time for anything except trying to get away, try to keep this short list of questions in your mind.

Why?

Why you are bugging out can be a long list or just a particular reason. It does not matter. Just make sure you have taken a few moments to really assess the situation and make sense of it.

When?

The timing of when to bug out is more important than most people want to believe.

SELCO ON WHY TIMING MATTERS

First shootings and killing already began, but it was still confusing, which is shooting on who and what is going on. You could still see the police force on the street, but at the same time, rumors were that police is robbing and shooting people too.

My friend was inside the town when all that started, and he wanted to leave the city because his family was already out. He had no real info about what was going on. He started the car to move through the city. Streets were already pretty congested with all kinds of stuff, abandoned cars, and things that people dragged from the stores and left there. People were walking, some yelling, others carrying weapons, some still trying to hide them, others carrying them openly.

When he came to the outskirts of the city, he found a barricade and ten or twelve police officers on a closed road. He remembers that they had police uniforms, but they looked dirty, and uniforms looked like they do not care. One of them even had cowboy boots that he probably took from some store. When they stopped him, he understood that it is not about regular police issues, it is about robbing him.

Then he started to yell at them that he is a personal friend to a local police department head and that when tomorrow police force comes from another town to solve the problems, he is gonna take personal care that they all lose their job and be punished for what they do to him at that checkpoint and so on.

At the first moment, they all laughed at him, but when he persisted with his attitude that he has friends in high positions (police head) and correct and true information (that the police force comes from the other region to solve problems and bring back law and order) they started to think deeper about that.

Then after some of them started with „OK sir, we are sorry, you can go."

He remembers that few of them still wanted to rob him, and who knows what else. A guy with cowboy boots was pretty drunk and kept saying, "f#ck the police and your friends in high places and get out of the car, " but others calmed him down and almost dragged him from the car.

They tell him that he can go, and he says that while he was passing the barricade, they were still arguing behind him what they should do with him.

For the next 5 kilometers he was crying and screaming because fear got him and laughing like the idiot at the same time because he had so much luck. He chooses (by luck most probably) the right moment to run. Groups of those police officers still were somewhere between police officers and gangs.

Some of them already had a mob mentality and did not care anymore for consequences, but most of them were not sure if the situation will come back to normal again, so maybe they will be *punished for what they are doing. Nobody had correct information about what's going on at that moment, so my friend uses that and lied.*

And it worked.

If he chooses to run only 2-3 days later, they probably would just shoot him and rob him immediately because they would have had a clear idea that everything has gone to hell, and they are „free" to do whatever they want.

The time of day when you are going to bug out depends on your particular situation. It is not always better to bug out during night time.

For example, if the guy would have come to that checkpoint during the night, the odds that he would have been shot would have been dramatically increased. In situations like that, people react differently when it is night, and there are not too many witnesses around.

Also, if you have kids and plan to bug out in the middle of the night through some densely forested area, this can easily turn into a disaster when someone gets lost in the dark.

Problems like these show that theories are fine, but you have to practice bugging out with the people you are most likely to go with when the time comes. Get to know your area and the route to your BOL at different times of the night, in different seasons, and in different weather conditions. You might be surprised how quickly small streams become vicious little rivers if it rains heavily for a few hours.

The nature of the disaster you face does not matter. It does not have to be an armed conflict – it can simply be a matter of some people finding a way to take advantage of others.

Every SHTF scenario has a few phases. While there are different types of scenarios (pandemics, terrorist attacks, climate-related disasters, etc.), if you choose to bug out, you need to recognize what phase you are in.

Different Phases of Anarchy

There are gaps between the different phases of chaos on the streets.

In the beginning, you might have sporadic violence, rioting, and looting, but most people will behave themselves because they still believe there is some sort of order. Most people also do not realize how bad things might get. In this phase, there are still periods of time that can be called "confused peace," which means that **things are peaceful simply because people are not aware of how much life has just changed**.

After people realize how severe the situation is, all hell will break loose. The violent people will feel like they are on a big playground, the greedy people will try to take advantage of others as much as they can, and the desperate people who are not prepared will start doing ugly things just to survive and because they do not see alternatives.

If you run into gangs or criminals, how intoxicated they are can also make a difference, not only on their desire to hurt and kill but also on their ability to fight.

If you did not make it out of your area before SHTF, try to get out when the confusion is greatest, and people are still not sure what is going to happen. Things will get only worse once people realize they are now living in a lawless area where everything goes.

How to Bug Out?

Plan your route in detail and check it for any changes, new shortcuts, and other improvements on a regular basis. Have at least two alternative routes and learn about the nearby areas along your primary route. That way, if you have to make a detour, you will still feel confident and be able to make informed decisions.

Be ready to change your route or even walk back on some of it at any time if you have to. In other words, your plan is just a plan. Do not get killed because you felt you had to stick to your "plan."

Survival is about considering all options at any time and being flexible when you have to.

Worst Case Scenario Philosophy

Always consider the worst-case scenario. If you are prepared to take the challenge on in the worst-case scenario, you are prepared for everything else as well.

Here is an example situation:

You have your BOL in the woods about 50 miles from your home, perfectly hidden and equipped with everything one could want for long term survival. Then disaster strikes:

emergency servicemen and women head home to care for their own families. Law and order are gone. SHTF.

You are taking your family with their bug-out bags to your BOL, and because you are all trained for packing and bugging out from your house before, you are pretty fast.

You also understood the severity of the situation right away and bugged out before the roads were clogged with traffic, so you just needed 10 minutes to get in your 4×4 and 45 minutes to reach your BOL.

And that's it, you are a winner and live happily ever after at your BOL!

The problem is it usually doesn't work out like that. When you learn about survival, you learn about dealing with plans that go wrong.

So what is a more likely scenario?

Most probably SHTF when your kids were in school, your wife was at the hair salon in a different neighborhood, your 4×4 is getting its yearly checkup and is not available, and you just find out that the kids played with the bug out bags, and you can't find them.

To be truly prepared to bug out, you need to be prepared all the time.

That means that you need to have a clear plan for every situation:

- Besides bug out bags, make sure everyone has their EDC with them at all times. ? Have a clear plan on what to do and where to go in case of some sudden disaster. Create a communications plan and practice it with all members of your family or group. Bugging out begins with a plan and not fancy gear in a bug out bag.
- Have multiple means to get to your bug out location (if you are planning to go there with a car, they also have a plan to get there with bikes or by foot if the roads close down).

Bug Out Vehicles

It makes sense to keep your vehicle in good condition. Always have a full tank of gasoline and have some extra gasoline canisters in your garage ready to take along. It also makes sense to have a bigger version of your bug out bag in your car with some extra things like a shovel, water, weapons, a change of clothing, a sleeping bag, some shoes, a bigger first aid kit, food, and, of course, stuff to fix your car.

The main reason we are not big fans of dedicated bug out vehicles is that some bug-out vehicles look like they are straight from the Mad Max movies and are the opposite of low profile cars.

If you depend on a vehicle to get to your BOL, it is probably a bit too far away or hard to get to anyway, and you might want to find another place in a better location. Also, if you depend on a vehicle, the chances are that the biggest problem will be the last couple of miles before you get to your BOL. In this case, consider parking or hiding something like an ATV (all-terrain vehicle) in a remote location on your way to your BOL.

If you are living out in the countryside and keeping a low profile does not matter, you can plan differently, of course. Don't get me wrong, in the city, it is good to have an armored vehicle, but for 99% of us, that money could be used to get more important stuff, stuff that you are really going to need, such as solar systems for your BOL or other investments that make your BOL a better place to live at.

Help on Your Way to Your BOL

Consider hiding some things on the way to your BOL. These hidden caches can have a variety of things. You can hide supplies or even a very basic set of survival tools in case you were not able to take your BOB or had to leave it behind. These caches are meant to help you when you need it most.

The idea is not to hide a huge amount of supplies at a certain spot but instead **hide sets of smaller, important items at different spots.** Make sure you use common sense when you decide where to hide what. Hiding caches with ammunition only on your primary route and first aid items on your secondary route does not make much sense.

Mix things up. A great way to store things is to use PVC tubes from your local hardware store. Cut them to the desired length and use end pieces to seal them. All items inside should be put in Ziplock bags as well, and you can use duct tape around the end pieces to keep them in place and add another layer of protection. Temperature changes can deform PVC pipes and make them hard to open after some time. Consider burying a screwdriver or similar tool in a plastic bag next to the pipe to help you open it.

Depending on the soil in your area, the earth might settle and stick to your cache, so it becomes hard to get out of the ground. Consider using a bigger pipe with a smaller pipe inside so you only have to dig to the pipe opening, open it up and pull out the smaller pipe to get your supplies.

Store your caches away from places heavily frequented by people. To avoid detection by treasure hunters with metal detection devices, you can bury some scrap metal on top of it so that they simply move on when their metal detector indicates it has found something.

Storing some ammunition close to your home is also a smart idea. You do not know how fast you might have to leave the house, and to have some extra ammunition can help you to get your house back or make your way to your BOL safer.

Remember the location of caches according to the natural environment, such as distance to nearby trees or big rocks. Also, record the GPS coordinates and store them as abstract numbers if you write them down, so people don't get curious if they find this information on you. You can also place your own natural markers such as stones on top of your caches to mark the location or place several stones around the cache to mark the right spot. Just like with everything when it comes to survival, have backups and multiple ways to find your cache locations again.

It also helps to mark the locations on a map and write what you have stored where to keep track of it, in case you set up several caches. Just make sure to keep the map in a truly safe place that it does not fall into the wrong hands.

Another idea is to take pictures of your family at these places and create an album with it. The "family fun in the forest" album is, in reality, the "family members on top of my hidden caches" album. You can write codes on the back of photos or mark them otherwise to indicate what a certain cache contains.

Another possibility is to create a code for the pictures: have your wife always standing on top of weapon caches, your daughter standing on top of wilderness survival caches (with fire and emergency shelter supplies), and ammunition caches are simply "nature" pictures without anyone standing there. There are many possibilities to get creative with your caches so that you have another added layer of security in your bug out plan.

Bugging In

One of the first things you have to understand when you are bugging in is that life will not be the same anymore. Forget about all your old habits. You will be living in the same place but with completely different rules.

Your neighbors might not be those nice friendly people anymore that you get together with to discuss sports events. They might be those guys who come knocking on your door to demand help and might even come at night to take what they need if you deny help to them.

Your house will be your fortress and prison at the same time when the world outside has turned ugly, and you will have to do many things differently.

You basically have two ways to protect yourself. Make your home look undesirable and empty (if you are alone or just two people–this doesn't work if you are with a big group), or you make it look like a hard target that would take too much effort to attack.

The Mind of a Criminal

Few criminals and even fewer desperate people who are struggling to survive will bother with challenges when they want to get something. They will always go for the easiest target.

Understand the "crime triangle" in the image above. It shows the major factors that lead to people committing crimes. You do not have any influence on the *skills*, *tools*, or *weapons* attackers have, but you can make attacking you *less desirable* and give them *less of an opportunity*.

SELCO ABOUT A MAJOR PROBLEM OF BEING ALONE

It is not if, it is WHEN you get sick because you WILL get sick in the period of collapse, no matter how prepared you are, it is simply like that.

People normally get sick today at normal times, so they will when SHTF, just much more because of the stress and more dirty conditions.

Without a system to care for you, it gets much complicated. Simple diarrhea in a collapsed society can kill you if there is no one to care for you.

You need to expect much more than diarrhea from some bad food. Bigger and smaller wounds, rashes, illnesses caused by poor hygiene, bad food, and water, or psychological problems induced because of new hard reality, all demand people to care for each other.

Another thing is that you cannot function properly when you are sick or injured. In other words, if you are sick and injured, and alone you are becoming easy prey. You make more desperate decisions or simply wrong decisions because you do not have another perspective.

It is very hard to be alone in an urban setting and survive when SHTF. If you find yourself alone in a city when SHTF and you do not want to or cannot bug out, I recommend that you try to join another group (relatives, friends, etc.). It is possible to survive alone, but from my experience, people who tried that more often than not paid a very high price.

Low Profile Look

The first and, in many cases, the most important defense of your home is to make it look uninteresting to potential attackers.

A great majority of attacks during my time in the war were simply because **attackers saw a good opportunity** to get something. Do not offer people an obvious invitation to stop by.

Your home needs to look uninteresting, that does not mean without defenses, but as if there is nothing to get.

For example, if you live in an apartment complex and your apartment is at the end of a floor, pile some trash and block the whole path to your apartment. You can still have a steel door or door secured with several deadbolts that are hard to breach, but attackers would only get to that after they get through all the trash.

A well-defended place looks like a place that has lots of valuable resources. You might surprise the first group of people with how well your defenses are set up, but after the retreat, they might simply come better prepared or with more people the next time, and sooner or later, you are going to be overwhelmed.

You can do a lot of things quickly once SHTF in order to make your home look less interesting.

Some examples are:

- If your area is struck with a pandemic, a good idea would be to

just to paint some signs on your home, for example, biohazard signs or "do not enter – infection" signs, etc. – Use other original signs, such as "do not enter" or "mines," or whatever makes sense for your particular situation.
- In most SHTF scenarios, there will be violence and looting. Simply make your place look like it has already been looted and destroyed. Use some fake or animal blood on your porch, break a few windows, take some stuff out and just throw it everywhere on your lawn. Make it look like it is not worth bothering with.
- Consider burning parts of your place that you don't need. Make sure your house blends in with neighbors' houses (or looks worse).

Home Modifications

There are many obvious things you can do to make your house harder to enter in good and bad times.

Doors

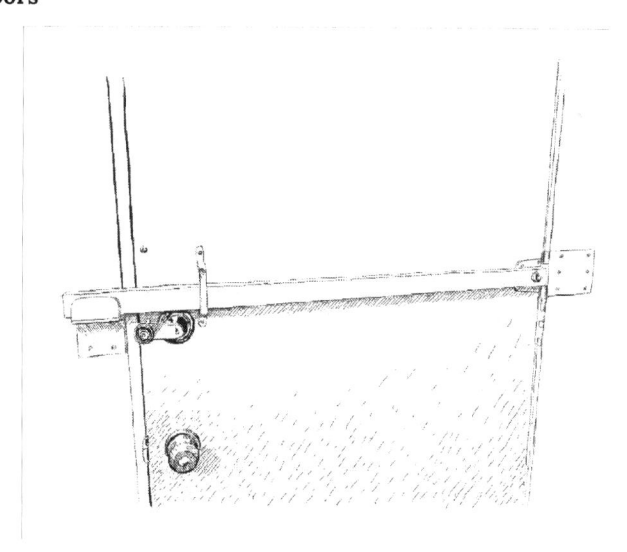

- The first thing is to reinforce your doors so that they can withstand kicks. Many wooden doors are easily kicked in. If you cannot afford to get a new door, attach plywood boards or sheet metal on the inside to increase the sturdiness of the door. Also, check that the hinge pins of your door are on the inside or replace the pins with pins that cannot be removed.
- Regular knob locks are bad and easy to break. If you have one, add a single cylinder deadbolt lock to the door. You can get your knob lock rekeyed to only use one type of key for both locks. The bolt-on, the new lock should stick out at least 1 inch when extended and should have a tapered cylinder guard.
- To avoid key bumping, a very popular and easy way of opening regular locks, get a high-security ANSI grade 1 deadbolt (Schlage and Medeco offer those, for example).
- Look for locks that come with a strike plate (like the Schlage B60N619 Deadbolt) and hardened steel inserts to make drilling the lock more difficult. The strike plate screws should go at least 1 inch into the door so that they do not break when the door is kicked, so you might have to make an extra trip to your hardware store for longer screws.
- It goes without saying that you should get doors without windows.
- Door chains are easy to break, so forget about them. For extra protection, consider getting a door club, a buddybar door jammer, or a door stop alarm.
- Get heavy-duty bike locks for tool sheds and gates and use a heavy-duty hasp that is installed so that all screw heads are hidden.
- Invest in an auxiliary patio door lock or lock sliding doors from the inside by jamming the rails they run on.
- If you have double-hung windows, pin them. Remove crank handles from casement windows and reapplying them if you want to open the windows.
- Install burglar bars on the inside of your house with quick-release mechanisms (if you do not want to do this all around

the house, consider doing this for an outside facing safe room).

Based on data obtained from the National Fire Incident Reporting System (NFIRS), on average, about 25 civilians are injured or die each year in fires where escape is compromised by unauthorized bars or gates.

The actual numbers may be larger than that, due to the fact that the presence of burglar bars is not always collected in a way that is recorded by NFIRS (e.g., written in the text but not coded). The most recent version of NFIRS, version 5.0, allows for the collection of data concerning burglar bars; however, data from the new version is not yet available.

Most fatalities/injuries involving burglar bars occur in residences when people become entrapped by the very bars that are supposed to protect them. Children, the elderly, the mobility impaired, and firefighters are especially vulnerable. The bars also can hamper rescue efforts, especially the efforts of those who arrive before public safety personnel.

Use tempered glass to prevent glass shards from cutting you or use foil or laminated glass to keep the glass in its place once it is shattered. Other options for more resistant glass are plexiglass or polycarbonate glass, which is more resistant and also lighter than regular glass. The disadvantage of this type of glass is that it does not hold up as well when exposed to the weather compared to acrylic glass. If you want to go all out and have the money to get it, consider bulletproof glass.

Alarm Systems

Regular alarm systems are made for our current, well-functioning society. They are built to alert neighbors or security companies to come and help. That's why loud alarms that call for attention are great in normal times, but after a collapse, when no help is coming anyway, silent alarms make much more sense.

Keep in mind that every modern alarm system needs power, so when planning an alarm system, make sure it is energy efficient and still works when the grid goes down (at least for some time). There are many different alarm systems available today. Here are some things to keep in mind when installing one.

- Add motion detection sensors out of reach of attackers.
- Get alarm systems that work outside your house but also set up alarms on the inside.
- Consider adding gas and smoke detection devices.

- Place pressure mats at strategically important spots (good hiding spots in your yard and in front of windows and doors).
- Add door and window contacts that activate the alarm once they are opened.
- Consider installing glass break detectors that detect the shock wave or the frequency of the sound that is created when someone breaks a window.
- Photoelectric beams activate the alarm when someone breaks a beam of invisible light. They can cover bigger areas than mats but are also more expensive.
- Get panic buttons installed that can start an alarm manually.
- Consider getting complete alarm solutions such as Simplisafe or a laser shield system like Skylink.
- Instead of getting CCTV cameras installed, consider video webcam monitoring via software such as vitamindinc.com.

How to Deal with Threats in Normal Times

This is advice for regular people. If you work in law enforcement, you know what you can do and what you can't. mIn normal times you want to simply **avoid contact with any possible threats** and let the police handle this.

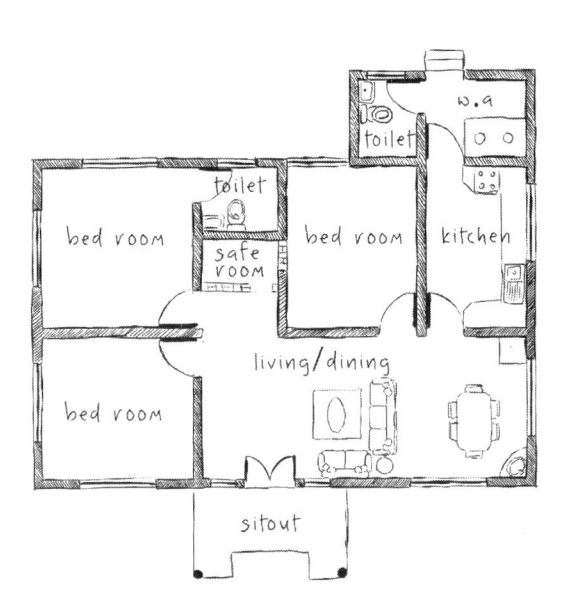

Why? Because you are in a big mess in most countries when you shoot or harm an unarmed burglar.

Most burglars leave when they realize someone is in the house.

If people still make their way to your house while it is obvious you are there, they are prepared to use violence to get what they want, and you should be too.

- If you see someone in your yard, do not confront him.
- Call the police and stay in the house so that the police do not mistake you for the potential attacker.
- If you suspect the threat is already in your house, do not go looking for him.
- Try to retreat to a safe room. Keep the room locked and wait for help to arrive.
- If you wake up with an intruder in your room, do not freak out and panic. Pretend you are sleep. If he heads your way,

64 | Chapter 2: Urban Survival

you can still surprise him, but hopefully, he will just pass through while looking for valuables.

What else helps you to stay safe in normal times?

- Make your house easy to find for emergency services, for example, by having illuminated house numbers.
- Get a fake tv and barking rex / electronic watchdog to scare people.
- Get curtains that do not let people see inside the house.

Creating a Safe Room

Safe rooms make the most sense for short term disasters. A safe room protects you and your family from the most common threats you could face in your area.

Consider the different scenarios you may have to face. Make sure the size of the room is big enough for people to lay down and sleep, in case you have to spend more than 24 hours there.

If you pick a room in your house, pick one without windows in the middle of the building. Reinforce the walls and doors. You can use metal mesh to make doors and walls harder to breach. Other options are simply plywood boards or metal sheets that you attach to the walls.

Make sure the safe room is easily accessible. If a crime is a common threat in your area or you are considering bugging in, consider a hidden safe room. A closet with a removable backplate can cover the entrance to a room, or if you have the money, consider adding sliding walls or build a staircase you can flip up.

Hiding Preps

If you plan on bugging in also consider hiding essential items for survival such as weapons, medicine, and emergency rations of food and water. Look for spaces on or in appliances that are not being used.

Consider spaces in your house or apartment where things can be hidden, such as air vents, fake power outlets, under floor tiles, or upon the ceiling (you can often remove drop ceiling tiles and hide something in the space above them). Install identical items with hidden supplies in them next to items that are actually used (e.g., pipes filled with supplies next to real water pipes).

Bury small items such as keys or memory cards in the soil of a fake plant, inside a child's toy, or in a hollowed-out space on top of a door.

Use diversion safes that look like regular household items (look for pots with double floors or rocks that are hollowed out and not anything that might be worth having in a long term disaster!). Add padding to your hidden items to avoid rattling sounds.

As important as hiding valuables is to keep a small bit of what people might be looking for in the places they expect. They see it is only very little, but that's better than nothing and leave, instead of tearing your whole place apart.

Perimeter defense

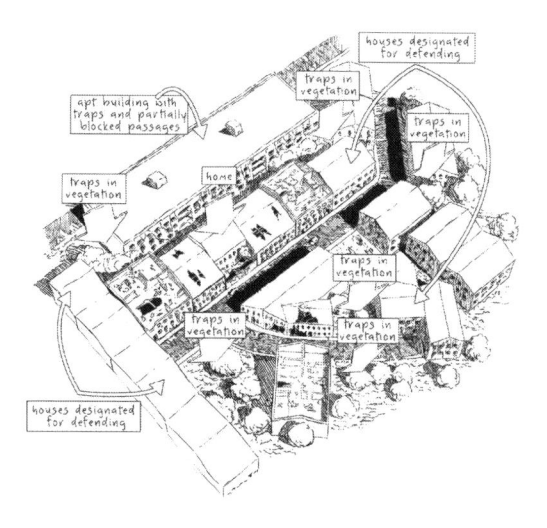

Think tactical when it comes to building your perimeter defense. How can you easily defend your home from potential attackers? Where would they go? From what side does it make sense to attack you?

Barricades, fences, and other obstacles serve the purpose to slow attackers down and guide them along a certain path and, in the best case, into a zone where you can trap, capture, or kill them.

Most of the yard modifications should be done months or even years before SHTF. You can make your life much easier by putting obstacles in the way of attackers, so planting trees or bushes at the right spots can give you a real advantage without making your yard look ugly.

Think about how attackers would approach your home. How would you get over your fence? Can people slide under it? If so, then add a ground barbwire to make it harder and not worth it for them.

Also, remove anything nearby that could help attackers to scale your fence. Create areas of denial by placing barbed or poisonous plants, trash, metal scraps, or other "unwelcoming" elements to funnel attackers along the path where you want them to go. Become

Chapter 2: Urban Survival | 67

aware of the best hiding spots in the area around your home, or even create hiding spots that just appear to offer concealment but not cover from bullets.

You want to get to the point where you know which path an attacker will most likely take once you have spotted them. Then you can either attack them in their hiding spot or wait until they have come to your kill zone, the area where they cannot hide or run for cover, and where it is easy for you to attack them.

Plan where lookouts will be placed to guard your home. These spots should not only offer concealment but also cover, so the lookouts are protected from incoming bullets. Sandbags are a good choice for cover because incoming bullets get stuck and do not ricochet.

If you live in a rural or suburban area, consider planting bushes and trees that conceal your house from any nearby streets or public places.

Stay Hidden Once SHTF

Think about alternative ways of entering and leaving your house without being seen. It can be a back door, basement window, or maybe even a small tunnel that leads to a bush nearby. It can also be a simple hole in the wall hidden from the outside with some bushes or junk.

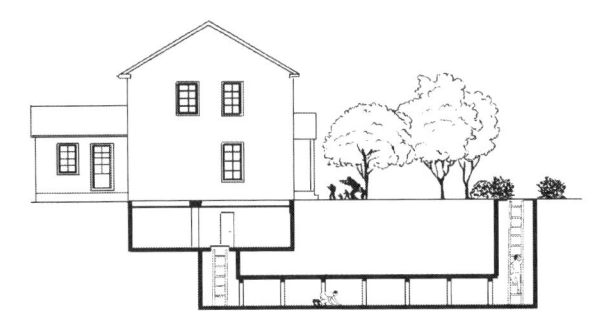

Barricade your main entrance, or set up a trap for potential attackers who try to enter. Make sure you have all the materials ready to cover all your windows so that no light from the inside gets out, so people do not know you are at home or anyone is even living in your house.

When you cook, make sure none of the smell gets out. Frying onions with bacon in a densely populated apartment building isn't recommended (as good as this might taste!).

Storage

Do not store all supplies at one place in your house or apartment, in case part of your home becomes inaccessible, gets destroyed, contaminated, or whatever else. Just like with everything when it comes to survival, this is risk management.

Maybe you have to leave your home or attackers break through your defenses and loot your place. Having your supplies stored at different places increases the chances that not all is lost once something goes wrong.

Some survivalists suggest you should poison food or water supplies before being forced out of your home by attackers. If you go for it, make sure you know what you poison and only poison a part of your supplies. Otherwise, you might be able to poison the attackers, and depending on what poison you use, even kill them, but then you won't have any supplies left for yourself. We cannot give you any recommendations for poison, but natural plants all around us have found ways to deter creatures from eating them. Every year you also hear about people picking mushrooms and killing themselves accidentally.

We suggest you stash your supplies at a few places throughout your home and have one place with supplies that is clearly visible once people enter your home. Get creative, and try to find hiding places in your area as well. If your neighbor's house is burned down or abandoned, for example, consider hiding some supplies there.

Do not hold onto your supplies at all costs. Remember that you need to SURVIVE. Resources can be obtained again; life cannot.

SELCO ON HOW THEY MANAGED THEIR WASTE

The first week or two, after all, services like waste management, running water, electric energy, and everything else was gone. The problem of garbage and waste disposal was a problem, of course, but it was like a "minor" problem comparing to everything else around us.

Then after that, we started to see that it is going to be an actual problem to take care of that. In the beginning, people burned trash, then after some time amount of trash that one house produces lowered drastically.

It is hard to produce too much trash if you do not take too much stuff in your house. Also, people stop to care to some degree for some stuff. So it was pretty normal to see junk everywhere on the street. People start just to throw away junk just to be sure it is barely outside their house.

We had the luck to had a small piece of ground (like a small park) close to our house, so we simply dig holes there in the beginning and later made primitive type latrine there. A lot of people did not care too much for that too, so one of the strongest memories from that SHTF time is a strong, very nasty, sweet, and smoky stench that was in the air all the time.

It was a mixture of burning, dead things, feces.

Think about a place where you keep your trash. Having too much trash is a sign you have stuff, and that is something you want to avoid at all costs. One thing that every survivalist needs to have in great numbers is garbage bags. They are very cheap but can be used for a wide variety of purposes.

If you have a lot of garbage bags, you have solved a lot of potential problems. They can serve as a sleeping bag, a survival poncho, a way to collect water, a way to dispose of garbage, or a way to fix a leaking roof.

When you are stuck in a location and have to keep a low profile, one of the things that get really problematic is the disposal of human waste. Again, garbage bags can help. To build a makeshift toilet, you just need a toilet seat, a plastic bucket, the size of the toilet seat, and garbage bags. Take the garbage bags out at night or whenever you venture out and get rid of them.

If you are in a city, you will be surprised how many fires will be burning after a collapse, so burning your waste is also an option to consider. In a large city, fires will burn for a long time after SHTF.

SELCO ON HOW A TYPICAL ATTACK LOOKED LIKE

In a perfect world, it is like cowboys and Indians, as a circle of wagons, the defense is on outside circle-houses, and they are heavily fortified and turned to "walls" with marked places for people on windows and doors and openings, etc., so in case of an attack, there is a plan where every man would be. In a perfectly organized neighborhood those houses would not (probably) be occupied (with non-combat folks).

This will be a perfect scenario if it works as most of the people imagine on forums when they discuss "neighbors work together." In urban areas, it is hard to achieve something like that, so it all ends in something like neighborhood watches" on few places in street, maybe few barricades, and some loose plan what to do when an attack happens (Jim needs to go there, the jack will be here)

But it is very loose and often chaotic.

Attacks happened in different ways. Sometimes from simple man (thief, scout, or simply nobody) or gang came to the door with some demand for people inside, or simply attack from nowhere. Sometimes some trade would go wrong and ends up in the full-scale shooting.

Sure, nothing too complicated, attacks were started almost always with hand grenades or RPG (sometimes) in house openings (if any openings were visible).

After that going in the yard and house, the idea was to clear out the area of people who maybe hide and cause some confusion. It did not happen in my case because we were organized pretty well and with pretty good firepower, so it always ended with some shooting without anyone entering the yard.

Group of guys coming into the street, cursing and yelling, looking for usable stuff. When you show enough force on your wall or defensive positions and shoot one or two, they usually left.

Other folks simply did not have that luck. They have been simply shocked or wounded with grenades, their places stormed, and they were killed and robbed. Few houses would just give what people wanted, and they would leave if they were lucky.

No rules, nothing like we knew what would happen. The thing is that in most of the situations, I even would not know at who I shoot in pitch dark and who is shooting at me, and I did not care if I saw something moving and suspected it was someone I shoot.

Leaving your home

Sometimes you will have to leave the relative safety of the place you stay in. I ventured out almost every night to find more resources, fuel to burn, or to trade for things we needed. Here are some things to consider when going out.

More gear means you will be heavier, slower, and less able to maneuver.

A lot of survival literature focuses heavily on equipment, and some so-called experts suggest you leave your home equipped like a Special Forces soldier. If you are comfortable with urban fighting while carrying lots of equipment, you should go ahead and carry it, but most of us are not.

Speed was often important for me because we had to cross areas that were under sniper fire, and constant shelling made jumping or sprinting to relative safety, something like a daily exercise as well. While your city is probably not surrounded by an army and under attack, urban fighting still demands a lot of agility and freedom of movement.

Your priorities should be your weapon, ammunition, a very small amount of food and water, a fire kit, and then everything else that is mission-specific such as products to trade or a crowbar to break wooden window frames out of the walls.

Do not sacrifice your movement speed and freedom for bulk items that you might or might not use. You can always come back with that folding shovel. In one period of time, I was forced to use only an old AK 47 bayonet for salvaging and dismantling stuff. In normal times I would have carried a big toolbox.

SELCO ON HOW HE AND HIS SMALL GROUP MOVED

Three was a good number for moving through the city, either going through the buildings or on "road" or what was left of roads. During the trade, one man would always stay hidden in case of possible trouble (scam, for example).

Simple moving was much easier with three people, and one guy is checking things while two others are clearing some problematic passage, for example. Even if you are just two, make one guy watch, and the other guy move or work or whatever needs to be done. This is also important for nights or when you cannot make it back to your save location on time. You want someone who can keep watch.

Routes You Take Through the City

Be prepared to use alternative routes to get from point A to point B. If the shortest way would be 3 km, expect to go 5-6 km in a post-collapse world. Safety is, in almost all cases, the main thing to consider when planning your routes. Avoid shortcuts if they expose you to any risks. I found out that splitting my route into several smaller parts and deciding on what to do next helped me to stay flexible in choosing where to go.

Exchange information about different routes and their conditions with others. Give different routes and specific waypoints certain names, draw maps (or even better, have copies of local maps at hand to give to everyone), so you can communicate any changes in your route or meeting points quickly.

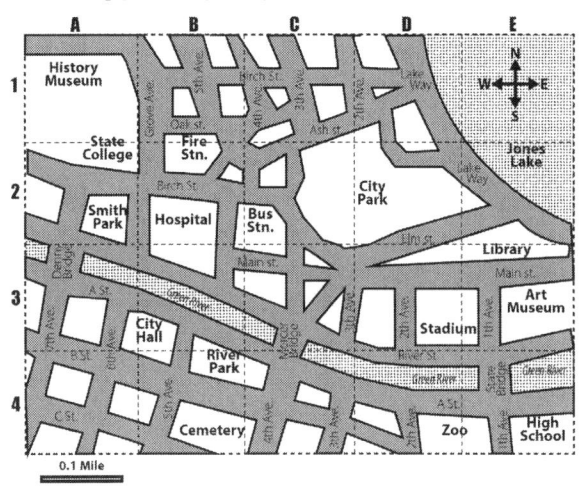

Most likely, you will move through other people's buildings, yards, and sometimes even use basements or sewers. When I started to go out at night (to avoid sniper fire), I often found myself asking, "where am I?" Even places that I was familiar with looked very

74 | Chapter 2: Urban Survival

different in absolute darkness. I later adopted a movement style in which I often took breaks to simply observe the environment. It helped me to remember things about different places and also to spot if other people were moving through the area. This way, I was often able to avoid meeting others who were out looking for resources as well.

The city is not just full of gangs or people who might rob or kill you. When services stop, other hazards such as junk, rubble, sharp things such as broken glass, and human waste can pose a threat to you too. Having well, sturdy, ankle-high boots help a lot. I prefer lightweight hiking shoes because they still enable you to run quickly and move but also protect your feet from dirt and rubble.

Movement at Night: Staying undetected

You can detect movement quicker in your peripheral vision, and in low light environments, this peripheral vision becomes even more important because of the "night blind spot." In the back of your eye, your retina has two different types of cells that send the images we see to your brain. The two types are rods and cones. They have different jobs. The rods see black and white, and it only takes a very small amount of light to stimulate them while the cones see colors, and it takes much more light to stimulate them.

In the center area of your retina that corresponds to the center of your vision, the so-called fovea centralis, you do not have rods and only cones. That means in low light, no, or just a few information is sent, and you have a night blind spot, which is an area from 5 to 10 degrees wide in the center of the visual field. As a result, if you want to see something more clearly in the dark, look right next to it and **let your peripheral vision do its job.**

Common sense is that you want to blend in with your environment. Use this information to no be seen and spot people hiding in the dark.

- Movement is one of the easiest ways to get spotted and spot others at night. Move either very slowly or take regular breaks and observe your environment to spot others. ? Contrast is

Chapter 2: Urban Survival | 75

important. Colors are hardly seen in low light environments but wearing a pitch-black can still make you stand out at night because most dark areas are not completely black. That's why dark blue, grey, or moss green colors are often preferred for urban camouflage.

- Shadows can make you easy to spot and give away your position. Always stay aware of what you are blending in with and what you have behind you when you approach another place. Watch out for lights that throw your shadow far ahead of you. With some creativity and if lights are still common, you can create some areas that will make enemy movement much easier to spot for guards by placing lights at the right places.
- Avoid everything that reflects light or use it with caution.
- Keep in mind that at night when people have less visual information to process, other senses like listening work better.
- If you hide in the dark, get down, and try to break your human outline apart. Just like camouflage tries to make you blend in better with the environment by making your human outline harder to see, try to hide at least parts of your body behind things to make your silhouette harder to be recognized as human.

Threats from Other People While Moving Through the City

The most important thing you have to keep in mind is that being curious usually gets you into trouble. Focus on why you left your place and do not get sidetracked because something else catches your attention. Stick to your plan and your route as much as possible.

Avoid people whenever you can. Not everyone is your enemy, but most people could be, and it is simply not worth the risk to find out. If you want to get into contact with someone, make sure you evaluate them first.

- Are they armed?
- How do they act (drunk, high, intoxicated, aggressive, tired…)?
- Do they have taken precautions to secure the area (for example, have one person on watch)?
- How do they move, and why do they move like that?
- How many of them?

Also, keep in mind that other people act to protect their houses as well or might even hide to ambush you. Whenever I was not sure if other people were around, I waited for 10 to 20 minutes to try to see any signs of movement.

Get used to crawling and hiding in dirty and unpleasant places. This is not pleasant but much better than being spotted if you don't want to be seen.

Your Neighborhood

There will be a big difference in your neighbors before and after SHTF. You have to accept that everyone except your family (or your group) could be your enemy. It does not really matter if you had a group of neighbors that used to get together and have a good time before SHTF. Once people are fighting for their survival, only the closest friends and family start to matter. Do not be that person who believes in the good nature of people for way too long.

Expect the worst.

Think of their situation in this way. Your neighbor's kids or wife is about to die. They are suffering. You, the neighbor, seem to have some food and some medication, but you told them you could not share your resources with them because that would put your own family in jeopardy.

So this guy sits there, and in front of him, the people he loves are dying… what do you think he will do? What would you do? Most of us would do whatever it takes to save our loved ones. So the nice neighbor might still be a nice guy, but life did not leave him many choices.

Do not get us wrong. It is good to help, and why not have a bit extra to give away to people you know and think you can trust. Just make sure that it appears you give them all you have, and they think it is a big sacrifice, even though you may still have a lot of more of what they need.

SELCO ON RECOGNIZING THE NEW REALITY

The perfect example is a story of a man who died simply because he gives his weapon to the police officers after the SHTF. Actually, police officers simply were people in uniform and weapon, no authority.

A lot of people died like that or ended up being robbed because they trusted in old symbols. The lesson here is once

SHTF trusts nobody and give out as little information as possible.

Defining Neighbors as Possible Allies or Threats

It is impossible to know what kind of people your neighbors will become once they are desperate. What you can do now is pay attention to how they act so you at least have a good shot at guessing how dangerous they might become.

How aware are they about the state of the world?

Is he a complete sheep, not looking left or right, and living his life as part of the system he relies on? Or is there some sort of awareness about the fact that we might face some very different and difficult times soon?

If he might be open to the idea of prepping or he might even be a prepper, try to talk to him in an indirect way. For example, mention one of the prepper TV shows and say how crazy those people are. Pay attention to his response.

Mention a recent disaster and how things could have been different if people would have been prepared and again, pay attention to his response. Your neighbor might be a prepper just keeping it a secret as every smart prepper should. Go slowly and check his attitude before you consider talking with him about forming a group once things turn ugly.

How dangerous could they be?

This is more than simply asking yourself, "are they armed?" You should also ask yourself: What are his views on life? Is he religious? Does he have strong family bonds? What kind of job does he have? Is he going along with the mainstream opinion? Does he hold his own views of what is right and wrong? Etc.

Hunter or Prey?

Once you have thought about how dangerous your neighbors might be, it makes sense to try to figure out if they will be either hunters or prey once SHTF.

Someone who has been helping others all the time most likely will try to continue doing so as long as he feels he can. Someone who is always about themselves is greedy, puts themselves first at all times, and feels entitled to things that will feel more desperate more quickly than someone who is happily living a modest life.

While there will be a few people who will enjoy the freedom of being able to do what they want to do, without any authority stopping them, most dangerous people you will come across are desperate. Make sure you think about who will be desperate first and if they have the means to become dangerous.

The bad news is that in today's society, people are as lazy as they can be, so they try to rely on the system as much as they can, which results in a lot of helpless people that become desperate quickly.

Create a "Trust Ranking" List of Your Neighbors

You might think this is too much or too extreme, but it makes sense to keep things organized and put them in writing. Over time you might forget the bad things a neighbor did and once SHTF feels good about him because he has been nice the last couple of months. You can use code words for the list or simply assign a 1–10 rating to your different neighbors. A higher number could indicate a higher threat, and a number below five could indicate they are most likely prey and vulnerable when things get ugly.

For example, if you have a neighbor who is a bank clerk, with a wife and three kids, drives a car with a bumper sticker that says "Ban Firearms," is a slave to TV and the mainstream media, most probably he will not be the most dangerous guy in your neighborhood. He might be desperate early on, but he does not have the means (weapons and being used to being violent) to be a major threat.

- You never know, but someone who was a sheep all his life rarely becomes a wolf overnight. Most likely, he will be dead very soon when SHTF.
- If you have a neighbor who is active in outdoor sports and is a hunter that goes camping with his kids, etc., we suggest you try to get to know him.
- That lazy guy who collects guns because it makes him feel powerful is selfish and always complains that he deserves better, might be one of the most dangerous people in your

neighborhood (besides criminals).

Keep in mind these are just examples. In war, there were tough guys crying like babies once real bullets were flying, and people who you would have never expected it from were fighting like vicious animals.

Do This Today

Assessing the risks of people in your neighborhood might seem like a low priority task, but it is not. Once you have done this, you will change your awareness of people and pay more attention to how they act. This information can become essential when you have to deal with these people once SHTF.

It is true that shooting a new weapon might be more fun, that so-called "survival experts" rarely suggest you sit down and make lists, and you never see Bear Grylls writing a list for half an hour on his survival entertainment show.

We are not giving you the "survival is fun. Let's go out and have a bbq and do some target practice treatment." We want you to understand that this part of sitting down and doing proper assessments is as important or, in some cases, maybe even more important than the fun action part of practicing skills.

Summary

Making the right decisions is the first part of survival; executing them comes after that. Even if you are older or have to deal with some physical restrictions, nothing stops you from being the man with the crucial intelligence to make the best decisions possible.

SELCO ON FINDING THINGS IN THE NEIGHBORHOOD

It is kind of about degrees. It is about what kind of things you are willing to accept, or how deep you want to go with things. Are you willing to kill in order to obtain food, or will you run and starve for days? Are you willing to steal things, or you want to stay man like you been prior to SHTF?

Of course, there was some kind of mental barrier when I wanted to go to other folks' deserted houses and look for useful things. But as the situation deteriorated more and more, I learned to do much worse things than taking things from ruins.

Also, it was about degrees, too, when it comes to the nature of useful things. First, it was food or weapon. We looked for places that we know ex-occupants were hunters or similar for extra ammo. Then after some time, it was about all kind of junk that was useful for anything. After some time, I learned what kind of wooden floor gives what kind of fire. If it is freshly polished, it gonna burned great but too fast, etc.

If you put a man in a hard situation for a prolonged time, you can be sure that he gonna do a lot of things.

If you are in a city during SHTF, you can be sure that sooner or later, there will be abandoned houses. You have to decide when it is the best time to take advantage of the resources around you.

If you run out to collect all flat-screen TVs in your neighborhood as soon as some people leave their homes, you will most likely have a different motivation than when you go out to look for some medication because your kid is sick.

Keep in mind you live in a different world, and your moral and ethical guidelines need to quickly adjust to the new circumstances.

Our Way to Think About Resources

This is just what we think about this topic. Keep in mind everyone's situation will be different depending on what kind of survival scenario or collapse happens to you and your area.

We do not encourage you to loot, but if you need some things to survive, and you have to take them to save your life, it makes sense to be clear about your priorities. Don't loot unless you have to, and when that's the case, it is always a personal decision.

Having said that, everything around you can be a resource. If you have abandoned houses in your neighborhood, they are resources.

When you experience total collapse, some people might call taking things from others stealing. We call it survival.

By the time most people will have adjusted themselves to the new reality, most houses will have little valuable items left, and often all helpful items that could aid you in your fight for survival are gone as well.

If you head outlook for anything useful (and forget about taking things you always wanted, like that big TV). Depending on the nature of your SHTF, you will probably look for different things, but some things like food, medicine, weapons, and ammunition are always useful.

Now knowing more about your neighbors becomes very valuable. It saves you time when you search for something particular and also helps you to set priorities about where to go first. We recommend you look for: weapons and ammo, food, tools, tarps (nylon sheets, picnic tarps, etc.), stuff for packaging (bags, plastic boxes, containers, bottles), all medicinal related things, ropes, and wooden or steel items for reinforcing doors and windows (steel plates, bars, plywood, etc.).

Do not be an idiot and take TVs, stereos, and other "valuable" things. Once SHTF, that TV or sound system is worth less than an old hood taken from a burned car in order to reinforce your door. Take what you really need and not what you would like to have in case life gets back to normal.

SELCO ON HIDING USEFUL STUFF

There's gonna be probably a lot of ruined and deserted places around you. Of course, choose places that are not gonna be attractive for others.

For example, burned or destroyed houses, burned cars, sewer openings... People used to bury interesting stuff under some rubble or ground on places where they find some dead animal, simply because the stench was repulsive.

For this purpose, also is good some signs independence of your situation (mines, chemical spill, UXO, and similar) but always keep in mind that it is better to make it hidden then to make it hard (dangerous) to get.

You need to have a few secret places in your neighborhood to hide useful things that you cannot take right away, are too big to carry alone, or that you want to keep for another time. These secret hiding places can also be used as temporary shelters if you have to leave your home in a hurry for whatever reason.

Value of Goods as Time Goes By

Different types of goods will have different values as time goes by. For example, one lighter does not have the same value on the seventh day after the SHTF compared to the seventh month. If you want to survive, you need to use common sense in determining what is worth having right now and what is going to be worth having in the coming weeks.

SELCO ON LOOTING

A lot of people were running on the street in the direction of the mall. I run with them too. I believe that the great majority of us did not have a clue why we are running at all and were but the sense of going somewhere to get something felt in the air. Later I found out that word came that the mall is getting looted, and we all want something from that, of course.

Sporadic gunfire was heard, and few explosions. When we get to the mall, we find some 150 or 200 people already in the mall and outside, dragging all kinds of stuff.

Some of them dragged technical stuff like TVs, stereos, and similar valuable stuff. Others kinda get lost in a whole that situation and tried to loot things that do not make too much sense. So you could see people carrying carpets, big lamps, etc.

I did not see at that moment that anyone was carrying food, like bags of wheat, or big bags full of cans—nothing like that. The reason is simple because it was the beginning of SHTF, and people still lived in „old-time values, " so it makes much sense to take the box of VCRs then the box of canned food.

The situation completely changed very soon. A few weeks later, people were plugging holes in the wall with VCRs, and with one can of meat, you could sometimes get a woman. If I knew at that moment what is gonna be and how bad it is gonna be, I would solve many of my problems with a few boxes of cans. But I did not know, so I took what I have the interest at that moment. I took a home computer; that kind was still a new thing at that time. Pretty soon, I even forget where I put it in my home. It becomes more than worthless.

Forget about old times and old rules.

First, you need to recognize the moment when SHTF and there is no more law.

Hopefully, by this time, you are ready to bug out, or even better, you saw the situation coming, predicted what was going to happen, and are chopping some wood at your BOL while listening to some HAM radio operators relaying events as the situation deteriorates.

If you have to stay in the city and everyone heads to the abandoned electronics store to get what they want, you should head to the abandoned hardware store and get what you need. Pharmacies are also places of high interest.

Just be aware that you will have to deal with plenty of junkies trying to get their hands on medication for their own needs and profit. Malls, stores, gas stations, and similar "places with stuff" will be looted very soon and in very efficient ways.

As time goes on, priorities will change, and more people will become aware of what they really need to survive. Things that people never considered valuable will become valuable. One example is steel covers for the sewers on the street.

They are very useful for reinforcing doors or windows or any other openings at your house. If you go near a gas station and find out that the gas has already been taken and the store has been looted, you can still take the steel shelves apart and use them to reinforce your home.

You can also be sure that people will go for cigarettes and alcohol first and might forget to take lighters. All those items are valuable once SHTF, but if you really know what makes sense to have and does not, you can take advantage of opportunities once they arise.

When to go out and scavenge for resources?

If you compete with others for resources, it is important to be one step ahead of them. It is simple: when SHTF, all resources that people really need are going to be very valuable, it is just a matter of when people realize what they need.

Here is some food for thought:

While others are getting all the TVs, computers, and kitchen appliances, you are getting the tools, tarps, sleeping bags, and other supplies you need.

When the malls are empty, and people realize their electronics are worthless, they will go out and try to find what you got in the first stage. At that point in time, you are already gathering fuel to burn for the coming cold months.

Once people realize they can't find sleeping bags, they look for fuel to burn to keep them warm. At that stage, you already got all the easy-to-get fuel in your area and are starting to make windows and door frames apart to use them as fuel (because you already have the right tools that make the job easier).

People will get smarter about what they need, but you will be surprised how stupid the majority of people are when it comes to what they really need in the first weeks after SHTF. It is no surprise. Most people are under extreme stress in a situation they never expected.

They have almost no time to get creative and think outside of the box, how to get things, what things to get, and where. Use your time now to think about it. It will help you a lot later on.

Trading

Trading is a big topic in survival forums, and while many speak about it, many myths and unrealistic ideas exist. Trading in good times is very different from trading in bad times.

Are people nice?

No, most people are not nice and friendly when SHTF. Even today, in normal times, people are "nice" because they are not starving and are not living with the constant threat of dying on their minds. Desperate people do desperate things, and when you realize how bad people react to everyday stress, imagine how bad it will be when they are fighting for survival.

Expect fraud, robbery, and all sorts of cons to get more of the scarce resources that are left. Hopefully, you will not have to depend

88 | Chapter 2: Urban Survival

on trading all that much because you will be prepared and have your own resources. Nevertheless, sometimes you might have to trade. Here are some basic things to keep in mind.

Basic Rules

When to trade?

Trading when you need something is not smart in a post-collapse world. Depending on where you live, heading out to find people to trade with can be dangerous.

In the first weeks after SHTF, the trade will be unregulated, and it will take some time before trade hubs are established, so you are dependent on what goods are available at that moment. Don't expect to go out and get what you need right away. Even at trade hubs, the variety of goods will change day today.

Having a steady supply of what we need is just a concept that we have gotten used to in the last 100 years. Smart traders think ahead. They get warm clothes in summer and medicine before they really need it. If someone knows you need antibiotics or your wife will die, they will make you pay dearly for it.

Value of Things and the Business of Trading

There is nothing wrong with getting something out of trading once SHTF. You have prepared and, hopefully, also prepared for trading, so it is absolutely fine to get the most out of it. If you trade smart, you increase your chances of survival and make your life easier.

Here are some examples:

Candles: Candles are very cheap in normal times, and it is pretty easy to store them. When SHTF candles are very good items to trade, but the most important lesson I learned was that they were more valuable in the first months after SHTF and less valuable later. The main reason for this was that people wanted to have light after they lost electricity.

Later they got used to living without light and realized it was not that important. People also learned how to make oil lamps and how to use them. We recommend you get candles, but be aware that you should trade them early if you store them for trading.

Antibiotics (and all other medical items): Contrary to candles, medicine becomes more valuable over time. Antibiotics, for example, were expensive all the time, but there is still a difference between expensive and very expensive.

One of the main reasons was that people did not realize how easily they can die from common problems because they were so used to having medical services and supplies around.

Once you see a loved one die from a scratch that got badly infected, you think differently about the value of medicine. In my case, antibiotics became almost like magical items that could and did make the difference between life and death.

Alcohol: People drink a lot, even folks who never drank before started to drink to simply escape from reality for a little bit and feel better.

It started to gain value after the first couple of weeks and later started to go down in value because people started to make their own alcohol. I was very aware of the alcohol prices because we "found" some larger amounts of alcohol in the days after the collapse.

Natural Remedies and "Mystic" Cures: The situation got worse and worse, and people got sicker as diseases were spreading, and people got weaker. At the same time, medical supplies and drugs became rarer.

At that point, herbal and natural remedies became more valuable. I am not talking about teas only, also all kinds of mixtures (cream for back pain, paste for wound cleaning, etc.). It stayed like that until the end of SHTF.

Skills: These days a lawyer is usually richer and more important than a welder or a person who works in a profession that demands physical labor. But just a few weeks after SHTF, people who had practical skills became more "important" and were in high demand and were able to barter with their services.

Some items had a stable value all the time. Items like coffee and cigarettes were expensive all the time, and cigarettes became something like a currency that almost everyone accepted.

Keep in mind that all these examples may only make sense in the region I was in and at the time, in the early 90s, when we were at war.

Think about what items are used often and in daily rituals where you live. People will want them even more once SHTF because it is that little bit of normalcy, that little bit of normal life that becomes a very beautiful and important experience.

Where I lived, many people smoked, and we always drank strong coffee when we meet. That's why those two things became good items for trading and were almost universally accepted.

Small Things, Small "Money," Small Steps

With every trade you do, you are actually going against the low profile policy. This means that you are getting attention because you are someone who has things to trade. So, to make robbing or killing you not worth the hassle, trade in small amounts. It is also better to trade smaller, less valuable things with different people than a few bigger, more valuable things with few people.

Also, keep in mind that most likely, you will have to carry what you trade. Generators, for example, are not only loud and too noisy for an urban environment but are also hard to transport.

Lighters are easy to store, easy to carry, and they will always be in demand, but you do not necessarily need lighters. Cigarettes, batteries, candles, and pocket FM radios are all things that will have some value and are easy to carry. You can always have 2-3 lighters in your pocket without raising any suspicion, and they will definitely not influence your movement or speed.

SELCO ON TRADING

One of the first trading's of my relative was about our need for wheat. He searches for the guy who (based on rumors) had enough wheat for trade. After he found him, they make an agreement to meet the next day on the place that another dude said was safe and secure. My relative brought some ammo, and other guys bring a bag of wheat, some 8 kg. My relative checked wheat. It looked OK.

Another dude was nervous because he "seen some guys looking suspicious, and maybe they followed him." At that moment, it makes sense to finish everything in a very quick way, because if someone following them, it may be dangerous because of the goods that they had with them.

So they finish the trade in a hurry, and my relative goes home in a hurry. He did not see any guys that other men mentioned, and nobody follows him home. When he came home, and when they want to make something from that wheat, they realized it looks funny.

It was not wheat at all; it was some mixture used in plastering walls or similar. Other guys cross my relative. And of course, he did not do trade in his home or even street.

Safe and Secure Trading

Never trade at your home or BOL

Can you imagine how a drug lord feels when he sees someone accidentally finding where his drug is grown or where his manufacturing operation is located? He feels threatened and most likely will try to make sure that person is not going anywhere to tell authorities what he found.

When SHTF, you might find yourself in a very similar situation. It makes sense to keep your home a secret from all the people that you trade with. Any trade can be just a scouting mission for a group of attackers. Try to pick a few places that you know well when you want to trade, so you know where potential threats could come from and how to escape.

Never Trade Alone

Never be alone when you trade. Going anywhere alone during SHTF is riskier, and this applies to trade as well. Send one person to scout the location and then have them fall back and hide nearby, observing the trade in case of any trouble.

If you want to raise your profile as a go-to guy for trading things or do not want it to be obvious that you are the source of all the goods, you can play the middleman and bring your friend, who plays the real trader, to the deal. This might even give you the chance to get an extra cut out of the deal.

Types of Traders

Of course, you will meet all sorts of traders, but there are some typical types of traders you will come across.

Some general types are:

The Desperate Trader

This is the worst kind of trader to be, but sometimes the best trader to meet. This is the guy who goes out and looks for something because he is desperate. His family may be starving, and this trade is his last chance to save them. That means that you can dictate price and all other terms of the trade. I know you think you will want to help him and not charge him as much as you could get from him. This is a good attitude, and I hope you keep it. Keep in mind that depending on how much SHTF affects you, when you meet this kind of desperate trader, you might have already changed your attitude and want to take what you can. But also keep in mind that his desperation means he has nothing to lose. Instead of not trading, he might simply turn violent because he knows this is his last chance. When SHTF, most of the traders will come from this group.

Trader Crook

This type of trader knows all the small and big scams and is someone who wants to make "money." He will mix grass with tobacco, water with milk, and coffee with barley to try to get as much as he can out of the trade. It is not much you can do about this. Try to check what you get, but that is common sense, and keep in mind that if something seems too good, it is probably a trap.

The "Real" Trader

This is the kind of trader you should be. This is someone who thinks about trading strategically and in advance. This trader also practices trading to have some experience with low threat traders, people they can most likely trust more than random people they do not know. This kind of trader keeps a cool head and calculates the risk, and does not get carried away by greed.

Pricing and Bargaining

If you have something like a flea market or garage sale in your town in the coming weeks, it is a good place to go to practice trading and bartering.

If you want to buy something there, bargaining is common. Here are some simple rules to help you get started, but everyone develops their own style over time. See what works best for you and work on your own techniques.

Summary

Never have more money in your hands than you are willing to spend.

If the price of something is $10, and you want to pay $6 for it, then it is stupid to have a $20 bill in your hand when bargaining. It makes much more sense to have exactly $6 in your hand and to say, "OK, all that I have is $6."

This is also a lesson you should never forget when trading after SHTF. Prepare for trading. Make sure you only pull one item out of your pocket if you want to sell one item or trade with it.

How to Look and Act

Look and act confident, and like you know what you want. Depending on how far you want to go, you might want to convince people that what they have (and what you want) will not be worth much in the coming weeks, and it is better to trade now.

Some people also offer obviously weak people a bad trade or threaten to simply take what they want without paying anything if they do not accept the bad trade. Never show weakness or what kind of bad/desperate situation you are in when it comes to trading.

If everything fails and the other party simply demands too much, you can try to get on their sentimental side by telling them your story and hoping they feel compassion for you. In the worst-case scenario, you have an opportunity to strike when they don't expect a crying, broken man to strike.

Dangers

The flexibility of thinking and acting is one of the most important survival skills you can develop. Understanding when priorities have changed, when it is time to take action, and when not to can have a much bigger impact on your chances of survival than the best gear you can buy.

Not all stages of a collapse like I experienced are the same.

Understanding the different stages can help you to better judge what you should do. All stages can last different amounts of time, and sometimes you only experience the first stage. For example, after some dodgy election or controversial sports event, everything may be over after 2-3 days.

The most important thing is to understand the transition between regular rioting and looting and a full-blown collapse. That's why the second stage matters, as this could be your last chance to bug out in relative safety.

The Starting Stage

When SHTF, you will first experience a stage of chaos and confusion. People are out on the streets, rioting, and maybe the first looting starts.

It is a wild, chaotic, and violent period of time, and if you decide you need to go out and look for more resources, this is the best time to do it. If you are well prepared, the best idea is, of course, to simply stay at home or bug out but not get involved in the mess on the streets.

Law enforcement will still work to a certain degree, but more and more bad things like murder and robberies will start to happen, and because of this, the next stage arises.

The "Calm" Stage

This is not a really "calm" stage because things get worse, and the streets are still dangerous and not peaceful, but in this stage, people realize things are not going to get better. They hear about the murders and robberies on the streets, and most people will try to stay at home and decide what to do.

Law enforcement may have stopped taking care of things at this point. If you missed your chance to bug out before SHTF, then this is your best bet to still get out of the city. Gangs and those who will later control parts of the city are not yet organized as they will be in the days and weeks that follow.

"This is a New World" Stage

Clearly, this stage is the longest lasting one, and you should prepare for it the most. It starts from the moment when even the most simple-minded people realize that the old "civilized" world is gone and there is no system in place that tells people what is right and wrong, and rules can be broken without any punishment.

There are many dangers in this stage, and you have to come to terms with the fact that nothing but your own actions will protect you from getting hurt or killed.

Dealing with Trouble

Most of us don't enjoy being violent or hurting other people. In our current society, we learn to negotiate, compromise, and find solutions that benefit everyone. In a post-collapse world, you have to forget this way of thinking.

You have to accept that the reality of survival is unfair. Good people might die first, and people who absolutely do not deserve bad things to happen to them may experience the worst. Don't fight all this; just accept it because fairness is a concept that we humans just made up and want to believe in.

Once all rules are gone, there are three steps for how to deal with trouble:

1. Avoid trouble
2. Avoid trouble
3. Deal with trouble in a quick and efficient way

You prepare and learn about survival to avoid danger, not to embrace it. Every time you engage in violence, there is a chance you might get killed or hurt.

Avoid trouble as much as you can, but when you cannot, act brutal and follow through to make sure any trouble won't come back to you again. There is no place for mercy in a post-collapse world.

SELCO ON FINISHING THE JOB

It is a world where any kind of hesitating will be very bad for you. I am not saying here that you need to act like a mad dog, but there's gonna be a time when you gonna need to act very fast and almost without thinking.

For example, in urban combat, in a situation where you need to clear some building, you just need to adopt that your reflex will do the job and you gonna think later. You need to think is they are a sense of going into that building and starting close combat in order to achieve something.

But once when you inside, you need to act fast and efficiently. It is a rough example, but you get the point. There were people who could not do it, but those people either die or stay home when jobs like that need to be done.

Gangs

Gangs exist today, and they will be much more powerful once all rules are gone. Expect gangs to be the first organized group after SHTF. Many weaker people will join gangs because many people look for leaders in times of uncertainty. In my experience, it was also not uncommon that single mothers offered themselves as "companions" for the gang entertainment to give their kids a better chance to survive.

Do not think how you can defeat the gangs in your area unless you have a large group (your own gang) and want to control the area. You will most likely cooperate with gangs from time to time because guys like them will own the black market and extra resources.

Try to keep any contact or deals to a minimum. Gangs quickly realize that they rule the new world and operate from a place of power, so even if things worked out the first few times when trading with them, there is no guarantee it will keep working out.

If you happen to find yourself with a mob or unorganized group of people that could loosely be described as a gang, try to blend in and act as they act. Be angry when they are, loot when they loot, and try to get away from them whenever you can.

"Common" People

This could be your neighbor or someone you got to know in your neighborhood. There is not much to be said about common people except do not trust anyone. In a post-collapse world where people fight for survival, trust has to be earned step by step, and even then, everyone will think of their own family first.

"Mad Max" Guys

If you read survival forums and blogs, you might start thinking that those Mad Max, lone wolf hardcore survivalists will be all around us once SHTF.

In reality, most of them will be dead a few days after SHTF because a real collapse is nothing like a collapse in Hollywood movies. Those who survive the first days and weeks are probably smart enough to understand that they have to adjust their idea of what matters for survival.

They might look impressive and have great gear and maybe even skills and ask if they can join your group because they realize they will have a hard time surviving on their own. Do not fall for this. Before SHTF, they planned to survive on their own, which shows they aren't aware of what really matters. Even though their gear and expertise might seem like good contributions to your group, that they planned to do things alone is a clear sign, they are bad team players.

The harmony of your group and having people that are willing to sacrifice for the good of the group are more important than someone with great gear and amazing shooting skills.

Group Building

For a sense of order, to prevent panic, and to begin work on a new and organized society, it is important for a leader to begin by working with the group to organize the community.

SELCO ON HIS GROUP STRUCTURE

In the beginning, it was formed in a way that we did not have something like voting who is leader, it was more like most "stronger" guy step out, and we agree with it.

That my relative had something like most "real-life experience," a lot of us had some other skills and knowledge that he did not have, like medical skills and similar, but none of us had his "organizational" skills. In short, he was a good manager, a booth with easy and hard decisions.

Work was distributed based on our knowledge and skills. It was not a democracy. We could discuss everything, but he would be made a decision at the end.

The Leader

For some, leadership comes naturally – for others, it does not. A leader has to make tough decisions and has to have a bond with the rest of the group–but also has to be willing to send members of the group off to do things where they may be hurt or killed.

The leader has to be well-respected and powerful in order to prevent anarchy.

To organize the community, the leader must:

- Establish a working micro-democracy, with a clear structure that everyone can understand ? Provide a framework of rules and laws, and punishments for those who disobey them. The rules must be strictly enforced from the beginning–if people are allowed to do whatever they want without consequences, then both the leader and the rest of the group becomes untrustworthy. Rules and clear procedures that are followed when someone breaks the rules are at the heart of well-functioning survival experience. ? Set up routines. Besides creating order, rules also help the group by establishing routines. Routines not only help to get things done, but they also keep people busy, and this helps to prevent worry within the group. If people worry too much or are under too much stress, then their self-control is impaired, and both anti-social tendencies and conflicts within the group increase.
- Use any access to influential and well-respected community leaders to their advantage, and use them to help establish new laws and a sense of order. Network with other leaders and present the group as an organized team that knows what it wants. ? Be willing to, and have the power to, enforce sanctions if one of the groups ignores the rules.
- Keep the group informed about long-term goals and how they will be achieved. ? The leader also has to make sure that every member of the group understands that immediate gratification isn't going to happen in most survival scenarios and that getting to that long-term goal may mean discomfort and suffering, while at the same time assuring the group that it is all for the greater good and future survival of the group.

The Group

Many people can be valuable assets once SHTF. Most likely, you will be with a smaller group of people who can hopefully do a variety of things.

Valuable group member professions:
- Nurse, doctor, paramedic, dentist, veterinarian, medical professional
- Soldier, sniper, explosives expert, communications expert

- Mechanic, carpenter, plumber, seamstress, leatherworker, blacksmith
- Farmer, butcher, herbalist, hunter, fisherman, wilderness survival expert

SELCO ABOUT HOW A DENTIST PROFITTED FROM HIS KNOWLEDGE

He was a dentist in the health center before SHTF, and he also did some private jobs. When SHTF in the beginning, he did not try to work, but later, when things deteriorated, he (like everybody else) offer his skills for whatever useful he could take.

It was nothing like real dentist ordination. He had the knowledge and some medical tools. Mostly he would take food, but actually, he would take whatever for his skills.

As time goes on and the situation deteriorated more, every skill was useful. Some were valuable more than other, but as the things get "worn out" and destroyed, people tried to fix it or make new, so how something looks become not important, important was how it works (Jay, trying to say that often those things that people made looked ridiculous, but if they worked it was fine, for example, I remember some handmade mills for wheat that looked like from stone age, but nobody care as long as they worked.)

Forming a Survival Group

For long term survival scenarios, good group size is 150 people. Research shows that groups bigger than that tend to split into two.

In the military, there is one leader for every 150 troops. This number is not only manageable, but it is a good amount of people for a group because, with more than this, it is difficult to maintain social connections—members of the group must bond in order to endure and overcome hardship.

The group of 150 should be further divided into three to six smaller groups of 25-50 people (platoons), and these groups can be divided into even smaller groups with three to ten people (squads), if necessary.

Most likely, you will find yourself in a smaller group of 3 to 20 people.

In a group consisting of people with diverse racial and social backgrounds, or made up of several families, tasks should be planned out that use a mixture of diverse people and families, so an "us vs. them" scenario doesn't develop, and so that bonds can form. From these bonds, trust develops, and so does an ability to solve problems effectively, as a group. A tight-knit group is a key element for long-term survival.

It is important that whatever group is formed, a leader is always assigned. A leader must ensure peace within the group, or there is a chance that people will take violent steps in order to protect their self-interests.

If you have other coordinated groups in the neighborhood that seem to be trustworthy, try to establish alliances to deepen mutual trust. This will not only prevent violence, but it will make the group stronger in case you have to face an outside force.

Honor and Mutual Respect

Systems for problem-solving must be devised that prevent discord within the group.

An example of a system that works is one that uses the principle of honor, often a system found in tribal societies. In these societies, male honor and noble conduct were idealized and became a guiding principle for every member of the group.

Those who acted with honor and nobility were granted more respect and a higher social status. Those that didn't obey rules and the code of honor punished themselves by feeling shame and were ostracized from the group.

The set of values that is considered "honorable" should be high—honor is pointless if it is easy to obtain. Although living by this code may be tough, those in the group should be inspired to strive for honor—otherwise, people become complacent and even lazy.

The group of warriors who have acted honorable becomes a more or less exclusive group. The few people who are in this group should be idealized, so that new (or young) members in the group have someone to model their behavior after. This also applies to any other profession, of course, and not just people who fight.

Mutual respect is at the heart of a code of honor. Even enemies and people you disagree with should get a certain amount of respect—disrespect of any kind is shameful. This also means that in the interest of honor, atrocious acts can be avoided.

When a strict code of honor is enforced, it has many benefits. A code of honor in the group creates a peaceful and organized culture, one that will help the leader recruit valuable new members to the group and deal effectively with enemies.

A code of honor may also help the group to function even if it has a controversial leader, as group members want to be seen as a noble warrior with strict adherence to the honor code.

SELCO ON WHY HIS GROUP SUCCESSFULLY WORKED TOGETHER

There are a few reasons why my group worked. First, and I think the most important is the thing that we were closely related, we were family, or we were of the same blood. So that fact makes us more compact, and that is very important.

Another thing may be that we had enough "people with force"- that means enough people capable of giving a good fight. Also, we had other folks with other knowledge (traditional knowledge, like edible plants, tea, etc.).

Also other things like facts that we had weapons on time, good position of the house and in the street.

> So group members knew and trusted each other, had diverse skills, important tools (weapons in our case) on time, and our house was in good to defend the location.

Building Your Team

In the best-case scenario, you build the group you plan to be within the case of collapse before it happens. When you look for people that fit into your group, look for those who have offered you help or assistance in the past without conditions attached.

You want to be with people who understand that the greater good of the group comes first and who are willing to make sacrifices if it helps the group.

Pay attention to people around you and how selfish they are. Selfish people will not change overnight once you find yourself in a survival situation. In the worst-case, their feelings of entitlement cause not only disharmony but even a group to break apart.

SELCOS ADVICE ON HOW TO FIND OTHER PREPPERS

> In short, you need to find other preppers but at the same time keeping for the secret fact that you are a prepper too. It may sound stupid now, but revealing to another man the fact that you are a prepper needs to be the last thing in the whole process of finding another prepper. And to make it more complicated than another perfect prepper (probably) will keep his prepper "status" secret too.
>
> So actually, it is like a game of finding the people that have the same goals as you, and those goals may be secret.
>
> There is no sense of going to a local hunting club (or gym, shooting range...) and saying," I am a prepper, and I am looking for more preppers."
>
> By sharing the common interests (hiking, for example) or views, you need to find people and over the time, check what

kind of people they are, and are they "deserving" to be in your group, with you when SHTF, remember that you are probably gonna need to trust that people with your life, because that process of finding it needs to be slow and careful.

Of course that when SHTF, you may find by luck perfect friend or group of people and join them in a matter of a day, but it is a matter of luck, not planning.

How to Find Preppers in Your Area

Get involved in local clubs and associations related to survival and preparedness. You will not only improve your skills at the shooting range or getting more knowledge of living in nature while hiking and camping, but you will also meet people with similar interests. Get to know people and see how they react when you mention a survival TV show or recent natural disasters. In this context, you can also mention that it probably makes sense to be a bit prepared. If some people agree, they might be good candidates for your survival group.

It is a personal decision if you let people who do not prepare know you do. Just keep in mind they will remember this when they run out of food and come knocking on your door.

But Out Bags (BOBs)

A bug out bag is like life insurance, only that you benefit from it before you die. It is an important piece of the puzzle in the prepper or survivalist scene because with a well-planned bug out bag, your chances to make it through a survival situation can increase dramatically.

A lot of businesses that cater to preppers sell the illusion of buying safety in the form of food items or fancy tools. The weapon industry also tries to come up with new weapon types that are best suited for different situations to make people buy more. Do not fall for all their marketing messages.

At the end of the day, you have to know how to use each piece of equipment to get the most out of it. Unless you get injured or sick, nobody can take the skills you have learned from you. That's why having quality equipment you can rely on when you need it matters and your skills in using them.

Assembling your bug out bag

Keep it simple

Your BOB should help you to get to your bug out location (BOL), nothing more and nothing less. Usually, a bug out bag should simply provide you with all tools and means to get to your bug out location within 72 hours. The most important thing is to stay mobile and move quickly with your BOB. Your BOB is not made for living off the land forever.

Know Your Equipment

Know every item in your BOB, use it, and check it on a regular basis. Keep in mind that if you need it in a real-life situation, it can be a life-threatening situation. You need to be sure that you can use it quickly and in a proper way. You do not want to learn how to use your fire starter for the first time during a cold and wet night while on your way to your BOL.

Shelf System

One BOB simply cannot cover all SHTF scenarios, so for example, in some scenarios, it might make sense to have a gas mask in your BOB. In other scenarios, it could just add extra weight.

It makes sense to have all items for your BOB organized on shelves, so you can quickly and easily assemble the right bag based on what you need. Store smaller items in groups in zip lock bags so you can grab everything you need quickly.

It also makes sense to have several bags ready to take so you can pick the right size depending on how mobile you want to be or what you want to take along. Make sure your shelf system is organized that you can **pack your BOB within 30 seconds or less**, so keep all the essentials close together and then add all extras such as additional medicine or weapons on top of that.

Test different "loadouts," so you already have an idea what kind of configurations you want to take and what fits where best.

SELCO ON HIS BOB SETUP

When you plan to go and bug out with your bug out bag, keep in mind that you actually do not know what situation will be at the moment you are bugging out. In other words, scenarios could be different than you imagine right now.

Military-style BOB with machete attached and other gadgets attached too, make sense maybe in the total apocalypse, but if you noticed that S. Is going to hit the fan, and you want to bug out during a (still) peaceful day, then some more casual bag makes more sense.

The best option is to have several different types of bags ready (including that military-style) next to your stuff, so you can grab whatever bag you think makes sense—sports bag, hiking rucksack, traveling bag, etc.

Have your stuff packed in a way that you have some items ON you, important items. There is a chance that you are gonna be forced to lose your BOB, so it makes sense to still have something with you after that.

First aid kit, the communication device (cellphone, radio…), some food (power bars, snacks…), water, weapon and some ammo, basic shelter (like a tarp, trash bags or space blanket), and fire kit need to be separated from your BOB and attached to you in some way (pocket, pouches…).

For example, you may have a sleeping bag in your BOB, but you still need to have a tube tent or similar inside your pocket, same with a fire kit and everything else.

Buying Your First Bug Out Bag

You will want to make your **bug out bag as light as possible** to be able to move quickly and even run.

You also have to be able to carry the bag for several hours and even days at a time. Make sure that you pick the right bug out bag for your body and personal fitness level.

Light and casual (to keep a low profile) 30 – 50-liter internal frame backpacks, with padded straps and hip belt are the right choices for most adults.

You want to keep a low profile, and therefore having stuff hanging outside of your backpack should be avoided. It attracts attention, and it might even get tangled up in some bush in a moment when you least want it.

If you do want to have the option to camouflage your bag, consider a camouflage rain cover you can pull over your bag.

Before you buy the backpack, try it. Most outdoor or sports stores can add a bit of weight into the backpacks and let you walk through the store to get a feeling of how the backpack suits you.

Your backpack also needs to stay organized.

Either you get one that is already compartmentalized if you want to keep the bug out bag packed, or you get different colored dry sacks if you stick to the shelf system, which we recommend. Get waterproof dry sacks instead of regular pack sacks and label them with a permanent marker so you can get quickly to what you need.

The red sack is for first aid, a blue sack for small tools, and so on.

Also, make sure you get a rain cover for your backpack. Keep in mind you can also collect all your bug out gear first and then later decide on a backpack.

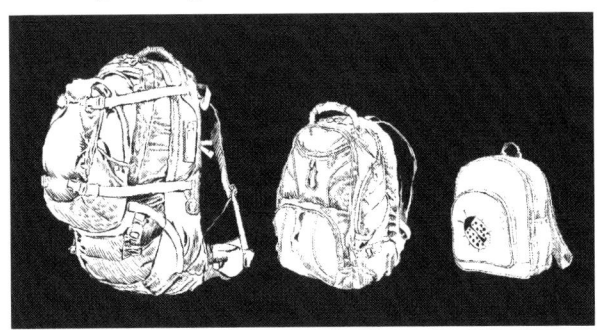

Different Bug Out Bags for Different Family Members

Even if you have a family, you will want to **have all the most essential things in one bag**. After that, other family members can have their own bug out bags with personal items and, if not too heavy, some backup items that you also carry in the main bug out bag.

If you are bugging out or even better, when you do a bugging out practice with your family, and you realize that some family members struggle with the weight of their bags, just let them get rid of less important things.

Mobility is the key to move as a unit.

If you have small children, get an off-road stroller that you can also take off paved roads into more rugged terrain.

A great multi purpose alternative is a rugged bicycle trailer that can later also be used to transport other gear or resources. This is obviously not a very low profile anymore but is often the better solution.

If you can fit everything in your main bug out bag, you could also consider a child carrier for yourself or your partner to carry small children.

If you take care of elderly or disabled family members, make sure you have a more rugged push powered wheelchair. Electric wheelchairs are hard to move without being charged.

BOB FAQs

Where to store your bug out bag?

Your bug out bag has to be in an easy to get to the location, **in the best case, close to the exit of your home**. Make sure you camouflage your bug out bag to evade curious questions from people who don't need to know that you are prepared.

Should I buy a readymade bug out bag?

Most readymade bug out bags come with cheap equipment. A proper bug out bag is also full of equipment that **you enjoy using**, so assembling all equipment yourself is highly recommended.

How much does a bug out bag cost to create?

A good bug out bag costs some money. It makes sense that you **have the equipment you can rely on** in an emergency situation.

Think of it like a mountaineer. Nobody would buy cheap ropes or climbing gear if, literally, your life depends on it.

I have a limited budget, what items should I spend more money on?

You definitely need a reliable knife, not only in your bug out bag but as a tool for a multitude of outdoor and survival-related tasks.

If possible, also invest in an easy to conceal the handgun. It does not have to be fancy. It is a tool and just has to work. Well maintained second-handguns are an option.

If you still have some extra money to invest after planning your budget, invest in a high-quality sleeping bag and bevy bag. That is, of course, after you have the proper clothing and shoes to make it to your bug out location.

Hydration

Carry enough water to sustain yourself for your whole journey to your BOL.

Three liters should be fine unless you have to cross very dry or hot areas. Use multiple containers in case one break. Even if it is just another container, you carry as a backup. Keep in mind you can always stuff some equipment into the empty container to use all space (or, for example, wrap paracord or duct tape around the bottle to take it along). Different containers also have different added benefits.

- Nalgene bottles are durable and not overly expensive. We recommend that you get the 1 liter (32-oz) wide-mouth hard bottles. You can screw them onto many common hand pump filters, and if you get the clear version of the bottle, you can expose the water you have gathered to UV light and kill off some bacteria and viruses in this way.

- Metal bottles or canteens (such as the popular Klean Kanteen) are durable and don't weigh much either. The big benefit is that you can cook water in them. A 1 liter or 32-oz version is a great addition to your bag.

- Collapsible soft bottles weigh almost nothing, and you can carry a lot of extra water whenever needed. We recommend you get the 3 liter or 96-oz Platypus bottle version to be more flexible about how much water you want to carry. They can also be used as camping showers. Again, it makes sense that you get the clear version to be able to kill off some bacteria and viruses by exposing them to the sun.

Water Filtration and Purification

Water is so important for survival, so it makes a lot of sense to have several options to filter and purify your water.

• Water purification tablets are a must-have for every bug out bag. They are rather cheap and take almost no space or add weight to your BOB. Get silver ion/chlorine dioxide tablets because if used properly, they are, unlike iodine or chlorine-based tablets, also effective to eliminate giardia and cryptosporidium. The only disadvantage is that it can take 30 minutes to 4 hours to be effective.

• Straw filters are also a great addition to your BOB. They are lightweight, compact, inexpensive, and get the job done.

• Bottle purifiers are similar to straw filters, only that they come attached to a bottle.

• A portable water microfilter can filter up to 1 liter (32-oz) of water per minute. They are a bit more expensive and take up some space in your BOB but offer a solid choice to quickly filter larger amounts of water (if you bug out with several kids, for example, this might become important). The rubber tube that comes with most of these filters can also be used to get water from hard to reach places or even as an emergency tourniquet.

• Portable electronic disinfection devices such as the Steripen are also good choices to have another option to get clean water. Because they rely on electricity and can break easier than other solutions, **they should only be added as another additional option.**

Carrying food is optional. You can go for a few days without food, without any problems. If you have just limited space in your bug out bag and want to carry some food, simply get some high calorie and carbohydrate-rich energy bars or granola bars, and you are good.

Keep in mind that when you are bugging out, most likely, you will want to be fast and rest little. So do not take food that takes a lot of time to prepare. We even recommend you do not take any food that takes any time to prepare. Open and eat food is the best.

There are MREs (Meals Ready to Eat) or dehydrated camping meals, but they add weight or need time to prepare, so they are not the right choice for a bug out bag.

SELCO ON THE FOOD HE TOOK OUT WHILE SCAVENGING

On my trip out of the town, my main source of eating was tea and soup. I had some cans with meat but not enough. Sometimes those soups were only hot water with some plants inside, sometimes with some meat.

The important thing is that it was a hot meal, and that was very important. Hot soup in that situation probably meant more on a psychological level than anything else. It raised my moral more than the energy level but at the end, that is almost the same.

Today I store a lot of instant soups and energy bars, they can give you a quick meal in the short time when you need it, and you are bugging out.

Cooking

While we do not recommend you to take a food, you need to prepare, having a lightweight metal cup or even a more expensive but lighter titanium cup and means to make a fire and cook with it does make sense. The metal pot can also be used as a container to carry water. You can purify water by cooking it, and the wildest food you can find on your way is best prepared in a pot.

Cooking wild meat or plants in water also offers you the ability to get the most nutrition from them. A lot of the fat or other rich sources of nutrition leak out of the food when you prepare it. **If you consume the water in which you boil your food, you maximize the nutrition you get out of it.**

In the best-case scenario, you will not need to boil or prepare anything with this cup. But carrying a container that you can use for boiling water offers so many benefits for the little weight it adds, it is a must-have.

As mentioned before, if you want to save some weight and space, you can look into getting a metal drinking bottle or canteen that you can also use to boil water and/or food with.

If you plan on cooking or even carrying dehydrated meals to prepare, you can add a "spork" (half spoon, half fork) to make consuming your food more convenient.

As a heat source, we recommend you carry a small solid fuel stove such as the tried and tested esbit stove. They weigh little and can heat up water and food with a hardly noticeable fire.

If you run out of solid fuel tablets, you can also use twigs and other natural fuel with these small stoves. The next best option is a small alcohol stove, such as the Trangia. If space is not an issue in your bug out bag, you could also consider a backpacking gas stove, but the fuel will be rather bulky.

Fire

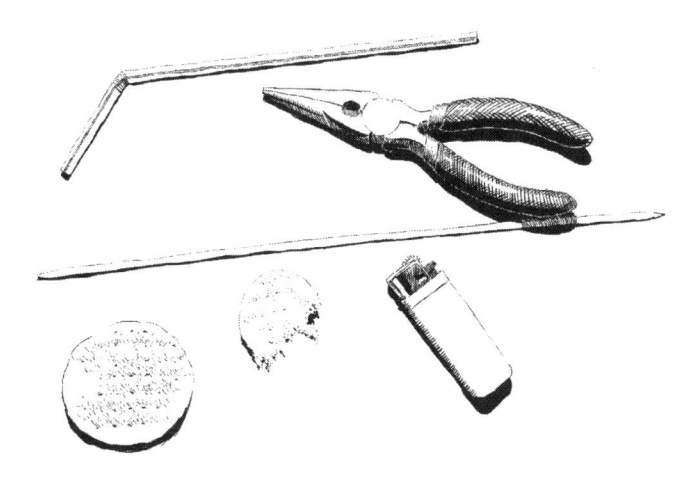

You will want to have at least three ways to start a fire.

We recommend you carry two mini Bic lighter and a small plastic bag or container with some cotton balls soaked in Vaseline or any other petroleum jelly.

You can also stuff the soaked cotton into plastic straws that you seal by heating one end of the straw over a flame and then sealing it once the plastic starts to get soft with some pliers. When you want to use your straw fire starters, simply cut one of the sealed ends of the straw, take some cotton out, and light it.

Most likely, this is all you need. Collect some more fuel for your fire, sort it according to size and build a small tepee with the smallest kindling. Light up one of the cotton balls and put it into the tepee. Add the bigger fuel once your fire gets going.

As additional options to start a fire, we recommend you take a pocket magnifying glass (you can even get a credit card sized magnifying cards) and a magnesium fire starter.

Store all your fire, making tools in a waterproof container or bag.

As with everything we recommend , **try all items** to make sure you know how to start a fire in difficult conditions.

SELCO ON HIS FIRE STARTING KIT

I had a few disposable lighters with me all the time. Actually, they were not disposable because we refill them by lifting the flame opening with a thin steel guard from the same lighter and then refilling it from the bottle. It was pretty valuable to have lighter at that time. Sometimes it was actually two disposable lighters, one to make spark other with enough gas inside, flint was too small to replace it in other lighters. The best solution is the simplest solution always, so disposable lighter makes a lot of sense.

Clothing

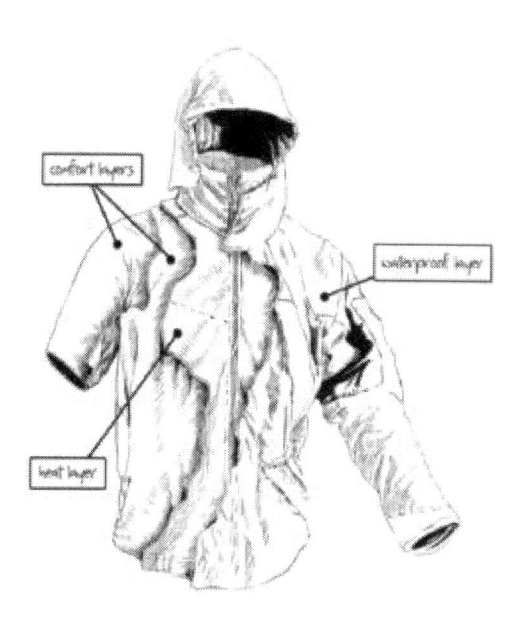

Take clothing that is appropriate for your climate zone. You will want to layer your clothing to get the most versatility for different times of the day and night from the clothing you take along. Get durable clothing in muted colors. You do not want to stick out with camouflage patterns but have colors that are well for hiding, such as olive green or dark navy or grey colors.

First Layer Underwear:

- Take two pair of wool hiking socks. Wool is durable, maintains insulation properties when wet, breathable, wicks moisture away from the skin, and is non-flammable. If you spend a bit more for merino wool socks, you will also benefit from the antibacterial properties of the wool. Just like shoes, do not go cheap on socks. If you walk for days, the wrong socks can hurt your feet as much as the wrong shoes.

- One more change of underwear. Merino wool underwear is great for this too and available in different thicknesses for a variety of climates.
- Carry a moisture-wicking t-shirt or top in hot and temperate climate zones. Sweat is transported quickly away from your body and can evaporate and cool you down. If you live in a cold climate, wool undershirt and long johns are what you want to have.

Second Layer Insulation / Warmth Layer:
- In hot climates, just carry a light long-sleeve shirt that can protect you from sun exposure and insects. In temperate or cold climates, carry a light or heavy fleece jacket. Fleece clothing packs down to a small size and does not weigh much.
- Loose cut outdoor pants. The pants should be rugged and be able to withstand some abuse and dry quickly (forget about jeans, they do not dry quickly!). The loose cut does not restrict your movements in case you have to hide or jump for cover or make any other quick movements.
- A lightweight, crushable Boonie hat for warm and temperate climates or a wool beanie for cold climates. We also recommend you carry a thin balaclava in any climate because they can be used as a scarf and keep your head warm during the night when you sleep (beanies can be too warm for this).

Third Layer Protection Layer:
- A rain jacket with hood or poncho and/or rain pants. Invest in a good rain jacket with a waterproof but breathable membrane such as Gore-Tex, eVent, Sympatex, or Omni-Dry. Look for rain protection that does not have any insulation inside to remain flexible. If the weather is cold, you can wear more insulation layers over each other, or in hot climates,. You just wear your underwear and rain protection.
- Good quality hiking boots. If you wear shoes that are unsuitable for bugging out most of the time, consider keeping good quality hiking boots along with your bug out bag. These ankle-high, waterproof, and durable shoes are some of the most important pieces of equipment you have. You will want to keep your feet

well protected and working. They are your very basic means of transportation, and if you have to fight for your survival, you might not have the luxury to simply relax and not move for a couple of days. Test the shoes and make sure they do not cause blisters when walking all day long.

- Heavy-duty gloves either insulated for cold climates or not. Just like your feet, you want to keep your hands well-protected. Get some gloves that you can wear and still do the most common things while keeping them protected.
- Shemagh or large bandana. You can use it to build water filters, as head and face protection, as a first-aid arm sling, as a pouch to carry twigs or kindling you have collected, or to simply tie things together. It is a great multi-purpose item that does not weigh much and does not take much space to take along.

SELCO ON WHAT KIND OF CLOTHES HE WAS WEARING

I was wearing clothes that I had at that time. I did not have too much choice, so most of the time, I had military-style (but not military) black jacket and work pants and boots. I was paying attention mostly to blend in, to look not interesting. Most of the time, I actually looked very poor like everyone around us.

Today I would choose similarly but more quality stuff, still without looking too „tactical" but actually being tactical.

Clothes in layers, waterproof, with enough pockets and „room" for running and similar footwear that is durable but still allowing fast movement (running, squatting, etc.).

Shelter

You lose body temperature through conduction, convection, evaporation, respiration, and radiation.

Conduction: You do not want to touch cold surfaces and exchange your body heat to the cold of the surface. Some insulating material absorbs your body heat and radiates it back to you. If you plan on lying or sitting down somewhere, make sure you have a proper insulating layer between you and the ground to keep your body heat.

Convection: Stay protected from wind to avoid the body heat that stays close to your body or trapped within the layers of clothing be blown away. Your outer layer or shelter should protect you from the wind.

Evaporation: When you sweat, or water evaporates on your skin, you cool down. To prevent yourself from losing water and energy, you will want to always stop and change to the appropriate amount of layers of clothing you are wearing to avoid sweating. To stay warm, your goal has to be to stay dry at night.

Respiration: You lose a bit of body heat every time you breathe in cold air and breathe out warm air. You can minimize this by wearing a light Balaclava over your face and pre-warm the air.

Radiation: Our body radiates heat, and we use insulating layers to trap this radiation and keep us warm. Down feathers work so well for that because they have so many fine hairs that can trap the heated air very effectively. Your head is a major source of heat loss through radiation so keep it covered whenever you are getting cold. Also, keep in mind that heat rises up when you build your shelter. To preserve this heat, some snow shelters let you sleep elevated and give the colder air a place to sink into.

Shelter Options

The most basic shelter is your clothing. You can cut a cheap sleeping pad just big enough to sit on and simply lean on a tree or rock to rest. You use your clothing to protect you from the environment.

If you look for insulating sleeping pads or mats, you can get versions that are air-filled or made out of foam or combinations of both.

The air-filled versions are very comfortable, pack down to small sizes but are not very durable. The foam pads cannot be packed down to such small sizes but also cannot be pierced and lose their ability to insulate you like air-filled ones. Foam pads also offer the advantage that you can cut them to a size that is suitable for you.

Many lightweight backpackers simply uses a pad for their upper body. Hybrids are also interesting options. They offer the comfort of air-filled mats as long as they work, self-inflate almost completely, and still offer some insulation if the shell is pierced.

A space blanket can be used to help you keep your body heat. There are also emergency bivvys made from space blankets that you can get your full body in just like sleeping bags. But keep in mind, **the material of space blankets is very thin and breaks easily**. They are really just an emergency option as shelter and good for just a few nights.

A sleeping bag and a waterproof liner or bivvy bag is another option for sleeping outside. You can also get more expensive sleeping bags that already have some form of water resistance in the outer layers.

If you live in an area with a temperate or cold climate, you might want to add sleeping in any case. Different sleeping bags come with different temperature ratings. A good year-round rating is a 30-40F degrees (or 5-0C). To carry less and save some space, go for a mummy-style sleeping bag that gets tighter in the leg and foot area.

Use compression sacks to make the sleeping bag as small as possible when carrying in your bag but keep in mind **for long term storage that you want to store your sleeping bag uncompressed** to avoid harming the down feathers or insulation fibers.

Down sleeping bags offer better insulation with less weight and can be compressed more than sleeping bags filled with synthetic fibers, but they lose their ability to keep you warm once they are wet.

Sleeping bags filled with synthetic fibers are cheaper, heavier, need a bit more space but can still keep you a bit warmer when they are wet. We recommend you go for a down sleeping bag stored in a waterproof compression sack if this is within your budget.

The next step up is using a poncho or tarp to create a basic lean-to shelter, ridgeline lean-to or center ridge line shelter. You will want to have an insulating layer you can rest upon. You can use the sleeping pad, space blanket, or use some dry twigs, moss, or leaves to create a layer that insulates you from the cold ground.

Practice setting up tarps and practice sleeping outside with this minimal equipment.

You have to be aware of the direction from where the wind comes and know how close or far you can make a fire to keep your shelter warm throughout the night.

A tarp is a great multipurpose item, does not weigh much and does not take much space to carry. You can use it to catch rain, as a groundsheet to sit or sleep on, as a sling pack to carry things, create makeshift hammocks with it, or even emergency stretchers.

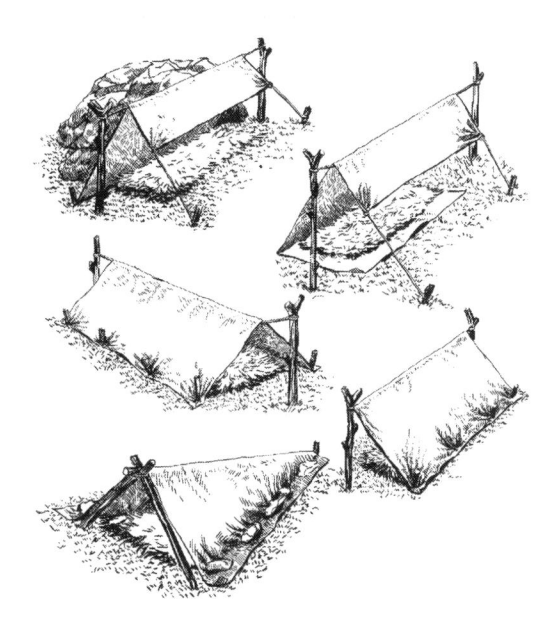

A tarp or open shelter does not prevent insects from getting to you, and during heavy rain, your space might also get flooded. A lightweight tent is another option.

Try to get a tent that is easy to set up, even in low light conditions. Freestanding (most of the dome tents) tents can help you to set up your tent in areas with loose or rocky ground. As with everything, practice setting up your tent under difficult conditions such as during rain, heavy wind, or snow.

Another excellent solution are hammocks if you stay in an area with trees. The big benefits of hammocks are, you do not need a flat ground to create your shelter, you do not leave a footprint of your shelter behind, and they are easy and fast to set up and pack. Depending on the climate, you will still need an insulating layer or quilt for the hammock.

Getting a quality hammock with an insect net and a tarp you can put above it is a great solution for people living in areas with trees. The tarp itself can be used in case there are no suitable trees to set up the hammock.

Summary

Picking a shelter depends on your budget, the level of comfort that is acceptable for you, and space and weight.

Just keep in mind that you want to keep your bug out bag small and lightweight. If you have to decide to either take a sleeping bag or a tent, pick the sleeping bag. We recommend you carry at least a tarp, some paracord (or nylon rope), and a space blanket in your bug out bag and practice setting up a shelter with them.

SELCO ABOUT HEAVY DUTY TRASH BAGS AS SHELTER

You can use heavy-duty trash bags as a tarp, poncho, groundsheet for your shelter, water collection device, floatation device if you fill it with air, and a sleeping bag if you fill it with isolation material such as dried leaves.

Have several of them, and it is important that they really heavy-duty ones. Sometimes you will use a trash bag simply as a primitive raincoat or cover for your backpack. But also it can be a life saver as a membrane between you and wet ground, for example.

Heavy-duty trash bags are for shelters; what Leatherman is for small tools.

Bug out Bag Checklist
Food

- Snacks
- Energy bars
- MREs

Shelter

- Trash bags
- Survival/space blankets
- Poncho type shelters, tarps
- Sleeping bag, bivvy bag

Fire

- Lighters
- Survival matches
- Firestarters
- Fuel tablets

Water

- Canteen or bottle (wrap paracord and/or duct tape around your water bottles as a convenient way to take them along.)

- Water treatment solution
- Hydration reservoir
- Purification devices such as a straw filters or hand filters.

Miscellaneous

- Signal mirror
- Headlamp
- Whistle
- Paracord
- Survival Knife
- Multi-Tool
- Duct Tape
- Spork
- Compass
- Backup batteries for your phone (or battery pack for charging it)
- Small (hand crank) AM/FM radio
- Sewing kit
- Superglue
- Map(s)
- Important documents (or copies of them)
- Kindle tablet charged and loaded with reference books (such as drug information and survival manuals)

Weapons

- Handgun(s)
- Pepper spray
- Ammunition
- Rifle(s) (if being low profile isn't important, another option are collapsible rifles such as the AR-7 or M6)

First Aid

You can start with a store-bought first aid kit and then add more things to it. Here are some things you should have:

- Adhesive bandages in a variety of sizes
- Antiseptic wipes
- Sterile gauze pads and roll bandage
- Medical tape
- Moleskin or other blister patches
- Tweezers (to remove splinters and dirt from wounds)
- Elastic bandage with Velcro closure (for muscle sprains and strains, can also be used to fix splints in case of broken bones)
- Battle dressing
- Sterile gloves
- Sunscreen (if you might be exposed to the sun while bugging out)
- Tourniquet
- Blood stopper (such as quick clot or celox)
- Chest seal (for penetrating trauma wounds of the chest)
- Trauma shears / EMT scissors (to cut clothing)

You can use medical tape and antiseptic wipes and not take adhesive bandages. A high-quality medical tape can be used in a variety of ways, and it lets air get to the wound.

The antiseptic wipes usually dry out within hours of putting them on a wound, and the medical tape can hold them better in place than most adhesive bandages can. Another benefit is that you can create big or small adhesive bandages with this system and also cover areas that are usually hard to get to.

Medicine

- 1-3 month supply of any personal medication (depending on size)
- Antibacterial cream, Iodine drops, Cream to treat burns
- Antihistamine cream

- Antibiotics: Ointment to treat cute and wounds, Amoxicillin, Ampicillin, Ciprofloxacin, Azithromycin, Cephalexin, Doxycycline, Metronidazole. Some of those may be hard to get. Google for fish antibiotics and other antibiotics for animal use. Make sure to educate yourself before taking any medicine without medical supervision.
- Anti-diarrhea medicine such as Imodium is good for short term scenarios, do not use it in long term scenarios. Diarrhea should come out because the body tries to expel some microorganism.
- Pain relief: Ibuprofen, Aspirin, Acetaminophen
- Enhancement drugs: Vyvance
- Wet wipes (great for cleaning yourself on the road)
- Small soap bar
- Hand sanitizer
- Roll of toilet paper (remove the cardboard and put it in a Ziplock bag)
- (Female hygiene products)

Conclusion

A bug out bag is an important part of a survivalist arsenal of preps, and assembling your bug out bag will help you to think through a lot of scenarios that might happen to you.

This guide shows you the main thought processes you should go through while getting your equipment but every personal situation is different, so make sure you tailor your BOB to your needs. A BOB for hot weather might have extra mosquito nets, while a bug out bag for cold weather needs more space for a better sleeping bag.

Make sure you practice bugging out with your bug out bag.

SELCO ON PRACTICING TO BUG OUT

Practicing run with your family is something like finding the perfect balance between speed (being with less equipment) and being very well prepared (dragging a lot of stuff along and being slower).

Lots of preppers keep forgetting one more important thing – common sense or, in other words having stuff that you need to have instead just more weight.

I recommend that you plan for several different scenarios (pandemic outbreak, rioting, chemical attack...) together with having the shelf system and several different empty BOB.

The next thing is that you say: OK, it is chemical attack practice today, so you go and pack your BOB quickly and get to BOL location. You would monitor the speed of the group and items that they pack in BOB.

For example, if they forget to pack disposable gloves and masks and more hand sanitizers (in the pandemic scenario, for example), then you might have a problem

Or in a scenario where you have info, that s. will hit the fan in a day or two, the good point is to take some casual bag and keep the casual look, together with a hidden weapon

The point of the drill is not only to get from point A to B with your bag. The point is to know how you will look, what you will have, and how fast and efficient you will solve problems on your way with what you packed in your BOB (for the scenario that you practice for).

3. Chapter 3: Wilderness Survival

In this chapter, you learn what we deem the most essential survival skills. Regardless of what environment you are, you need water very soon, most likely shelter as well, and if you plan to stay more than just a few days, you need to eat.

For this Chapter, we are happy that **Toby Cowern** joins us.

ABOUT TOBY

To say the outdoors for Toby has been a lifelong passion would be an understatement. Constantly researching, refining, practicing, and sharing skills, Toby is committed to cutting through the myths, misunderstanding, and unfortunately, outright fantasy, so prevalent in today's Survival Marketplace by delivering applied skills that have been thorough 'pressure tested.' Toby has a fusion of teaching background, risk management qualifications, military training, and outdoor experience that allows him to deliver Wilderness Survival Skills training of the highest caliber.

Now, based in Scandinavia, deep inside the Arctic Circle, Toby draws on his 25 years of training and experience to share his expertise in Extreme Cold Weather Wilderness Survival Skills. In addition, he travels extensively to deliver applied Survival Courses internationally.

When not teaching or studying aspects of survival, Toby also deals with Risk Management Consultancy on outdoor-related activities and runs various highly applied self-defense/unarmed combat camps and seminars. Working firmly with the mantra 'Always a student, sometimes a teacher' Toby strives to continuously learn and share knowledge on all things survival related. He is exceptionally excited to join Selco's team and have the opportunity to develop and grow within the SHTF school community.

Finding Water

The average human can only live for 3 days without water.

Sixty percent of the human body is fluid, and it only takes a loss of 2% of bodily fluids for the human body to start having problems. The human body needs fluids to keep blood from becoming too thick, which can impact your ability to function and make the right decisions.

One liter of fluid is lost per day, even if that day is spent just lying in bed. That is why, in hospitals, adult, bed-ridden patients get 2.5 liters of intravenous fluids every day. If you do physical exercise in a hot climate, you need to replenish your body with 5 to 6 liters of fluid, or even more.

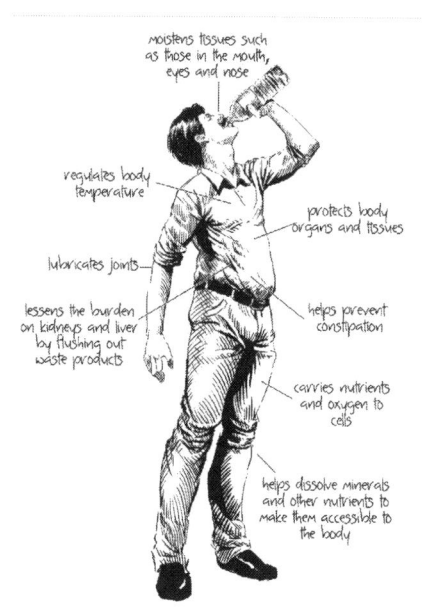

Just like with the data about how many men lives without food, there is a misconception here about living without water too. While it is correct that man can live without water for 3 days, that info can misguide you in the SHTF situation.

Lack of water will strike your abilities right on the first day of being without it, so for example, on the second day of being without water, you are not going to be able to think clearly, or run fast, or simply to recognize a probable ambush 100 meters ahead of you.

Being without water when SHTF does not mean that you are going to lay down inside your home waiting for rain. You are probably going to need to go out fight for resources, scavenge, or similar, so you need to think in new terms.

Dehydration

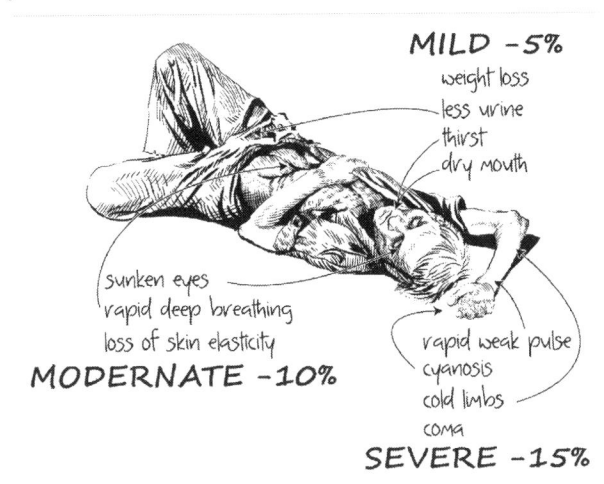

MILD -5%
- weight loss
- less urine
- thirst
- dry mouth

MODERNATE -10%
- sunken eyes
- rapid deep breathing
- loss of skin elasticity

SEVERE -15%
- rapid weak pulse
- cyanosis
- cold limbs
- coma

Here are the first signs that you are dehydrated:

- Thirst
- Headache
- Heat cramps
- Reduced endurance
- Dark yellow, almost brownish, urine
- Pain during urination

- Decreased urinary output
- Light-headedness or dizziness, fainting when standing up

If you do not intervene at this point, things get progressively worse:

- Fatiguing
- Loss of appetite
- Severe heat cramps
- Loss of strength
- Your body fluids stop working (dry eyes and mouth)
- Body temperature rises
- Nausea and vomiting
- Constipation
- Tingling in the limbs
- Loss of feelings in some limbs
- Skin becomes less elastic
- Hallucinations
- Coma, unconsciousness
- Death

All of this sounds really bad, and it is – but do not get caught up in the details. If you become aware of any of these symptoms in yourself or someone in your group, take the necessary steps to avoid the worst.

If you are involved in physical activity, are ill, or are in an area where there is high heat, high humidity, or extreme cold, you need to increase the amount of water you drink.

If you work outside, try to work at night or whenever the temperatures are the best for your work. Pace your work and take a break when you start sweating. If you are walking, make sure you get rid of insulating layers of clothing that make you sweat. When you take a break, and your body cools down, add warmer layers of clothing while you rest that your body does not get cold.

Do not talk or open your mouth if you don't have to and breathe slowly through your nose to minimize the amount of humidity that can escape your body.

If you have to talk, just do it, as this can also boost your morale in moments when you need it. Digesting food also takes water, so do not eat unless you have enough water. Stay away from alcohol and cigarettes because they tend to dehydrate you more.

If you can obtain about half a liter of water, you should be able to stay alive for weeks (unless you face other circumstances that make you lose fluids rapidly).

Every little bit helps. A cup of water a day is better than no water at all – just make sure the effort in obtaining the water is worth it if you have to ration your water.

Finding Water

You first have to think about the energy expended – resources gained ratio of getting water. If you lose 2 liters of water from sweating while you dig a hole that might give you 1 liter of water, you are fighting a losing battle. The priority is not to lose too much water when trying to get new water.

Here are some tips for making sure you have water:

- Before you go anywhere, make sure you have enough water with you. If you are in a new country and are going hiking, ask the locals how they find water or if there are any plants that store drinkable water and how to find them. ? Learn about plants that need a lot of water–this indicates that there is water close by. Willows, elderberries, cottonwoods, poplars, and cattails require lots of water.

- Before you start digging holes, think about how and where you could get water. Just walking in a certain direction in the hopes of finding a river or stream isn't the best course of action.
- Look out for animal trails that can lead you to water, or watch swarms of birds to see where they land. If groups of birds fly fast and low, they are heading for the water. If you find several animal trails headed for the same place, you are most likely heading in the right direction. If you find animal feces, chances are there is water within walking distance because most animals drink several times a day (usually in the morning and evening).
- Insects such as flies or mosquitoes also indicate there is water nearby because most of them breed in water and rarely travel far from it.
- When you look for water, also consider unlikely places such as holes, cracks, and on big leaves after rainfall. Keep in mind that this water is most likely cleaner than stagnant water or water from pools on the ground, but it should be still cleaned.
- Look for low-lying areas, valleys, and creeks. Follow the terrain to its lowest point where water is most likely to collect. If you don't find water at these lowest points, look for dried-out streams or creeks. You can follow these dried out small streams up if you are in the mountains and try to find the spring they came from since they still might carry a bit of water.
- Keep in mind that right after it rains, a lot of openings in the mountains will look like springs but simply carry the rainwater from a few hours before. It is easier to find proper springs if it hasn't rained for more than one day.
- Look out for plants as indicators of water.

- Water can often be found on the outside bend of dried out riverbeds where the water flows fastest, and the riverbed is deep.
- Study any maps you may have or come across and look for water sources indicated ? Look for other water indicators in the area such as seepage of water on the surface of rocks. If you cannot find water on the surface, only start digging a hole if the ground is moist, you are very confident because of abundant plant life around, or as a last resort. You don't want to waste your energy on nothing. If you do not find water after digging down 2 feet (60cm), even if the ground is moist, you are not likely to find water. If you stay in the area, check the holes, later on, to see if water has seeped in.
- Cacti, such as a barrel or the prickly pear, and other plants can be a source of small amounts of water. Get rid of the spikes on the outside and cut out some of the pulp to chew it and suck out the moisture. This will not give you much, but it is better than nothing. Save the chewed pulp and put them in a primitive solar still.
- Fruit trees are another option. If you live in or travel to a certain area, make sure you know how the local edible fruits look.
- Because humans need water to survive, any abandoned buildings or other areas where humans have been and that you consider safe to go to our areas of interest too. Also, look into gutters, drainage ditches, rainwater collection barrels outside, hot water heaters, toilet tanks, or even waterbeds inside houses and apartments. The water in hot water heaters should be safe to drink, even if it was used and heated. Purify all other water.

- Getting water out in the ocean is a much more difficult challenge without a desalinization kit or a reverse osmosis pump. Try to catch rain or dew or build a solar still. Fish eyes also contain some drinkable, jelly-like water, and some fish

also store freshwater along their spine.
- As a last resort, drink seawater. The salt concentration is high, but it will give you a few extra hours, and if you are lucky, even 1-2 days, of survival. Start drinking seawater after 24 hours of having no water because later on with more severe symptoms of dehydration, it can deteriorate your situation more quickly, and you won't be able to function. Mix it up with fresh water if you still have it or simply take sips every once in a while. Do not drink big gulps of seawater. Just sip it and never drink more than 200 mL over a period of 24 hours.
- At the beach, you can dig a hole in a low lying area a few meters after vegetation starts and wait for the water to seep in. The sand and soil should filter out enough salt to make it drinkable. Dig multiple holes to speed up the process of gathering enough water. ? Also, look for coconuts because they are an excellent source of water and food. Go for the green nuts, as they contain more water. The darker, brown nuts are milkier and cause diarrhea if you consume too much. Coconuts have very hard shells, and if you do not have a knife or machete, they are tough to crack. One way of doing it with primitive tools is to grind down the shell with a stone and then pierce the coconut with a sharpened stick or stone. Some types of coconuts also have softer spots. Try to find them and pierce the coconut at the soft spot and let the water drip out.
- In warm and humid climates with jungle foliage, you can often find water vines or other plants such as banana trees that you can use as sources of water. Water vines should be cut at a higher point first and then at a lower point because a cut makes the vine suck water up. Then you can take that piece of water vine and hold it up like a canteen and let the water drip into your mouth or a container. If you cut a banana tree near its core, water from the root system accumulates in the hollow trunk.
- The same technique works for other trees such as sugar, coconut, nipa, and buri palm trees. Try to find younger trees

that aren't that high and cut them at the top. Bend the tree over and let the water slowly drip into your mouth or container. Cut more off the top when the first cut dries out.
- Bamboo is probably the most amazing survival plant as it can provide food, a multitude of tools, or shelter. Of course, it can also provide water. Just like with the palm trees, find some younger green bamboo and cut it at the top and bend it over to let water drip out of it. If you find bigger bamboo, there might be water trapped in some of the segments of the tree. Shake it and listen if you hear the sound of water in it. Then pierce each segment to drain the water.
- If you are in a mountain area, look for terrain that is sloping down. Rock walls and cliffs often also have small springs at the bottom.
- Study any maps you may have or come across and look for water sources indicated.

TOBY ON WHEN YOU HAVE FOUND WATER IN THE WILDERNESS

If you discover water and you are already in a state of dehydration, there will be a huge temptation to drink copious quantities of water quickly. Do everything you can to resist that urge, and drink water in small sips over a longer period to avoid any 'shock loading' of your body and vomiting reflexes being triggered.

SELCO ON FINDING WATER IN A CITY

Finding water in the city SHTF was mostly about waiting for the rain to come down in order to collect it and to use water from the river.

A better option was to use collected water from the rain because of its purity. We used simple filtration through gauze and boiling. Tarps helped us a lot collecting the rain.

In some worst period, I drank actually whatever water I could find. Sometimes only quickly filtrating it through the fabric of my sleeve.

Sometimes without even boiling it. It was sometimes a matter of functioning properly, so you just have to do it. Of course, we suffered from diarrhea and similar problems many times because of it.

Any available source is good when you are in need of water because you cannot "teach" yourself to live without it.

TOBY ON FINDING WATER IN A CITY

Many people are completely unaware of the waterways that are flowing, channeled, and contained or diverted through their cities, obtain maps and research in advance where the waterways are, which way they flow, and at what points they become accessible.

Natural Water Collection Rain collection (Rating 5)

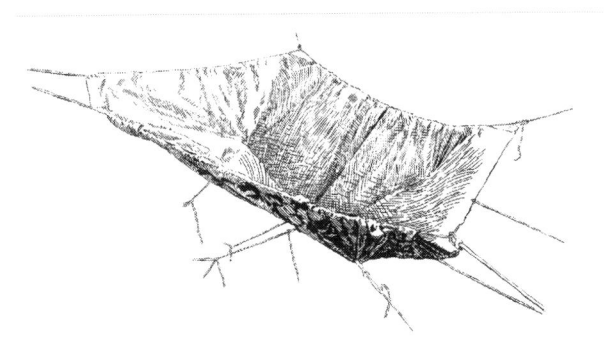

If you live in the right area, rain can be an excellent source of water. **Rainwater is safe to drink before it comes into contact with anything.**

The problem is that rain is unpredictable, so having this as your only solution doesn't make sense. Do not forget to camouflage your rainwater catchment systems if you don't want to attract attention. Watch out for clouds, so you are ready to collect as much as possible.

The easiest way to collect rain is to have a clean tarp set up to catch the rain. You can also collect rain from roofs, but the water will be contaminated. A less-efficient way to collect rainwater is to take bed sheets or towels, let them get drenched outside, and wring the water out in a container.

You can use the same technique to collect morning dew from plants if you live in an area with an appropriate climate. Dew can also collect on the side and bottom of rocks when the cold air of the night condenses as the sun rises. Flipping over rocks to look for water won't give you much, but at least it's something.

Melting snow (Rating 4)

If you get a bucket full of snow, after the melting process, the bucket will be 1/10th full. Always compress the snow as much as possible before melting it to get the best yield.

As an alternative, if you want to melt snow a bit faster or don't have a container, you can gather snow in a pillowcase or tie the legs of trousers and shovel snow in it. Then you can hang it directly over a heat source and collect the dripping water with a bucket underneath.

If you do not have a container or cloths, you can spare, dig a hole, fill it with snow and add some stones you have heated up in a fire into the hole to melt the snow. Remove the rocks and sip out the water.

If you have only sea ice, use the more blue parts of it because they contain less salt. Melting snow in your mouth needs more energy than what water gives you back, so this does not work as a long-term solution unless you have a proper shelter and clothes. Melting snow in your mouth lowers your core temperature, and your system has to work harder (and consume more water) to raise it again.

SELCO ON EATING SNOW

> *I made the same mistake as most of the guys that found themselves thirsty and exhausted while on a long walk through snow without water. You can find lots of info about how a man gets exhausted and dehydrated and how eating snow is a bad idea because you cool out and waste energy.*

I had some bottles with water with me, but it was a way too small amount for the length of the trip and my condition. After some time, I tried to melt snow in the bottle by pushing it inside and keeping it in my jacket, but it works way too slow, and I could get an only a small amount of the water at once. I needed much more. Then I started to eat snow. First, by melting it in my mouth, later was more like swallowing it.

And of course, it was a bad idea, later simply felt like I am dying, I was constantly thirsty, and my mouth and throat felt like I was drinking boiled water.

TOBY ON HYDRATION IN COLD CONDITIONS

It takes a lot of time and effort to process snow and ice to make it drinkable. In a cold environment, however, the elements are working against you to try and turn your liquid (water) back to a solid-state (ice) try and insulate your water containers with items you have or can scavenge. IF you choose to keep liquid containers within your clothing system to slow the freezing process, do so only in your mid-layers, DO NOT keep containers by base layers or next to the skin.

Transpiration (Rating 2)

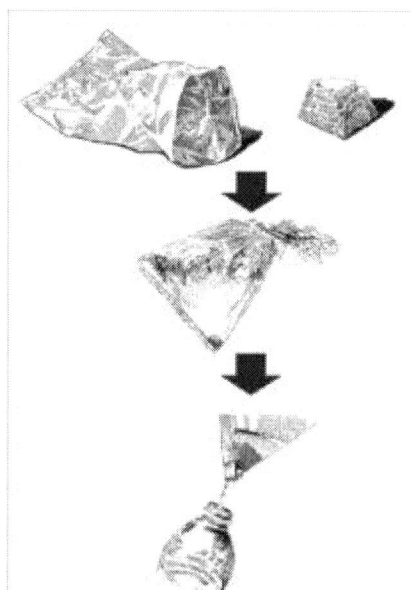

If you happen to have several large clear plastic bags, you can put them over branches of non-poisonous plants and trees to collect water vapor.

Pick plants that have large root systems for the best results. To make this work, the plastic bags have to be sealed airtight with some rope or tape. The vapor will condense and accumulate on the bottom of the bag, or you can add a pebble on one side of the bag to weigh it down so that water collects at one spot.

With a higher temperature and lower humidity, your yield increases. This sounds like a good technique to get clean water (which you don't even have to filter if you use clean bags), but in reality, the yield is rather low, and you would have to place quite a few bags to make this work.

Solar stills (Rating 3)

Setting up a solar still

this cross section of a survival solar still illustrates how heat from the sun vaporizes ground and vegetation water. then this vapor condenses under plastic, trickles down, and drops into the container.

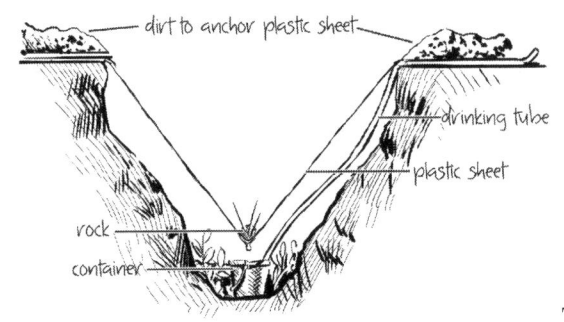

- dirt to anchor plastic sheet
- drinking tube
- plastic sheet
- rock
- container

There are several types of solar stills. The most commonly used solar still is simple, and all you need is a container to collect water and a clear plastic sheet to cover a hole in the ground.

(Here is one problem with this method—you need to dig a hole and precious energy is wasted on this.) After you have the hole, you put a cup in the center of it and add green plant matter, urine, dirty water, or whatever else is the source of your water.

If you add plant matter, crush it or break it apart so that the stored humidity can escape more easily. Cover the hole with the plastic sheet and add a stone in the middle of the sheet above the container so that the plastic bends down slightly and the water can collect. The solar rays heat up the air inside the hole, and humidity condenses on the underside of the plastic sheet. It drips down to the middle where you placed the stone and drips into the container.

If you do not want to wastewater and humidity, you should have some tubing that you can use to drink directly from the container without moving the plastic sheet and letting humidity escape.

The big benefit of this technique is that it produces pure drinkable water from urine or saltwater. Make many solar stills if you can get enough water.

As a last resort, you could also improvise something similar to a solar still by simply digging a hole in the ground, covering it with clean, big leaves, peeing in the hole, waiting until the sun heats it up, and licking some droplets of condensed water from the leaves. It still has to be airtight, so use big leaves if possible.

Drinking Urine (Rating 3)

You can drink urine, which is perfectly safe if you drink it right after you urinated. However, only drink the first passing or the second one, because after that, the waste in the urine becomes too hard for your kidneys to handle. This can result in death from kidney failure.

Making Water Ready to Drink

Always purify water from unknown sources before you consume it!

It is estimated that 90% of freshwater on our planet is not safe to drink. Of course, if you are about to die from dehydration and have no means to purify your water, you should simply drink it and hope for the best.

Just keep in mind that just because water is clear, looks good, and smells good, that doesn't mean it is good!

Before the French chemist Louis Pasteur discovered germs in water in the mid- 1800s, people drank mostly tea or fermented drinks such as beer and wine. The alcoholic drinks were mixed with regular water, and the alcohol worked to sanitize the water.

In general, what people knew back then still holds true today. Well, water is usually much safer than surface water, and spring water is often safer than well water. So if you have to drink without purification, then go for spring water, if possible, and drink from the source, where the water comes out of the ground.

Water can contain a range of nasty organisms you would do well to avoid. The consequences of ingesting them can range from a slightly upset stomach to death.

For example, after major flooding in densely populated areas, the main concern is cholera because the drainage systems overflow and contaminate the drinking water supply. One infection can spread quickly and contaminate the water supply of whole areas. Cholera has a fatality rate of 1%, but in a complete collapse, this can be much higher if the necessary medical supplies are missing.

About 4% of all human illness stems from waterborne diseases, and it is estimated that about 2 million people die from unsafe water each year. Ninety percent of these cases are from unsanitary conditions in the affected areas. These figures do not include the multitude of mosquito-spread diseases that can be fatal as well, such as malaria or dengue fever.

The problems are microorganisms that inhabit the water. They fall into four broad categories:

- Bacteria
- Parasites
- Protozoa

- Viruses

Running water usually contains fewer protozoa and bacteria, but the threat of viruses and parasites remains.

Bacteria

Bacterial infections from water are most common, so whenever you can, get water from a running water source before you begin the purification process. Usually, bacteria are introduced into the water through an outside source. Common waterborne bacterial diseases is dysentery, cholera, botulism, salmonella, and typhoid.

Signs of bacterial infections usually show up within 6 to 72 hours after exposure.

Parasites

Parasites are small animals that you ingest along with the contaminated water, and they create all sorts of problems in your body. Tapeworm is parasites that live inside of you and feed off the food you digest to keep growing.

This leads to gastrointestinal problems and weight loss. Other parasites such as Echinococcosis can cause an enlarged liver and cysts that put pressure on your bile tract. If those cysts rupture, they can cause a serious allergic reaction that is rapid in onset and may cause death (through anaphylactic shock).

Protozoa

Cryptosporidium and Giardia intestinalis very common protozoa in untreated drinking water and cause problems such as diarrhea, stomach cramps, and nausea/vomiting.

Protozoan infections can take a long time to show up, from a few days to months. They are rather hard to treat once they have spread through the body.

Protozoa are categorized as plant life and include fungus, amoeba, and algae.

Viruses

Viruses can spread through the water as well. Hepatitis A, SARS, and polio are just a few of the many very dangerous viruses you can get by ingesting infected water.

The most common source of contamination of water in disaster scenarios is through human waste, so make sure you never let feces come into contact with any of your drinking water sources.

Some differences you should be aware of when talking about water. To **filter** means basically just removing bigger particles from the water. Unless you use something like a micropore filter or other special filter, the water is not necessarily ready to drink. That's why usually, after you filter, you **purify** the water and remove smaller particles and make it safe to drink.

Water that is safe to drink is not necessarily safe for wound treatment, so when you take this one step further than purification, you **sterilize** water. Sterilized water is absent of any life (including bacteria, fungi, virus…).

Water Filtration and Purification

Use the cleanest water you have for all hygiene matters and clean your eating and drinking utensils with purified water only if possible.

TOBY ON STERILIZING GEAR

Often you simply do not have enough purified water. I recommend you use metal cookware and eating utensils extensively on the basis they can be 'cleaned' with any water and then sterilized in/with the heat of the fire.

Items often can be 're-sterilized' just before using them, to ensure any dirt collected during activities is eliminated prior to eating. Of course, often, we find we are eating with our hands only and therefore having sanitizers or similar is a distinct advantage (can also be used in fire starting).

SELCO ON PURIFYING WATER

When the danger of being without water goes way over the danger of drinking dirty water, you just stop to think about some things, even if you aware of it.

We used simple filtering of water through gauze. If we after that noticed that there's more pollutants in it, we continued with filtering, then after that, we boiled it, and that's it.

Of course, sometimes it was not enough, so we constantly more or less had problems with diarrhea, but we simply were not ready for anything more than those methods.

You can either use heat, UV rays, chemicals, or filtering to purify your water. The option that is best depends on water quality. Often it makes sense to go through several steps. For example, filtering water to remove the biggest particles and then boiling it to sanitize it.

Here is some advice on how to get the best water:

- Let dirty water settle for at least 12 hours before filtering it. This way, the bigger pieces of dirt can settle on the bottom of the container and won't clog up your filter system. Use a coarse filter to remove large impurities.
- If you come across a stream and decide to collect water from it, you can walk up the river for about a quarter-mile or 300 meters to look for any obvious contamination such as animal feces or dead animals floating in the stream. Then walk back to collect your water.
- Whenever you have the chance, filter the water. This should always be step one. The water will taste better and will be safer than unfiltered water.

Commercial Filters

If you have a portable water filter, you are lucky (or well prepared). They come in two types. There are the bigger gravity-fed filters such as AquaRain and British Berkefeld, and much smaller ones, popular in the Trekking scene, that is used by pushing a hand pump.

If you look for a hand filter besides the popular MSR and Katadyn filters, we recommend the Sawyer Micropore Filter System that is used all over the world for water treatment.

These filters usually work with either charcoal or silver elements to help clean the water. Silver is a natural sanitizing agent and destroys any pathogens it comes into contact with. Charcoal does not destroy pathogens, but because it is a very fine porous material and has a high surface area, it is perfect for filtering water.

Modern filter systems remove everything, even radioactive particles and harmful chemicals, except for a few specific viruses. If you combine a modern filter with another form of treatment such as UV exposure or chemical treatment, you have a great setup to get clean water.

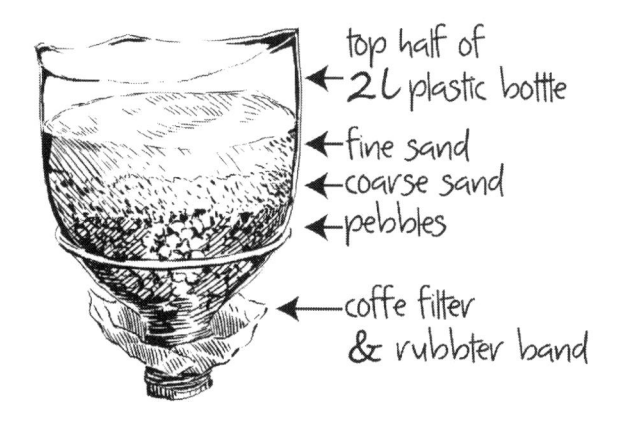

Diagram labels: top half of 2L plastic bottle, fine sand, coarse sand, pebbles, coffe filter & rubbter band

If you want to filter out, bacteria, make sure the filters are rated at 0.2 microns or less (to give you an idea how small that is, the thickness of an average human's hair is 76 microns).

Parasites are larger and, therefore, easier to filter out. Protozoa are usually 3 to 10 microns and can be filtered out as well.

Viruses are the smallest at 0.004 to 0.06 microns. They cannot be filtered out, and to make sure you avoid viruses, just filtering will not be enough. You might remove a lot of the viruses during the filtering, though, because they tend to attach themselves to larger particles.

Improvised Filters

If you do not have a proper filter, try building one. Get creative when it gets to filtering your water. You could try a sand filter or simply use a piece of cloth to filter out the biggest impurities before boiling it.

Use your socks or several layers of cloth to get rid of the larger impurities in the water you are trying to make drinkable. You can also stack several filters over each other. The top filter should filter the largest particles while the filter on the bottom filters the finest.

Primitive filters do not kill or remove impurities, but they reduce them and make the water taste better.

If you use the filter on a regular basis, clean the filter by leaving it out in the sun every few days.

If you don't have anything to use as a filter, you can dig a hole at least one foot away from the body of water and wait until it seeps through to the hole.

Remember that commercial filters often use charcoal?

This is important information because you can create charcoal yourself (by burning wood at high temperatures) and therefore build your own filter.

Every campfire creates a bit of charcoal. To create a DIY water filter that is a step up from the sand filter, boil some rocks and sand, find a suitable container that has an opening on the bottom, and fill the container with a layer of rocks. Then add layers of sand and charcoal and repeat until the container is filled (or you run out of material).

To make this filter even more effective, use some silver dust sprinkled in with the charcoal and use some cloth in the last layer on the top.

If you do not have a proper container to create a filter, crush the charcoal into the water, stir it and let it settle and drink it through a piece of cloth to filter out most of the charcoal.

Using Heat

If you really want to make sure you get clean water, boil it for 10 minutes at a temperature of at least around 185 degrees Fahrenheit (85 degrees Celsius).

The temperature will differ if you are higher up in the mountains – you will need more heat and a longer boiling time. Don't get obsessed with the temperature.

If the water boils properly it is hot enough.

Of course, you will lose a lot of water during that process and use a lot of fuel for the fire or cooker you use. So, if you just have a little water, boil it for a shorter amount of time and hope for the best.

Usually, cooking it at a rolling boil for 1 to 2 minutes will do the trick unless it is heavily polluted water.

The boiled water will lack taste. You can get some of the taste back by aerating it. Stir it vigorously with a clean, sanitized spoon or put it in a sealed container and simply shake it.

SELCO ON BOILING WATER WHEN HE WAS OUT SCAVENGING

> *I always carried water with me, sometimes when I was forced to spend more time out, I used a small raincoat for collecting rainwater when raining. In some worst situations, I collected it from the pools after the rain, sometimes filtering it just trough the sleeve, I used old can for boiling it over the fire, and that's it.*

TOBY ON BOILING WATER

> *Our aim to make water safe to drink is to bring it to a rolling boil. If we have a cooking pot or purpose-built container to heat the water in, that is great.*
>
> *But we must maintain our adaptive mindset and be able to identify and embrace other containers, that with the right technique, can be used in which to bring water to a boil. Empty food and drink cans are excellent, but even glass or plastic soda bottles, or certain types of food pouches can be used.*
>
> *It is not enough to know the 'theory' of how to boil water in these containers. We must practice and understand the nuance of doing so. This is an indication of how vital (and taken for granted) water is.*

Selco often talks in this section of being forced into making very bad choices as there was no other alternative, do not find yourself in the same position, ensure you know and can execute as many different water sterilization methods as possible.

Chemicals

Tablets for water purification are small, not very expensive, and should be part of everyone's BOB. If you didn't plan ahead, you probably don't have access to these.

An alternative is a bleach (also known as liquid chlorine), which can be found in most households. Just add a teaspoon of bleach for every 4–5 liters of room temperature water. Please keep in mind chlorine is ineffective in cold water.

Smell the water after treatment and let it sit for 15–30 minutes. It should have a faint smell of chlorine. If it does not, add another dose of bleach, and if it then still doesn't smell like bleach after 15–30 minutes, discard the water, as it is too polluted to be cleaned.

The best bleach is calcium hypochlorite in granule form. It has a much longer shelf life compared to liquid bleach and is easier to store.

Another option is to use iodine to make your drinking water safe.

Iodine is a great multipurpose item that you can use to treat and disinfect wounds as well. Most iodine tinctures come in 2% strength and are available at your local pharmacy. Just add 5–10 drops per 32 ounces (about 1 liter) of water into the water, mix it well, and let it sit for 30 minutes. If you are unsure about how much to put in the water, just use a few more drops to be on the safe side.

Many water treatment tinctures also come with two solutions or tablets. The first helps to purify the water and the second usually contains vitamin C or ascorbic acid to remove the chemical taste.

You can also get iodine tablets containing tetra glycine hydroperiodide. They provide the added benefit that they also reduce the uptake of radioactive iodine in humans. This can help to treat water after a nuclear fallout or attack, where radioactive iodine ingestion is a concern for internal radiotoxicity.

Just be aware that unlike chlorine dioxide tablets, that we recommend, iodine tablets are only partly effective against giardia and not against cryptosporidium.

Protozoa can transform themselves into cysts that survive even harsh chemical treatments. These cysts become active again once they are in the proper environment (such as your digestive tract). That's why a multistep treatment of water, such as filtering it first and then using the chemicals, makes sense.

UV Rays

A clear container or plastic bag can also help with water purification. This is also known as SODIS (Solar Water Disinfection) and is promoted by the World Health Organization (even though other treatments are safer, this way of treating water is available almost everywhere).

The UV rays of the sun kill some of the nasties in the water. UV rays can penetrate only about 4 inches (10cm) into the water, so do not use containers or bags that are too big. If you only have a big container on hand, just double the time you let it sit in the sun and shake the bag on a regular basis to mix the water.

First, filter out all the sun-blocking particles before you put it out in the sun. After that, shake the water in the container to oxygenate it and then top it off with some more water to make sure there is no air left. Putting the container onto a dark surface increases the heat and can also help to make the water safer to drink. Leave it like this as long as possible. If the sun is shining and it's hot, it can take just 6 hours to have safe drinking water.

If it is colder and sunny, it takes 12 hours. If it is cloudy, then let it sit outside for at least two days. Detailed information and training material in a variety of different languages can be found on the SODIS website.

The problem with this technique is that bacteria is only reduced to a safe amount and is not completely eradicated. That means it can build up again overnight, so you will want to consume this water in the evening right after you treated it.

There are also commercial ultraviolet water purifiers available (such as the Steripen). They work great and are easy to carry, but of course, you have to rely on them to work, and you need to have enough batteries to power them. The UV rays have to penetrate the water, so only reasonably clean water can be treated.

Emergency Administration of Water

If there are no other options, and you enter the lethal stages of dehydration, consider giving yourself or people in need enemas with water. Enemas are the fastest way to rehydrate.

The colon tissue absorbs the water but not the bacteria. You can only absorb a little amount, but that can mean the difference between life and death.

You will also want to use slightly salty and sweet water so that the person who suffers from dehydration won't get hyponatremia, which is an electrolyte imbalance in the blood and can be life-threatening condition.

Here is a recipe for a makeshift electrolyte mix for enemas:

- 33 ounces (1 liter) of water
- ¼ teaspoon salt
- 6 teaspoons sugar

Storing Water

If you plan on bugging in, it makes sense that you store some water. At a minimum, you should store 14 gallons (52 liters) of water for every person, every week. Make sure you store enough calcium hypochlorite in granule form to treat your stored water before you consume it because bacteria will grow in water if it is stored over time.

Get proper food-grade plastic containers for storage that can be tightly sealed. We recommend you get multiple smaller containers that you can still lift when filled with water. You never know when and if you might have to move.

If disaster strikes, but your tap water is still running, fill the bathtubs, sinks, and all other containers you have at your disposal. There are big bags you can seal and place in your bathtub that can store water as well.

If you have a reason to believe that the public water will be contaminated (for example, after flooding), cut off the utility water supply. If you know where the water pipes are in your home, you can drain them as well for more water.

Our Recommendations

Filtration and then boiling the water is the best way to clean water.

JAY ON WATER PURIFICATION

When you prepare yourself for possible survival scenarios, how to get and purify water has to be on top of the list. If you get filters, have at least one or two backup filters. Water is life. How to obtain and purify water is one of essential survival skills you need to master.

If you have to clean large amounts of water over a long period of time, boiling might consume too much energy or become too tedious. That's why we recommend you use a bacterial (smaller than 0.2 micron) filter and, after that, use a chemical treatment on the water.

We recommend you get a portable filter with a ceramic or ceramic / carbon hybrid filter element (which lasts longer than those with just carbon-based elements) such as the MSR or Katadyn filters. The Sawyer Micropore Filter System uses proprietary technology that is also certified and has proven to work well.

You should also get some chlorine dioxide tablets and for treating larger amounts of water calcium hypochlorite in granular form. The benefit of MSR and Katadyn filters with activated carbon is that they also remove most chemicals, bad taste, and odor from the water.

If you want to bug in, we recommend you get a reverse osmosis system and a bigger gravity-fed filtration system such as the Berkefeld or Aquarain.

Keep in mind that all filters clog up after some time, so proper maintenance and care makes a huge difference in how much mileage you get out of them.

Having more options is never wrong. Add a Steripen for UV sterilization as well if your budget allows it. Getting things in order to build your own filtration systems with silver dust and charcoal, and finding a reliable way to produce charcoal, makes also sense if you are prepping for long-term survival scenarios.

Shelter Basics

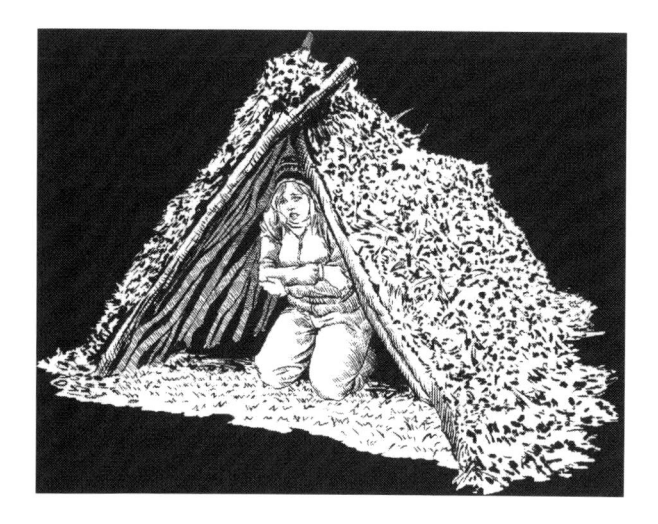

The importance of finding shelter

Never underestimate how quickly a mild day can turn into a dangerous situation. You do not have to be in snow or freezing temperatures to have cause for concern – cool weather combined with wind and rain can cause hypothermia, and before you know it, that short day hike could become a life-threatening situation unless you know how to find or build an adequate shelter.

The primary aim of finding shelter is to ensure that your body temperature will remain in the healthy range regardless of weather conditions so that you can fight off the earth's biggest killers of outdoor enthusiasts – hypothermia and hyperthermia.

Having a shelter does not only help you to avoid or conserve heat and regain energy, but it also gives you a mental boost, a sense of security, and a lift immoral, which are essential to sustaining your ability to think clearly and strengthening your willpower and your resolve to continue the fight to survive.

Depending on your environment, finding or building a shelter can be one of the first and most important activities in a survival situation. The urgency of seeking shelter depends mostly on the weather, time of the day, and your physical condition.

The art of survival is all about decision-making skills and prioritization. Ask yourself: Are you in immediate danger? Is the temperature extreme, is it about to rain or snow, or are you showing symptoms of illness? Are there predators or enemies in the area from which you must hide, or are you somewhere where it is likely you will be rescued? How much time do you have before the sun goes down? Are there enough of the right building and fire materials in the area to match your needs? Read on to learn the answers to these questions and more. **Dangers of not having shelter: Hypothermia**

Hypothermia is one of the biggest threats for humans trying to survive in the wilderness. Through a process called thermoregulation, the human body has a remarkable ability to maintain its optimal internal temperature, which fluctuates just 2 °F (1 °C), between 98–100 °F

(36.5–37.5 °C). The lack of a proper shelter can cause a drop of just 3 ° F (1.5 °C) in body temperature, which triggers the onset of hypothermia and can rapidly deteriorate into a life-threatening situation.

Keep in mind that you do not necessarily have to be exposed to extreme weather conditions to get hypothermia. Water is denser than air, so it absorbs more heat and can steal up to 32 times more heat from your body than air can. If your clothing becomes damp by either rain or perspiration, the insulating properties can drop as much as 80%. Therefore even when you get caught in the rain shower or if you are sweating and the temperature drops, it can rapidly lead to hypothermia because of how quickly water cools your body.

There are several different factors that contribute to heat loss that you should be aware of in wet or cold weather situations.

1. **Conduction:** You lose body heat when you touch a cold surface. Therefore you should try to get as many layers between you and whatever cold surface with which you are in contact, for example, the surface on which you are lying down overnight.
2. **Convection:** Convection is the process of losing heat to something in motion, such as wind. Air currents transport heat away from your body. Try to stay out of the wind and minimize airflow through your shelter.
3. **Evaporation**: We evaporate heat and moisture every time we exhale and sweat. Be mindful of how much energy you exert when building or locating a shelter.
4. **Radiation:** Your body constantly emits heat as a part of our metabolic system, and you ordinarily use your clothing to trap some of this heat and keep you warm. Use your shelter to trap air within insulating layers and prevent yourself from losing more heat through radiation. Simply putting a roof over your head will help reduce heat loss through radiation. Insulating materials can include sticks and branches, vegetation such as leaves and grasses, and snowflakes.
5. **Respiration:** You lose some heat every time you breathe out. Try to stay calm and have a steady slow rate of breathing will help you to not lose unnecessary heat. Talking less can also decrease your heat loss from air coming out of your body.

Signs and symptoms of hypothermia

The following table demonstrates the rapid deterioration of the mind and body as your body temperature falls. You should be very aware of these so that you are alerted to the onset of hypothermia, and you can locate or construct an adequate shelter before your mental faculties are affected. In particular, you should make shelter your immediate priority if your shivering becomes intense, and you notice numbness or a bluish/grayish skin tone.

1. **37 °C (99 °F)** – Normal body temperature.

2. **36 °C (97 °F)** – Mild to moderate shivering (body temperature may drop this low during sleep). Maybe normal body temperature.
3. **35 °C (95 °F)** – (Hypothermia) is less than 35 °C (95 °F) – Intense shivering, numbness, and bluish/grayness of the skin. There is a possibility of heart irritability.
4. **34 °C (93 °F)** – Severe shivering, loss of movement of fingers, blueness, and confusion. Some behavioral changes may take place.
5. **33 °C (91 °F)** – Moderate to severe confusion, sleepiness, depressed reflexes, progressive loss of shivering, slow heartbeat, shallow breathing. Shivering may stop. The subject may be unresponsive to certain stimuli.
6. **32 °C (90 °F)** – (Medical emergency) Hallucinations, delirium, complete confusion, extreme sleepiness that is progressively becoming comatose. Shivering is absent (subject may even think they are hot). Reflex may be absent or very slight.
7. **31 °C (88 °F)** – Comatose, very rarely conscious. No or slight reflexes. Very shallow breathing and slow heart rate. Possibility of serious heart rhythm problems.
8. **28 °C (82 °F)** – Severe heart rhythm disturbances are likely, and breathing may stop at any time. The patient may appear to be dead.
9. **24–26 °C (75–79 °F) or less** – Death usually occurs due to irregular heartbeat or respiratory arrest

SELCO ON HYPOTHERMIA

From my experience, I can say that hypothermia can play games with your mind.

During my trip out of the town, over the mountain, I experience a touch of it. I was badly prepared for the trip, and with no experience in the wilderness. The temperature was around -15C, snow blizzard, deep snow.

Something around 50 km through the mountain. I had military boots on my feet, not made for snow, military jacket, and homemade poncho over everything; I carried around 30kg of stuff with me. I drink alcohol all the time and eat small amounts of sugar "to keep myself warm." Due to heavy trips, I think I did not even notice that my feet are wet or that I am not feeling cold anymore.

I was just walking like in the dream; I did not feel anything; actually, just walk and walk. But on one point on a mountain path behind some pine tree, I have seen a wolf. It was standing some 10 meters from me. I was surprised for a moment, then in the next moment the wolf just disappeared. I mean, he did not run or go. He just disappeared.

At that moment, I realized I am hallucinating, and I am going to die there from "cold death." Again I did not feel cold, pain, or anything. I was numbed completely. Guys from the group found me, I guess, after 20 minutes, sitting in the snow, all white, but with my eyes open, I do not remember that.

They took me to some shack and rewarmed me next to a fire, with hot tea, and gave me dry clothes. They said I was cold as death, and completely wet.

TOBY ON HYPOTHERMIA

There are a number of concerning things about hypothermia that are very difficult to anticipate unless you have frequently treated it or suffered from it.

One of the biggest issues is that early stages of hypothermia take away the things you (as a casualty) need the most, small motor skill and elevated brain function. Once you're not thinking straight and clumsy in your actions, your condition can deteriorate much quicker than you anticipate.

Every person I have treated that was truly hypothermic, first and foremost denied they were, and secondly were unable to commence re-warming actions without assistance. Had intervention not occurred, they would allow their physical condition to deteriorate until they realized they were in serious trouble and then would be unable to help themselves.

This is why preventive practices and early diagnosis (as in realizing you are on your way to hypothermia, not waiting until you have it) are essential skills to develop.

Further to this, it is common to find worsening symptoms occur exponentially. I often refer to the 'cliff-edge' stage of Hypothermia treatment, if a casualty crosses a certain point of deterioration in the field, it is very, very difficult to manage beyond that point.

What to do? Don't let it get that bad! There are a number of deeply flawed 'accepted truths' around managing hypothermia in the wild. These will be covered in more detail, separately.

Lastly, a casualty who has recovered from a hypothermia episode is extremely vulnerable to relapse and should be very closely monitored for at least 48hrs after any treatment, if remaining in the field.

Shelter versus Fire

One of the most common dilemmas faced by people in survival situations is when the night is approaching, and the weather is dropping, do you invest time in building a fire or a shelter? In such a situation, you must evaluate how soon you want to build your shelter, where and with what materials. If rain is approaching, every minute counts. Drops in body temperature caused by exposure to rain and wind can lead to an inability to function physically and mentally, and ultimately death. Starting a fire without being able to think clearly or use your hands properly can be impossible.

I recommend the following steps:

1. Take a few deep breaths and try to relax. Decisions made in a state of panic are usually bad ones.
2. Look for immediate shelter that could be found, for example, under a spruce tree or some form of natural cover. Assess if it is adequate to give you sufficient protection or to block the wind and moisture to help you start a fire.
3. If the answer is no, look at your surroundings and consider these crucial questions: What materials do you have to build a shelter, and how effective will that shelter be? Do you have enough of the right type of fuel to keep a fire going through the night and enough time to gather it, or will it run out and leave you freezing in a basic or no shelter when your fire has extinguished?
4. A good shelter can keep you dry and warm enough to survive overnight without a fire. Remember your priority in cold or wet climates is to stay out of the snow, wind, and rain. If fuel is not readily available, or there is not enough time to gather enough wood before night fall, build a shelter to protect yourself. A debris shelter or snow cave can save your life by keeping you protected from the elements without a fire.

5. Remember, the clothing you are wearing is a part of your 'shelter.' If you are adequately clothed for the conditions you are in, then finding additional shelter becomes less of a priority. Conversely, if your clothing is inadequate, the additional shelter will be a higher priority.

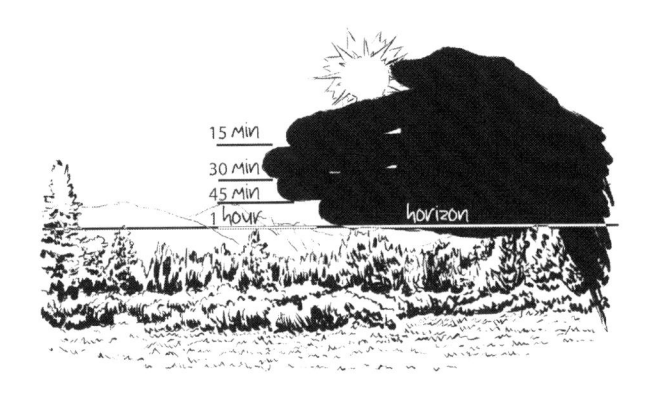

Follow these simple steps to figure out approximately how long you have left before darkness falls:

1. Locate the sun without looking directly at it.
2. Raise your arm in front of you and then turn your hand inwards 90 degrees, with your fingers parallel to the ground, your thumb tucked into your palm, and the back of your hand facing you.
3. Position your hand so that the little finger runs along the line of the horizon.
4. Place your other arm out in the symmetrical position. Count the number of times you have to place one hand on top of the other before you see that your hand is sitting just beneath the sun. Each hand width (e.g., 4 fingers lined up) represents approximately one hour until the sunsets.
5. Swap to using fingers if there is less than one hour until sunset. Each finger typically represents approximately 15 minutes.

Dangers of not having shelter: Hyperthermia

In hot weather, hyperthermia can quickly kill you in a similar manner to hypothermia, and when mixed with dehydration almost certain death without an adequate shelter during daylight hours. Many landscapes will provide you with natural shade but if you're planning a voyage by sea or through deserts, for example, be sure to familiarize yourself with the signs and symptoms below and the shelter building techniques that follow.

Signs and symptoms of hyperthermia

1. 37 °C (99 °F) – Normal body temperature
2. 38 °C (100 °F) – Sweating, feeling very uncomfortable, slightly hungry.
3. 39 °C (102 °F) – Severe sweating, flushed, and very red. Fast heart rate and breathlessness. There may be exhaustion accompanying this. Children and people with epilepsy may be very likely to get convulsions at this point.
4. 40 °C (104 °F) – Fainting, dehydration, weakness, vomiting, headache, and dizziness may occur as well as profuse sweating. Starts to be life-threatening.
5. 41 °C (106 °F) – (Medical emergency) – Fainting, vomiting, severe headache, dizziness, confusion, hallucinations, delirium, and drowsiness can occur. There may also be palpitations and breathlessness.
6. 42 °C (108 °F) – The subject may turn pale or remain flushed and red. They may become comatose, be in severe delirium, vomiting, and convulsions can occur. Blood pressure may be high or low, and heart rate will be very fast.
7. 43 °C (109 °F) – Normally, death, or there may be serious brain damage, continuous convulsions, and shock. The cardio-respiratory collapse will likely occur.
8. 44 °C (111 °F) or more – Almost certainly death will occur

Building Shelters

Shelter Location

Be aware of your surroundings and possible threats before choosing your shelter location, and keep in mind the following tips.

Watch out for dead trees, branches, rocks, or other debris that might fall onto your shelter.

Look for dried out creeks and think about the way water will flow once heavy rain sets in.

If you want to stay undetected in an area, make sure that your shelter site isn't easily spotted (including any light sources at night).

If you want to be rescued, try to stay at a high up vantage point or in a clearing (but beware of overexposing yourself to wind or deprive yourself of a water source).

Be aware of hilltops exposed to wind and the wind direction before setting up your shelter. Move down from windy hilltops and look for shelter on the lee side.

Avoid hillside terraces, valley bottoms, and deep hollows where the ground can hold moisture. Avoid setting up shelters on animal trails. Try to find a flat surface to sleep on to ensure you get the best rest possible.

A lot of effort can be saved by thoroughly searching in your immediate area. Fifteen minutes spent finding a 'pre-built' natural shelter can save hours on 'starting from scratch.' Locate your shelter as close to the resources you found as is safe to do so, instead of constructing a shelter and carrying resources to it.

Equipment

It is always useful to carry a good amount of strong cordage (a minimum of 30 meters is recommended) with you in order to assist with erecting a shelter, as well as a large, sturdy piece of material. For a light shelter, a tarp or army poncho is the most versatile and is also strong and cheap.

These can be easily erected in a variety of ways using improvised pegs and cords if necessary. Gore-text bivvy bags have become popular as they are lightweight and simply fit over your sleeping bag, but they are very expensive for what they are. Tents are more specialized shelters which should be carefully chosen with the help of specialist advice to meet your needs.

You can also place a poncho liner on a military poncho (close the head opening with paracord or the hood string of the poncho) and roll yourself up in both (you may have to do it diagonally if you're taller). When it is raining, even having a wet poncho liner will allow you to stay warm enough to sleep as the wet liner will warm up from body heat.

When you decide on a shelter, you always have to balance the amount of comfort you want with the work you have to put in or the weight you have to carry.

Type of Shelter

TOBY ON NATURAL SHELTERS

> *It's a dream for the aspiring survivalist to spend a night sleeping in a shelter made from all-natural materials, and doing so is incredibly rewarding, but we need to avoid the romantic fantasy and appreciate all-natural shelters are time-consuming, require (often) a lot of resources and as much focus on insulation from the ground as building up layers of weatherproofing.*
>
> *Correct shelter type selection and sizing are vital to minimizing energy expended in its construction. You need your emergency shelter to be appropriate to your environment, big enough, and no bigger.*

There is an unlimited number of options for shelter, each of which is suitable for different requirements and circumstances. How do you choose which type of shelter suits you best?

Usually, the answer will be decided for you depending on your situation.

Consider the following:

1. Is your shelter for an emergency?
2. Can you find shelter in your environment?
3. Are you injured?
4. Are you alone?

5. What equipment and materials do you have at your disposal?
6. How much daylight do you have left?
7. Can you light a fire?
8. What kind of weather and natural forces do you have to shelter from?
9. What resources do you have to build a shelter?
10. How long will you stay?
11. How much energy do you have and want to spend on building the shelter?
12. Is it likely that anyone will start searching for you in the coming few hours?

These considerations will help you to identify your aim, your resources, and any potential obstacles.

The longer you intend to stay in one place, the stronger your shelter should be. However, a stronger shelter will need more effort to build and use more materials.

If your energy supplies allow it, use more time to build a shelter that can really offer you enough comfort to get some rest, instead of trying to cut down on time building the shelter and ending up having more time to rest in an uncomfortable shelter that does not help you to regain your energy.

If you find yourself caught without shelter, try to find terrain which will provide you with plenty of shelter-building materials, such as woodland. Even though it may take you an hour to walk back to where you last saw a suitable site, you will regain that time and effort in the reduced time spent building your shelter and the energy you recover by resting well.

Shelters fall into two categories: manmade and natural. Each type of shelter has its use, so always carefully weigh the benefits of each before making a decision. Remember that even natural shelters can require significant effort to make habitable and comfortable. A good option in the right circumstances is to look for an easily adapted natural shelter.

Most shelters consist of a frame and some sort of cover to protect you from the forces of nature.

The Framework

Use cordage to quickly set up frames if possible. The structure needs to be built as sturdily as possible from materials that you can easily gather in your environment. Cordage is easy to transport and help you to take your frame along with you and set up your shelter at a different spot the next day if you are on the move.

If you seek protection from rain, make sure the frame has at least a 45-degree angle that raindrops drip downs quickly. Remember, you want to create a (small – delete) shelter not too big and not too small, this way, it will warm more effectively with your body heat.

The Weatherproofing and Insulation

You'll most likely need insulation to keep you warm and protected from the elements. Try to build at least 6 – 8" / 10 – 15 cm thick coverage of locally available insulation over your entire structure. Use leaves, saplings/thin branches, leafy foliage, bark sheets, or a combination for the 'weatherproofing' on the outside of your shelter.

For insulation from the ground, build a 'bed' of leaves or similar 12-18" / 25 – 95 cm deep. Alternatively, you can lay down alternate layers of saplings or thin branches, event logs, and try to cover this 'raised bed' with a layer of leaves or foliage in order to insulate you from contact with the ground.

If you have man-made materials available such as a poncho, tarp, garbage bags, or plastic sheeting, these can provide excellent weatherproofing items to supplement your shelter.

Good insulation can not only keep you warm but also dry.

Recommendations

If you have time and money to prepare, perhaps a motorhome, travel trailer, station wagon, hand-cart, as well as a backpack kit, consider high-tech metalized bubble roll insulation. It's very light, only a little heavier than thick-mil plastic sheeting or even less than a sturdy tarp, and provides contact insulation (body heat on cold ground or stone), reflects heat to improve the function of small heating fires or huddling people, is a slight sound barrier, and a block against thermal imager devices.

If a tarp of okay quality is too expensive, go to a thrift store and look for a large tent (8-man) with a broken zipper or damage to the tent. Get a good price after pointing out damage, then cut the floor away, and you have a sturdy tarp with grommets.

I have used pieces of this to cover the windows of vehicles, as insulation inside bivy bag (USGI gore-tex), and on the floor and walls of a tent to keep warm and make shade. Good for cold and hot weather. Waterproof and wipes dry with no absorption does not support mold. Not as good as camping foam or Therm-a-Rest as a sleeping pad, but okay and cheaper. Cover with netting, dull sheet, local materials, or paint to reduce exterior shine.

Different Shelters

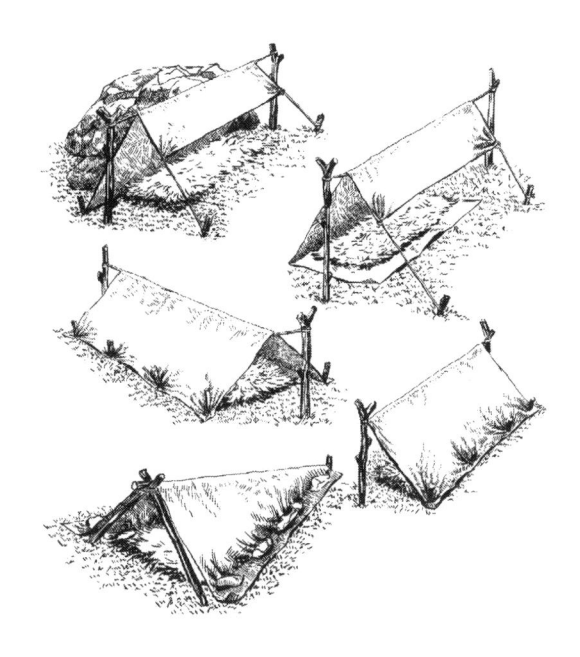

There are many different wilderness survival shelter types to choose from. It depends very much on the environment, circumstance, aims, the competence of the individual/group, and equipment carried in order to decide what shelter type is best.

A-frame

A-frame shelter consists of one or two A - framed openings and a cover. It can be built with very basic means. Having some cordage and a plastic sheet, poncho or tarp can speed up the process greatly.

A-frame with a poncho or tarp

1. In the best case scenario, you have cordage to construct the frame between two trees or between two sturdy sticks you push into the ground.
2. Make sure the openings of your a-frame do not face the wind (or you might get rain blown right into your shelter, and it will be way colder during the night).
3. You can add drip sticks to the cordage a few inches away from each of you a - frame openings. Drip sticks are 3-4 inch / 10 centimeter long sticks that will prevent water from running along with your cordage into your shelter.
4. Spread your plastic sheet, poncho, or tarp and use some heavy rocks or sharpened sticks to anchor it to the ground.

A-frame without equipment

Adding a supporting stick or cordage makes your A-frame shelter much more sturdy

1. Look for a sturdy, long branch, stick or cut a small tree that is

strong enough to hold your insulation.
2. Lean it onto a bigger tree or create an A-frame opening by tying two crossed sticks together and lean it onto that.
3. Add smaller twigs and branches onto on sides of your shelter. Cover it with (a lot of) leaves, debris, and other material to add insulation.
4. Add a supporting stick or cordage to prevent your frame from collapsing due to the added weight from the insulation.

A-frame shelter experiences and recommendations

If you have no trees or structure to support cordage with, use fiberglass or aluminum poles salvaged from a camping tent. They are lightweight and sturdy- easy to carry in the pack and good for many things.

If you build your roof or cover with branches, align them closely to keep debris from falling through. Adding another layer of branches on top of your debris/insulation layer will prevent it from getting blown away.

A little bit of money spent now will give more options in time of trouble. You want to stay home, not go out with guns and silver looking for rolls of plastic to trade for. These things should be stored in a 20L plastic bucket buried away from buildings so that fire will not harm it.

Add enough insulation to keep you warm and dry at night. Some more minutes spent on adding more insulation can make a big difference at night.

Try to finish the cover and insulation of one side of the shelter first, so in case you run out of the time, you can use the – frame as lean-to shelter.

Lean-to

A lean-to shelter is similar to the a-frame shelter but with only one side protected from the elements. Therefore you should pay attention to where the wind is coming from when you start to build your lean-to shelter.

Build the lean-to with the back into the wind.

Lean-to shelter work great when you make a fire next to them and catch some of the radiant heat from the fire in your shelter.

You can add more branches around your lean-to to prevent wind coming in from the sides.

Going underground

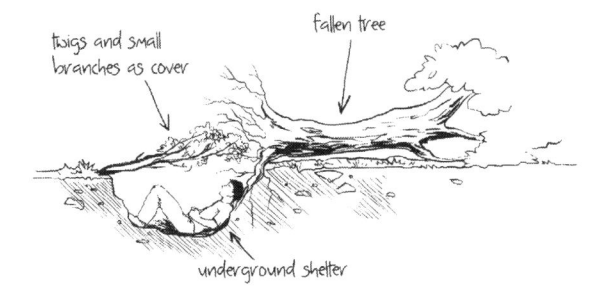

176 | Chapter 3: Wilderness Survival

You do not have to literally go underground. Natural obstacles such as big piles of snow or dense bushes that you can dig into are all good shelters of this kind too.

The best way to keep yourself and your supplies warm or cool are by going underground. The roots of a fallen tree often provide a good 'starter cave,' which can be further hollowed out, or you can simply dig a pit large enough to sit and lay comfortably in. Don't bother trying to dig a tunnel and chamber; it's not worth the effort unless you happen to locate some truly ideal terrain for such a thing.

Once your pit is of adequate size, simply lay large branches across the top as a frame to support surface cover/camouflage. If big enough, they don't need to be secured, or you can dig notches around the edge of the pit to hold them in place. Cover the larger branches with smaller sticks, twigs, and finally dirt, leaves, and other debris until your cover resembles the ground around it. If available, a net works great at holding twigs and such in place.

Usually you can find plenty of branches and debris laying around with no need for chopping wood, however, in heavily forested or permafrost areas digging a pit can be tough, and you may need to chop through roots/ice.

Given enough time and effort, this type of shelter can be quite secure and elaborate. It's easy to add on or connect chambers by simply digging more pits. Carefully choosing large, heavy framework branches, and using lots of them, the surface cover can hold a considerable amount of dirt and can be walked on. Given enough time, vegetation will grow on the surface too (or snow will fall on it), making it invisible.

The thicker your cover, the warmer/cooler your shelter will be, and a thick layer of dirt will even keep your supplies safe from wildfire (not you though, as there will likely be insufficient oxygen).

Improving your shelter

- Add living plants on top of it as camouflage if you want to stay hidden.
- Set a fire, fire can warm you, dry out your clothes and fire can make you feel safe. ? If you've got a fire going, capture as much heat from it as you can. A reflector built of logs, stones, bricks, or rubble on the other side of the fire from you will reflect heat back to you, increasing your comfort and saving fuel.

Urban shelters

In urban settings, there is something like the myth that man is going to be safe if he is just going in the basement and barricade in.

In reality, most of the people who did that end up dead after more or less time of siege.

One of the basic rules of sheltering in urban settings is to be safe in every moment that you can get out and run. No matter how hard your shelter is, everything can be penetrated and taken.

If you seek shelter in an urban environment, learns from homeless people in your area. Pay attention to where and how the homeless people in your area live. Most likely similar ways of seeking shelter in your area once SHTF will make sense too.

Good places are, for example, malls (with lots of different shops) once they are looted, abandoned, and empty. There are many places to hide and many exits. It is big enough to pick a place that you feel comfortable with, and you have many possible ways to escape. Set up small noise traps with debris or whatever trash you can find to get alerted once someone approaches.

Banks and police stations are good places as well after they are looted. Banks usually have many rooms inside and often rather hidden back entrances or exits. Police stations are worth checking out if you have to seek shelter because they are usually well fortified with reinforced glass and often thicker walls.

Another good idea is to find an apartment or room in a burned-out or otherwise destroyed apartment complex and fortify it. You can use the debris to block certain passages, knock some walls down or create other different entrances and exits, so you end up with a little maze that is hard to navigate for everyone who is not familiar with it. Again, make sure you do not make entrances and exits obvious. For example, use windows as entrance and block doors or break down complete staircases and have a hidden ladder to get to your shelter.

Forget about basements. They might be good to avoid gunfire, but once someone finds you, they can simply wait for you to come out, throw a grenade into the basement or smoke you out of your home. It's a death trap. A good urban shelter is hidden or has no obvious ways in but still offers many ways for you to escape, in the best case, undetected.

If you are alone, try to sleep somewhere inside a house a few rooms away from the entrance so you can set up noise traps and have some time to react. Sleep with your weapon next to you and facing the most likely point of entrance of potential attackers so you can react quickly. Higher ground is always preferable, but being on the higher ground without one or more ways to escape is dangerous.

SELCO ON URBAN SHELTERS

> *They need to serve you as protection and place to hide so you need to follow same rules. When I needed place to hide or to spend some time over the night for whatever reason I always look for same things, centered inside some building, no direct openings, always one more exit, on place where I could easy monitor what s going on, etc.*
>
> *It is a kind of compromise between being very well protected and being able to monitor what s going on or adapting it to your needs and still not doing anything too much to make it "stick out."*

There was a situation when I was forced to hide very fast because a group of armed guys was coming to me, and I did not have too much chance in confrontation with them. It happened inside ruined apartment building. I just dig myself in on a pile of ruins and dirt.

There was nothing else to do, and I did not have a fire going there, or blanket or anything else, but for several hours it was a perfect shelter for me.

Fire

Why Fire Is Important

When you are camping as a recreational activity, a fire is often nothing more than a pleasurable addition to your outdoor experience. However, in survival situations, fire is crucial to fundamental principles of survival (protection, location, food, and water) and could mean the difference between life and death.

Warmth

Even in temperate and desert climates, night time can bring a significant and potentially fatal drop in temperatures. In some of the hottest deserts of the world, throughout the Americas, Africa, Australia, and Southern Asia, the desert's surface receives a little more than twice the solar radiation received by humid regions and loses almost twice as much heat at night, meaning minimum temperatures can drop below 0° F (-18° C) and overnight freezes are common during winter. Retaining body heat is vital to prevent hypothermia, and in this way, being able to start a fire may well keep you alive in what could otherwise seem like hopeless conditions.

Morale

You cannot underestimate the importance of keeping your morale high in survival situations. Psychological factors play a key role in your endurance, your decision-making capacity, and ultimately, your ability to stay alive. A fire provides comfort and a sense of homeliness, whereas not being able to start a fire can add to psychological stress in already difficult conditions, which in turn can lead to being tempted to simply give up. People are fascinated by fires, that's why fire can also provide entertainment, creating a focal point and a sensation of relaxation.

Purifying Water and Cooking

Water gathered from all, but the most reliably clean sources need to be purified before it is safe to drink. Around 90% of water-borne diseases can be removed from water by boiling, and in order to do this, a fire is usually necessary. Also, while most foods that are safe to eat cooked are also safe to eat raw, fires can be used to preserve foods and slow them from spoiling, plus barbecuing your meal over a fire may provide you with a sense of achievement, satisfaction and that all-important boost of morale that is crucial to your success.

Protection

In regions where wild animals may present a danger for campers, a fire can provide protection. Most animals will avoid confrontations with humans where possible, and fire will deter many species such as wolves and bears. Smoke from your fire can also be used to deter flying insects such as mosquitoes, which can carry a range of potentially deadly diseases.

Signaling

Sometimes in survival situations, we want to be discovered, and sometimes we want to stay hidden – for example, if we are avoiding enemy forces. It is important to remember that in every survival situation, there is a chance of rescue, no matter how remote.

The international signal of distress is three columns of smoke, but remember that even your campfire will increase your chances of rescue by emitting light, smoke, and scent. Particularly at night, when both flames and smoke can be seen from a vast distance, fires serve as a clear message to anyone who is traveling by air as well as anyone within sight or smell that someone is there. It is important to remember that for this purpose, unlike cooking, you will want to create a fire with a lot of smoke, and therefore you will require more fuel. Damp wood is useful for creating smoke.

During the day, try to create a color of smoke that contrasts with your background. If you smother a large fire with green leaves or moss, the fire will produce white smoke, which is useful if, for example, you're in a jungle.

If you add rubber or oil-soaked rags to a fire, you will get black smoke, which is ideal for attracting attention when in the snow. If trying to stay undetected, try to minimize your use of fires and create a color of smoke that will blend in with your background. Dry hardwood creates less smoke than other types of wood.

Avoid anything with humidity inside if you want to keep your fire hidden. Slowly build up your fire by adding bigger pieces of wood or other fuel to avoid smothering the fire which would create smoke. Smoke is also created if your fire doesn't get enough air. Try to find the right balance between air/fuel / heat and flame.

In urban SHTF, fire does not have to be like a big bonfire, and most of the time, it is very dangerous to be like that.

We are talking here about making a fire outside of your home, on your way somewhere, and in improvised shelters.

It is not a big deal to find improvised shelter in the city when SHTF, there's gonna be a lot of ruins everywhere. One of the good places to make fire is close to the place where it was burning ruins (burned house or similar) because it hides the smell (also, these places gonna be everywhere when SHTF in the city).

People also make what we called "can fire." Actually, it is something that survivalist call today

"survival stove" or similar, just kinda inverted. It was a very small fire covered with can, with holes for venting. It was used for heat and fast cooking "on the road." And of course, it was a constant struggle between too much smoke or too much light.

The important thing is to understand that all you need in these circumstances is a very small fire that you can use for quick heat, quick-cook (boil), and fire that you able to extinguish very fast and without too much effort and noise.

Big fire in SHTF conditions when you outside of the security of your home is usually a luxury that can bring you a lot of troubles. It can be seen from very far, and you are gonna be very distracted by it and not able to react in the proper way.

Making Tools

A recent study by the University of Cape Town in South Africa found that 72,000 years ago, and perhaps as early as 164,000 years ago, early modern humans in coastal South Africa were using carefully controlled hearths in a complex process to heat stone and change its properties, the process known as "heat treatment." Previously scientists thought the first use of heat treatment occurred in Europe approximately 25,000 years ago.

This sophisticated human use of fire allowed our species to forge blades and axes and is thought to have assisted early humans who left Africa 50,000 to 60,000 years ago to cope with colder conditions and rapidly migrate across glacial Eurasia. A more simple method involves using fire to heat and harden the tips of wood arrows or spears for hunting or fishing. Coals from a fire can also be used to burn depressions into bigger wooden chunks and create simple pots and cups.

How Fire Works

In order to successfully build and sustain a fire, you need to understand how fireworks. Referring to the visual above, you'll see that a fire needs three elements to function: oxygen, heat, and fuel. If one of these elements is removed or not present, the fire will not work.

Oxygen

Lack of oxygen can occur when a spark is smothered by too much tinder at the early stages, or when fuel is heaped onto a fire without due care. This is one of the most common mistakes in fire-making. To increase oxygen, a blowing or fanning motion can help.

Heat

High temperatures are needed to ignite the fuel in a fire. Without heat, fuel will not burn.

Fuel

A continuous supply of fuel is needed to keep a fire burning, and without it, the fire will eventually extinguish by itself. Remember, the more oxygen on the fire, the faster the fuel will burn (ideal for creating smoky fires), and the more ventilation is reduced, the slower fuel will burn, and the more embers will be allowed to glow (ideal for cooking).

SELCO ON USING FIRE

Very soon after SHTF started, we realized that fireplaces and fire stoves need to be a little bit "improved" in order to meet our new demands. Since firewood becomes pretty much hard and dangerous to find, we "invented" some new ways of saving fuel.

Old steel plates from stoves are replaced with thinner material in order to make it easier and faster to cook food on it (and save fuel on that way).

Sometimes small homemade stoves that people used for heating looked more like cans made from thin metal then real stoves. But it worked.

Later, people made small stoves from pressure cookers and similar.

Preparing to Build A Fire

If there is one tip to remember from this entire section of the guide, it is to be prepared by carrying a fire-starting tool! Whether you are going for a single or multi-day trip, carry at least one ignition tool with you at all times (better two or three). Survival experts agree that one of the keys to a successful fire is to prepare thoroughly before you try to light it. Along with practice and equipment, planning the position of the fire and choosing tinder, kindling and fuel must all be considered.

Ignition Tools

It is much easier to make a fire if you have ignition tools at hand. If possible, carry a selection of these items with you. However, it can be surprising what can be used to make a fire if necessary.

Cigarette Lighters / Matches

The most reliable tools for making the spark needed to start a fire are cigarette lighters and matches. However, both of these items can fail if they are allowed to get wet, so take precautions by storing them in a small, easily-visible, and fully waterproofed container. Remember these useful tips for using matches:

- Damp matches can sometimes be saved by rubbing them in a rolling motion across dry, reasonably clean hair.
- The correct way to strike a match is by sliding it down the rough edge of the matchbox, away from your body. Strike down at 45degrees on the box held in a vertical position, and then the match not only has less chance of breaking but also lies directly into your cupped hands, minimizing the chance of being blown out directly after striking. Cup the flame in your hand to protect it from sudden breezes and allow the match to burn some way down the stem before trying to light tinder.
- Light a candle with the first match you strike. This will save you from having to use further matches. Tea light candles are ideal as they are small, portable, and burn slowly.

Flint

A fire-starting kit consisting of a steel striker and flint or magnesium rod works well in most conditions. Using modern fire steel is quite intuitive. For best and consistent results, it is essential you practice and master the correct techniques of using this excellent item. It should be noted the market place has seen a recent and concerning influx of 'fake' magnesium firelighters and exceptionally poor quality fire steels that do not spark well or light at all. We recommend you buy any and all equipment you may be staking your life on from a reputable brand! Natural flint is also found in many environments and can be used for the same purpose.

Powder from Ammunition

If you are carrying ammunition and have no other way of starting a fire, you can use the gunpowder propellant from your ammunition. There are two ways to do this:

- Empty powder directly onto tinder and use a flint or match to ignite it, or
- Empty part of the contents of the round and pack a piece of cloth into space, before reloading and firing into the earth.

Potassium Permanganate

Potassium Permanganate is a chemical that has multiple purposes in an outdoor situation. It has been heralded as one of the world's most valuable survival aids for its ability to purify water, create an antiseptic solution, act as an anti-fungal treatment, mark snow as an emergency signal, and to start a fire. It must, however, be used with the utmost care, or otherwise, you risk potentially dangerous adverse chemical reactions, causing burns or other injuries.

Potassium permanganate will start a fire when mixed with a couple of different compounds, Glycerin and Antifreeze being the most common.

After gathering all the necessary tinder and firewood to keep your fire going, place approximately a teaspoon of Potassium Permanganate on a flat surface. Carefully add the same amount of Glycerine or Antifreeze evenly on top of your pile. Next, stand back a couple of feet and wait at the ready with your tinder. It can take some time for the chemical reaction to start a fire, so if you decide to choose this method, keep a safe distance in the meantime.

Frankly, in our opinion, this method is risky and impractical when you consider the safer, cheaper, and easier methods available to start a regular fire. Regardless, you might find some creative ways of using it if you want to delay the ignition for a fire.

Magnifying Glass

The lens of a magnifying glass can be used to direct a ray of bright sunlight onto dry tinder. This will increase the heat and hopefully ignite the tinder. If a magnifying glass lens is not available, consider the lenses from a pair of spectacles, or even a fragment of broken glass. You can buy flat cards that are magnifying lenses to carry along.

Battery & Wire Wool

A battery, even one with minimal charge, can be 'arced' to cause a spark to form between two pieces of wire or heat a wire connected between both terminals, to the extent tinder can be ignited. The larger the battery, the stronger the spark or greater the heat output will be. Exercise particular caution if fire lighting this way.

Be wary of over-using and draining batteries, which are needed for other items of kit such as torches.

When you find yourself in life threatening situation, especially in a prolonged one like an SHTF scenario, you'll see that the saying "keep it simple" make so much sense. So most of the time, simple cigarette lighter will do the job of starting the fire very well.

You cannot beat the simplicity, availability, and cost of a simple, cheap lighter today. But also you need to use common sense and think about "what if," so you need to have knowledge about how to start a fire with other tools other than a common lighter. There is no too much sense in starting a fire with batteries or flints if you are having a lighter with you. Remember SHTF is not a reality contest. Nobody watching you in order to grade your skills. Keep it as simple as you can.

TOBY ON IGNITION TOOLS

I am fortunate to teach survival internationally and have a great deal of exposure to a wide variety of students and environments. Most students correctly identify fire lighting is an essential skill, and many carry equipment and materials for this, but there is also a deeply worrying trend in survival training towards over complicating fire lighting, or worse, convincing oneself that 'low percentage' techniques are more reliable than they actually are.

While I fully appreciate the satisfaction of creating a 'fire by friction,' it is also not lost on me that you 'fight as you train' and I have seen on a number of occasions, in serious circumstances, students focussing their fire fighting efforts in completely the wrong direction and manner.

Here in the Arctic regions, we will constantly carry, separately, at least three different fire lighting methods and also weatherproofed packs of tinder. Such is the importance of fast fire generation.

Master AS MANY fire lighting skills as you can, but DO NOT forget the fundamentals.

You want to be confident that you can get a fire going **quickly** in any environment if you need too. This leads to one of my cardinal training points – **There is no such thing as cheating in Survival!**

Fire-Making Equipment

As well as the obvious choices of several waterproofed sets of "strike anywhere matches" and lighters, there is a wide variety of items that you can carry to make starting a fire easier.

Cotton wool

Cotton wool is one of the easiest tinder to ignite. Store cotton wool balls in a waterproof container, a Ziploc bag or small sealable plastic container are fine (old 35mm film containers are excellent). Prior to attempting to light the cotton wool, tease it apart as much as you can to ensure good airflow.

A variety of accelerants (Petroleum jelly, alcohol-based hand sanitizer, some bug sprays, etc.) can be added to the cotton wool, in small quantities, prior to lighting, to make the tinder burn even longer.

Matchless Fire Tin

Matchless Fire Tins are widely used in the military and contain everything that is needed to start a fire. Typically, these waterproof tins contain a flint and steel, a hexamine fire-starter fuel block and cotton wool, a tampon, or alternatively lint from your clothes drier to use as tinder. We recommend adding extra waterproofing to the tin by sealing it with electrical tape, which can also double up like kindling.

Fire Can

These homemade fire starters are small, slow-burning, and will generally get a fire going with no leftover materials. Make a fire can using a small tin (shoe polish and tobacco tins are suitable tins), corrugated cardboard, and candle wax, by following these steps:

1. Cut a long strip of cardboard, around 4mm deeper than the tin.
2. Coil the cardboard into the tin, packing it reasonably tightly.
3. Pour melted wax into the tin until it is full. You can do this by lighting a candle and dripping it in, or by melting candles in an old tin or pan.
4. Allow to wax cool until hard.

A similar alternative to the fire can is sometimes referred to as a "magic muffin," in which the tin is replaced by cupcake liners and packed with sawdust or small scraps of shredded newspaper as well as melted wax.

Char-cloth

Make a char-cloth which can be used in difficult fire starting conditions by using 100% cotton fabric scraps and a small, portable tin, by following these steps:

1. Start by punching a small hole in the lid of the tin with, for example, a nail. Ensure the hole has a width of no greater than 1 cm.
2. Place scraps of fabric into the tin. Do not pack them in tightly and try not to place them evenly one on top of the other, but layer the cloth instead.
3. Replace the lid and place the tin on top of hot embers or at the edge of a fire, where it will not fall over.
4. Smoke will start to come out of the hole in the tin lid. This is the oxygen burning off.
5. When no more smoke appears, carefully remove the tin from the fire. Do not under any circumstances take the lid off straight away, since not only will it be super hot, but it is likely to set the cloth inside on fire if you let more oxygen in before it has cooled.
6. Remove the lid. Ideally, your cloth should be slightly soft but not fragile and completely black. If it is brown, replace the lid and continue the healing process. If it crumbles when you touch it, it has probably been overdone.
7. Test your char-cloth by applying a spark – you should get a red, glowing ember.

Magnesium Ribbon

We have not used this method in 'all conditions', but it has worked for us every time as a fire starting tool. You take a little bit of magnesium ribbon and wrap it around the head of a "strike anywhere" type match. You want tight contact with the match head. Then, you light that match with another match. The flare-up of the match will light the magnesium ribbon. You can rest this match in the middle of a pile of wood and tinder if you like, then light it up. Yes, it is a method that requires you to sacrifice two matches instead of just one, but it works very effectively. Give it a try. Making fire is about finding a way that works and knowing all options available.

Choosing Your Location

Time spent in carefully choosing the right position for a fire is time well invested. Shelter from wind and rain will make lighting a fire and keeping it lit much easier. However, signal fires should be positioned in the open and in the highest spot possible to attract attention.

Before making any attempt to build and light a fire, the first step is always to clear an area of around two meters in width to avoid unintentionally starting a wildfire.

Scrape away any leaves, twigs, grass, and other materials that could accidentally ignite. If you notice tree roots under the surface of the earth, choose another spot. Tree roots burn slowly, and fire can travel underground. Make sure you have access to means to extinguish the fire if you have to.

If you have to light a fire on wet or snow-covered ground, gather together branches of greenwood to form a platform.

If you are lucky enough to find a camping spot where previous visitors have built a stone fireplace, make use of it. The stones will prevent the fire from spreading, and keeping all fires in one spot reduces the environmental impact.

If you have time, it is worth setting up a firewall. This can be made using boughs of wood, branches, rocks, or whatever another material is available. Using a firewall will help to reflect heat and shelter you from the wind.

Most of the time, starting a fire outside my home during my SHTF means that it needs to be somehow hidden from not wanted people. Remember that when you are sitting next to the fire in pitch dark, you cannot see too much around you.

The best place for the fire was inside ruined buildings because few reasons: you could always find some junk for fuel, and also I was fairly hidden from view.

Of course, glow of fire would be visible from outside the building, so I choose rooms without direct openings to outside, and even then, I would carefully do only small fires without too much flame.

Also, smoke was not a big problem, as long as you disperse id a bit- again by not doing the fire direct next to the openings and similar. Some amount of smoke was OK, and smell too because the city was burning and smelling more or less all the time.

If the fire were glowing too much, I would just cover it with anything available, like build "walls" around it and cover it with wet cardboard or similar.

It did not look like a good camping fire at all, but it did the job.

Gathering Essential Ingredients

The second stage of preparing a fire is gathering your essential ingredients: tinder, kindling, and fuel. Ideally, you should gather around 10 times more fuel than you think you will need and keep a good supply close at hand so that the fire doesn't go out during the night.

For kindling, we used very thin pieces of the wood floor since it was dry and polished, it was a great source for that. People often carried pieces of wood in a pocket and made kindling with a knife if needed.

Also, we carried pieces of cardboard or small pieces of fat (hardened) extracted from canned meat (very low-quality meat, but a lot of fat, which was great fuel.

Today I like to have parafine cubes, cotton balls, magnesium rod, .and steel wool for starting a fire Simplest way of fire setup is tepee, but probably the smartest way outside the home is star fire, depending on circumstances (is it smart for a fire to be seen? is it good to have too much smoke?) I would again prefer to have something like "can fire", it is some kind of "covered fire" so I am able to control strength and visibility and being able to "kill it" fast. It does not have to be can. It can be rounded with rubble or building blocks and covered with some cloth (high) or cardboard or similar.

Step by step fire-making

- Tinder catches a spark or holds an ember and turns it into a

flame.
- Kindling takes a flame and turns it into a fire.
- Fuel keeps a fire burning and, if necessary, growing in size.

Tinder

Tinder is dry material that is easy to set alight and is used to start a fire. Dry grasses, leaves, cotton scraps from clothing, plant seed heads, abandoned birds' nests, and shavings from bamboo are all good examples of items that can be used for tinder. Since good, dry tinder can be hard to find, you should gather it up as you go, storing the materials in a waterproof container or close to your body, where your body heat will keep it dry.

In wet weather, try looking under trees that lean over to one side, creating a shelter. Often, by lifting the bark, dry material for tinder can be sourced.

In situations where a supply of suitable tinder is unavailable, you can try making feather sticks by taking the following steps:

Choose five or six pieces of dry wood measuring 20-30cm in length and around the thickness of three fingers.

Work on a flat surface and remove any bark from the sticks.

Practice running the blade of your knife down the length of a stick (always away from your body).

Change the angle of the knife blade to cut into the wood. The aim is to make shallow cuts, causing shavings to life away from the body of the wood without falling loose.

Work in a circular motion around the piece of wood, creating a cluster of wood shavings at one end. When complete, the end of the feather stick should resemble a feather.

Kindling

Kindling describes small dry twigs and sticks which are added to the fire after an ember has been formed using tinder. Initially, you should use twigs with the thickness of a matchstick, gradually working up to larger pieces around the width of a single finger. When gathering wood for kindling, it is important to choose dry wood, which can be snapped easily.

If the kindling available to you is not completely dry, remove the bark (which carries most of the moisture in the tree) and break into small pieces.

Fuel

Fuel is the material in which you feed the fire to keep it burning. Many different materials can be used for fuel. The important factors to get your fire started are that the fuel is dry, and the timing when you add new fuel is right.

Do not fall into the trap of building your fire with timber, kindling, and firewood and lighting it all at the same time, as you will risk the firewood not heating up in time or depriving the fire of oxygen. You should use a cascade effect, making sure the heat generated by the initial fire is being used to light and burn fuel that is just a bit bigger. As fuel is first added to the fire, the idea is to build a base of hot coals by slowly adding larger pieces.

If you cannot find wood to burn, you can try burning other items. Dried animal dung, peat, and animal fat will all burn successfully, while man-made materials, especially those containing oil such as petroleum and anti-freeze, will also serve as fuel in emergency situations.

In general, the denser the wood, the more heat it will produce. Dense wood is heavier, but heavier wood can also be an indication of higher moisture content.

Softwoods such as pine, cedar, spruce, and chestnut burn faster and tend to produce more sparks than hardwoods such as beech and oak burn. If you are not sure whether a tree is a hardwood or softwood, press your thumbnail into it – if the pressure of your nail leaves a dent, then it is softwood.

Use dry wood to start the fire. Once it is going, you can use some damp or greener wood, if possible, mixed with dry wood to make a longer-lasting fire.

SELCO ON THE IMPORTANCE OF FIRE

When SHTF, lot of things changed, so ways to heat yourself and cook food changed too. Even folks who used wood for heating prior to the SHTF needed to learn some new ways of cooking food, obtaining wood and fuel, etc.

I use to know the exact time and amount of fuel needed to cook something. For example, I use to know how much polished wooden floor tiles (parquet stripped from some ruined house) I needed to make wartime "bread."

Fuel was pretty much precious, and most of the time, it was dangerous to go out and look for it. First, people chop and take it from city parks, cemeteries, etc.

After that, anything was good, furniture, wooden floor, door frames...

Everything connected to fire was valuable, ways to start it, and fuel too.

TOBY ON THE IMPORTANCE OF FIRE

Fire lighting and management is as much an art as a skill. There is simply no substitute for time spent practicing not only lighting fires but keeping them burning in a sustainable, efficient, effective manner. In almost all environments, a fire is going to be an essential aspect to the likelihood of your survival, train accordingly.

Building the Fire

The type of fire that you build will largely be dictated by conditions such as location and availability of fuel. In windy weather, choose a fire type which makes use of a hole, or set your fire in a depression in the ground.

Teepee

The teepee, or wigwam, fire is one of the easiest types of fires to build. After igniting the kindling, the fuel is placed on top in a triangular arrangement. This type of fire is suitable for warmth and cooking but burns through large quantities of fuel.

Star-shaped campfire

The star-shaped campfire also called the Indian campfire, is built so that 5 or 6 logs lie in a spoke lie arrangement, meeting in the center. As the logs burn, they are pushed into the middle. This type of fire is good for cooking and heating water and conserves fuel.

Dakota Hole

The Dakota Hole is useful when fuel is limited, or it is preferable not to attract attention. This type of fire is made by digging one large hole and one small hole connected the two with a small tunnel which works like a chimney.

Long log type fires

Long log type fires are useful when large pieces of fuel are available, and conditions are extremely cold. To make this type of fire, a depression is scraped into the ground, and the logs are placed in position with the fire on top. If required, two long log fires can be built, one on each side of your sleeping area, to increase the warmth emitted.

Using Rocks

Using rocks to create a fireplace can help to radiate the heat produced by the fire. Stones used in and near fires should be non-porous and not sound hollow when banged against another stone. Flaky or wet stones should also be avoided.

Transporting Fire

If you have successfully started a fire, but need to move camp for some reason, transporting fire will save you time and effort at your new base. To transport fire, hot coal or ember is extracted from the remains of the original fire and placed on a piece of dry rotted wood. Certain types of hard fungus, such as the Tinder Fungus, can also be used for this technique.

The coal and wood are then gently wrapped in damp leaves or grass and enclosed within a piece of thick bark. The aim is to allow enough oxygen to keep the coal lit, but not so much that it will set the bundle alight.

Fire Safety

- When working with fire, safety should always be a priority.
- Never build a fire which is too big to extinguish and always keep water or sand nearby to use to put the fire out in case of an emergency.
- Before breaking camp, fires should always be completely extinguished.
- Always ensure that clothing, equipment, and personal items are kept at a reasonable distance away from the fire to prevent them from being set alight by sparks or otherwise damaged.
- Make sure that everyone in camp understands the dangers of fire and are aware of basic fire safety rules. Remember that is someone's clothing catches fire, they should stop what they are doing, drop to the ground, and roll. Throwing a blanket over the person will also help to stop the clothing from burning. Keeping the fire triangle in mind, running is the worst thing that you could do in this situation, as the airflow increases oxygen.

Useful Tips

Understanding the theory of fire-making isn't enough – this is a practical skill that can take many attempts to learn. Don't wait until you are in a life or death survival situation to practice fire-making.

When deciding which type of fire to build, the method which requires minimum effort in terms of energy expended should be always the first choice.

Although it may be tempting to build a huge, roaring fire which you will need to set some distance away from, you will enjoy more heat and burn less of your resources if you sit close to a small fire.

Alternative Ways to Start Fire: Friction Methods

Starting a fire by friction, either by the fire plow or hand drill methods, is one of the most primitive techniques. These skills can take years of practice to master and should be considered as a last resort, as the effort involved to produce an ember can drain energy and spirits.

The fire plow comes into play when no other tools are available. Using one flat piece of wood with a baseboard of around 5cm in thickness, make a long groove. The second piece of wood is the plow, which should be long and thick enough to grasp in your hand.

Sliding the plow up and down the groove rapidly with a high level of friction creates powdery sawdust, which should then ignite and form an ember.

The hand drill method works like the fire plow, but instead of moving the plow up and down the wood, it is twisted on one spot. A hole is made in the baseboard, and the stick (spindle) is rolled between the hands in a rapid motion.

Since your hands will naturally move up and down the wood as you work, blisters can form, and it can be hard to get into a rhythm. Modifying the method slightly by making a notch at the top of the spindle and adding a length of string with a loop at each end for your thumbs. This can make the work more comfortable and easier to sustain.

Food Basics & Plants as Food

Don't get lulled into false complacency when you see crowded supermarket shelves—most grocery stores only have a 3 day supply of food. When it comes to food, you have to think in two directions:

storing food for short- and mid-term survival situations and getting food for long term survival situations.

SELCO ON FOOD

In SHTF time the human body is under constant stress, physical and psychological too. Before SHTF, I eat not thinking too much about food. When SHTF, I have seen that what I eat and how much I eat have a great impact on everything. In other words, it can kill you. When you hungry, your performances are lower than usual. In the normal times it does not mean too much, you just lower your activities until meal, and that s it. But when you need to run, jump, fight, scavenge, etc., every calorie counts.

When I was hungry, when I did not eat for a day or two, I was very cautious, and I tried to avoid any hard physical activity or confrontation. But sometimes that was not possible, and those days were very hard and dangerous.

TOBY ON FOOD

It is very true, food, in a survival situation, is the first thing we think about, but the last thing we need. In modern society, we have become exceptionally accustomed to food security and oversized portions.

The psychological 'shock' (and it is overwhelmingly psychological) once we miss meals and start to feel hungry can be a significant distraction to our survival activities. The simplest way to avoid this is to train yourself to deal with missing meals and to work through hunger pains.

This is a training we can do anywhere. You don't need to be in the wilderness even to try it! I routinely, through each week, skip meals, and change meal times. At least every two weeks, make sure you try and go a minimum of 18hrs without eating. These are simple, easy, powerful practices...

Rationing Food

If you have a limited food supply, you can ration your food instead of eating a lot on some days and just a little on others. Estimate the number of days you will have to live off the food supply and divide the food by the estimated days and the number of people.

Assign slightly bigger rations to people who do more physical work and slightly smaller rations to people who do not (about 20% of the calories we burn are because of physical exercise). Keep in mind that sick and injured people need bigger rations too. Men need about 2,500 calories per day, women 2,000 calories per day, and children and older people about 1,600 calories.

Food as an Energy Source

One pound of fat is about 3,500 calories. Most likely, you won't just be eating lard, so another real survival power food is nuts, which provides 2,500 calories per pound. Regular milk has about 2,500 calories per gallon.

Beans are a great source of energy, too, with 1,250 calories per pound. Beef has about 1,100 calories per pound. Crickets (yes, the insects!) have about 550 calories per pound. Wild meat, such as rabbit, boar, and deer, have about 500 calories per pound. Seafood has around 350 calories per pound. The amount of calories for vegetables varies between 100 and 200 calories per pound. Fruits come in at around 250-400 calories per pound because of their sugar content.

Nutrition Facts

	calories
Handful of Beans	1,250
A Chunk of Meat	1,100
A Cricket	550
Wild Pig	500

Plants as Food

Here are some tips for safely picking plants to eat.

Ninety percent of plants are not edible for humans. This makes it absolutely crucial that you identify plants before you eat them. Get a guidebook for plants in your area and practice identifying them. ? You should always thoroughly wash plants before you eat them—they may be covered in pesticides.

- Always eat plants in moderation. Larger amounts might cause stomach cramps and diarrhea.
- If you eat plants growing in a stream or pool of water that you suspect to be contaminated, the plants themselves are probably contaminated too. Boil them before consumption. ? Do not eat any plants that show signs of going bad, such as mold or fungus. Some fungus can be toxic.
- Never eat mushrooms unless you have experience identifying them. The nutritional value of mushrooms is very low, so if

you're not sure about a mushroom, it is not worth the risk of poisoning yourself.

Always avoid plants with:

- Milky or discolored sap
- Bitter or soapy taste
- Mushrooms growing on them
- Shiny leaves, fine hairs, spines, or thorns
- Dill-, carrot-, parsnip- or parsley-like foliage
- Yellow or white berries
- An almond scent, which is characteristic of cyanide compounds
- Umbrella shaped flowers
- Grain heads with pink, purplish, or black spurs
- Plants with three leaves, like poison ivy **Universal Edibility Test**

If you need to find out if a plant is edible, you can use the **Universal Edibility Test**.

Before you even begin the test, make sure there are enough plants of this type around to make it worth the effort of testing.

If possible, fast at least 8 hours before you test a plant and test only one plant at a time.

1. Separate the plant into its basic components – leaves, stems, roots, buds, and flowers. Some plants have edible and toxic parts.
2. Test if the plant irritates your skin. Crush one part of the plant and rub a bit of the plant on the inside or your wrist or elbow. Wait for 15 minutes and see if any irritation occurs.
3. If that doesn't cause any irritation, take that part of the plant and proceed to prepare it for eating. Touch the prepared food with your lips and see if there is any burning, itching, or numbness of your lips.
4. If nothing happens after 5 minutes, put the prepared food on your tongue, and keep it there for 15 minutes.
5. If there is no reaction, chew the plant and keep it in your

Chapter 3: Wilderness Survival | 209

mouth for another 15 minutes.
6. If nothing happens, swallow the food.
7. Wait for 8 hours. If you start to feel sick, induce vomiting, and drink a lot of water.
8. If nothing bad happens, eat a quarter cup of the food and wait another 8 hours. If nothing happens, the plant (part) is safe for eating.

If you consider a plant safe, but it still tastes terrible (such as acorns), you can improve the taste by cooking them with something sweet. Sap from trees such as maple, birch, walnut, and sycamore contain sugar. Collect the sap and boil it down to get syrup.

Boiling also gets rid of any bacteria. You can also use the inner bark of many trees, such as birch and pine, to flavor your food. Scrape the bark out, dry it, and grind it into flour for easy consumption.

When SHTF and food become very hard to find, only, then I realized how much time actually I spend imagine and thinking about food. In the beginning, it simply occupied your mind way too much, and you are not able to thing clear.

Later we learned to eat what we have and somehow not to think too much about what we want to eat instead of what we eat in reality.

Food somehow becomes what it is in reality- a way tor getting fuel for your body, and we concentrated on that.

So people, just like with all other things, start to "invent" some food (because of lack of real one), all kinds of soups (actually some plants in boiled water), pancakes (again plants with small amounts of wheat), and some new types of pies etc. We eat it and at the same time laugh how bad it tastes.

There were a lot of tries with bad results and cases of diarrhea and vomiting.

Fishing, Hunting & Trapping

The characteristics of the water you are fishing in determine what fishing method makes the most sense. In pools that provide little cover for fish, a spear is great. In running water or pools with a lot of undercut banks and overhangs where fish can hide, using your hands might work better (spears can easily get stuck in cracks or roots that float in the water). In still water with lots of vegetation, using hook-and-line fishing is probably the best method.

TOBY ON FISHING

> *Fish hooks and lines are cheap, compact, and lightweight and have many additional uses beyond their intended purpose.*
>
> *Be sure to pack a good quantity of line in your kit or Bug Out Bag. I'd recommend at least 50 meters (150ft) of two different*

breaking strength lines, and a minimum of 20 hooks of varying sizes.

Be sure to wrap your line around something for storage as fishing line tangles very easily

Hand fishing

Hand fishing is most effective in water with vegetation and hiding spots because the fish are used to being touched by plants and other floating debris. There are different ideas on how to effectively fish with your hands. One approach is to slowly stroke the belly of the fish to mesmerize it. Another suggestion is to put your hands under the fish and quickly flip it up, throwing the fish onto land.

We recommend that you handfish in areas with slow water current. Before fishing, search for any hazards that can hurt you. Check carefully around large rocks, under undercut banks, in areas with overhanging bushes, and under fallen logs.

When you fish, move your hands slowly in the same direction, the water is moving. Keep your fingers limp and focus on the touching sensation. In most cases, you will not be able to see, and you will have to feel for the fish.

Once you have found a fish, stay calm, and slowly try to find its head and determine its size. If the fish is big, gently move your other hand in as well. Try to locate the gills and place your thumb and index or middle finger on the side of the gills.

Do not apply any pressure yet unless you feel confident you are at the right spot, in which case, apply a lot of pressure quickly. The fish will struggle and relax, struggle, and relax. Make sure you grip the fish properly before you remove it from the water. If you feel it is slipping, try to throw it onto land.

If you cannot locate the gills, but the fish is in a hiding spot next to a wall, you can also push the fish against the wall and then make sure you have a good grip before you remove it from the water.

If you are hand fishing in a stream, we recommend you start downstream and move upstream.

That way, the sediment you stir up will not obstruct your view. Also, fish face upstream, so they will not be in their field of vision when you approach. Even if the stream is rather wild, you can always find areas and pockets of still water where fish hide.

Spearfishing

It is easy to create a spear, and they are easy to use. To make a spear that pins the fish (instead of puncturing it), follow these instructions:

1. Find a straight sapling. It should be 8 to 12 feet long, and no thicker than 1-1½" inches at the base.

2. Cut off all of the limbs, then sharpen the stick to a point. It is a good idea to leave the bark on because it will act as camouflage.
3. Measure about 9 inches from the shaft. Tightly wrap some string or other material around this point.
4. Create a split in the sapling from the top to the tip of the string. Never remove the string –it will keep the split from running down the entire sapling.
5. Make a second split perpendicular to the first one on the tip of the sapling.
6. To keep these tips apart, jam a twig into each of the splits.
7. If you need a longer spear than the one you have, you can simply tie sharpened sticks onto a bigger spear shaft.

When you hunt fish with a spear, make sure the spear is already very close to the fish before you strike. Keep it underwater so you can factor in the refraction so that you know where your spear is in relation to the fish. Aim for the head or the front half of the fish. Once you have caught the fish, grab it tightly with your hand to remove it from the water.

Hook-and-line

Fishing hooks and a line weigh almost nothing and make a good addition to your bug out bag or maybe even your etc. If you fish in an area with large fish, attach the fishing line to a stick you can grab onto tightly to avoid getting cut if the fish pulls the fishing line out of your hands.

Fish usually simply swallow their food, so a simple pointed piece of bone with a line attached can be used as a barb. This barb can be held flat in place by the bait you use. Once the bait is swallowed, the barb turns perpendicularly and gets stuck in the fish's gullet.

Hooks are better, as they find some resistance within the fish more easily. Use whatever you have to make a hook. Safety pins, sharpened paper clips, or other pieces of metal or sturdy plastic all work. You can also create hooks from wood. When you don't have ready-made hooks, make sure you are always on the lookout for material suitable for creating hooks. Bones are great for that.

Different bait works for different fish and different places. If you use live bait, such as worms, maggots, or frogs, let it simply sit on the hook and move on its own. If you use dead bait or lures, such as dead worms, pieces of meat, shiny pieces of metal, or pieces of cloth, give it a tug from time to time to create the illusion it is alive.

To keep your hook at a certain depth, tie a stone a foot below the hook. Tie a wooden bobber that can float the stone and the hook 4 feet above the stone. This way, you can fish at a certain depth. Experiment with different setups.

You can either bring the hook with the bait over your head and release it to throw out the line or use a pole if you want to get the hook farther out onto the water.

The bobber will move when a fish has taken the bait. When this happens, simply draw the line in by applying constant pressure. Walking backward away from the waterworks well. Only stop when the fish is far enough from the water that it can't slip back in.

You can also use poison to make fish easier to catch. Acorns mashed up and dumped into the waterworks, and so does black walnut. There are many local plants that can be used. Speak with experienced local fishermen for advice about this.

Fish traps

If you have nets, use them to catch fish. If you do not have a net, you can try funneling fish into pools you have created in running streams to make them easier to catch, or you can create closed pools in which fish are trapped when the water recedes (due to the tides or weather changes).

Hunting for Meat

Meat is one of the best energy sources and, therefore, also a great food for survival. When you think about hunting animals, start small. Ninety percent of insects are edible and are great sources of protein, essential vitamins, and minerals such as iron. If you compare the nutritional data of beef and crickets, they are similar. In fact, crickets have more iron and vitamins than beef.

Insects can save you from starvation. However, as with plants, you have to be careful which insects you eat—some can be toxic. These insects probably won't kill you, but they will make you sick.

You can use the appearance of the bugs and their odor to help you decide if they are safe to eat. Don't eat brightly colored bugs—stay away from bugs that are red, orange, or yellow. Black, green, and brown bugs are safe to eat. And, stay away from insects with a strong odor.

It's a good idea to find a book listing edible plants and insects and keep it with you when you are spending time outdoors.

Basics of hunting

When you hunt for meat, it is a two-step process—you have to get close enough to the prey and then kill it. In the first step, you sneak up on the prey or disable or hurt it so that it can't move, and in the second step, you close the distance and move in for the kill. Snares, traps, and shooting weapons can do the job for you in one step.

Finding prey

Look out for animal feces and tracks in your area. Tracks usually lead to places the animal visits on a daily basis to drink, eat, and sleep—even if you don't find the animal, you might find a water source or something else to eat.

You can also look for chewed, broken, or rubbed vegetation (missing bark on trees, for example) and for the remains of food. Bigger animals also leave vegetation pressed down to the ground when they use it as bedding.

If the tracks have claw marks, you are most likely looking at tracks from a canine critter. Cats can withdraw their claws into their paws. If you look at the composition of the feces,, you can get more clues as to what animal you are dealing with. **How to be an effective hunter**

Experienced hunters know what animals in their area are up to at different times of the day. They learn their patterns of behavior, when they eat, and where they relax in the sun and hide during bad weather. Some experienced trackers seem to almost be able to read the animals" minds.

Here are some tips on how to be an effective hunter: ? Always be ready to hunt. Have your weapon ready to act quickly to strike or disable prey. You might run into an animal when you're not even looking for one. If you do, freeze. It might not recognize you as a human, and you can plan your next move. Bring your weapon into position and hope that it comes even closer (if it doesn't smell you). Move very slowly. If you run into any dangerous animals, slowly withdraw, keeping your eyes on them at all times. Be ready to use your weapon(s) and move in circles around them to make it harder for them to catch you.

- Conceal yourself. Wear dark clothes and camouflage your skin with mud or charcoal. Use smoke or smelly plants to mask your human scent. Stay downwind from the animal and if you see it, only move when it has its head down. Freeze when the animal shows any

signs of being alert. Use your surroundings to hide and break up your human outline by adding sticks and foliage to your clothing. If you hide behind something, look around it and not over it to make sure you blend in better with the background.

- Always track. Whenever you find fresh animal tracks that look promising, follow them. ? Ambush. If you find a watering hole or area with many tracks marks, simply hide and wait. Make sure you are aware of the wind direction as your smell might alert potential prey to your presence.
- Lay traps. If you have something, you can use it as bait, set up simple traps, or put the bait in a location that makes it easy for you to ambush prey.
- Driving. If you are with a group of people, you can "drive" or herd animals into an ambush, traps, or a location that makes it easier to kill them.
- Get down and dirty. If you are following the blood trail of an animal you injured, the tracks of prey you are stalking, or if you want to conceal yourself, get down on the ground if you have to.
- Consider all dimensions. Use the terrain to your advantage—you might be able to find a spot where you can hide and throw rocks from above to stun or disable prey.
- Hunt in the morning. This is the time of day when night-active animals head home, and day-active animals get up to find food. Hunting in the dusk is good too, but then more predators are around that might make the hunt harder or even more dangerous for you. Do not hunt in the dark. We humans aren't made for that, and most night-active animals have senses that

are far superior to ours. You can still layout the bait and wait to ambush prey, of course. If you have a fire, small critters might also be curious and come closer to check it out.
- Be realistic. Do not try to tackle animals bigger than you without the proper equipment. ? Learn the habits of local animals. This can make hunting much easier and can help you if you lose an animal's tracks when you are stalking it. If you want to take this to the next level, learn to mimic mating and other calls to rouse animals' curiosity. This way, the animal comes to you.

Tracking

Pay attention to the following factors when looking at tracks:

- Weather. If it recently rained, did some rain collect in the tracks? If there is water in other holes in the ground but not

within the tracks, that will help you to determine how recent they are.
- Shape and contour. Wind and weather deteriorate the shape and contour of tracks. If the outlines aren't crisp and clear anymore, the track is older.
- Vegetation. If there is some new growth within the tracks, they are old.
- Dirt that gets kicked up. Depending on the surface some soil might have become dislodged and sprayed in the direction the animal was traveling.
- Size and depth. This can give you ideas about how heavy and big the animal is. Compare it with your own tracks for a point of reference.
- Dead ends. If tracks suddenly stop, look for means of escape such as trees the animal could have jumped on. If you didn't find any, the animal might have used their own tracks to go back. You can try tracking the trail back to locate the animal's den or maybe find out which direction the animal has gone in.

Trapping and snaring

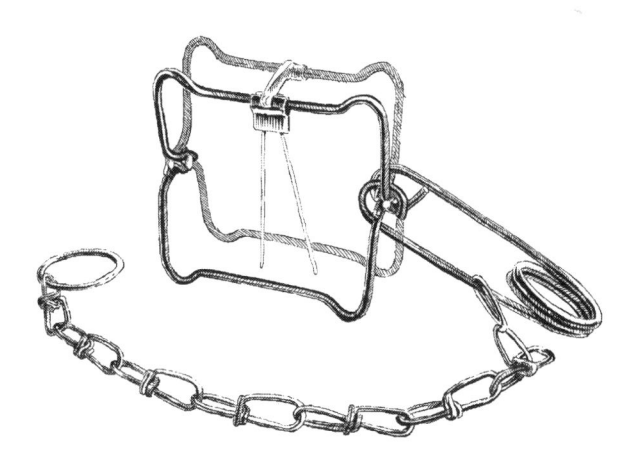

A great addition to every survivalist's equipment are small metal body traps. These very effective traps that are also often called "conibear" traps after Canadian inventor Frank Conibear kill animals quickly by snapping their necks and therefore minimize the time animals have to suffer or could escape.

Find out what kind of small game roams your area and get the appropriate size of traps. Check with your local authorities what kind of small game you are allowed to hunt.

Just like having a lighter beats starting a fire with a bow drill, primitive traps cannot beat the efficiency of commercial traps.

Besides small game traps, you can find even working bear traps that might come in handy for all sorts of bigger dangerous creatures.

Here are some tips for effective trapping.

- **Set up as many traps as possible.**
- Setting traps up properly and in the correct location are the deciding factors for success or failure. Set them upright outside of animal homes and next to watering holes or feeding grounds. Animal trails are also a good location for your traps–these can be found in heavy undergrowth and parallel to open areas and roads.
- If possible, add some bait next to the trap to lure the prey.
- Conceal your traps from animals and other humans.
- When setting up a snare along an animal trail, look at what kind of animal tracks you can find. If you find marks of several different animals, you have an animal trail; if you find just marks from one species, you have an animal run. Keep in mind that bigger animals that pass through a trail can destroy your snares.
- Create obstacles on the sides of the path leading to your trap or snare to funnel animals into it. These obstacles do not have to be impassable. They just have to make it inconvenient for the animal to head in that direction. Set the snare or trap up at the most narrow part of your funnel.

- There are a few things you can do to mask your human scent. If you can, wear gloves or rub your hands in mud before handling the snare. Smoke is also a familiar smell for most animals, and they only become alerted if the smoke comes with fire.
- Avoid human scent in the area around the snares or traps by building the traps somewhere else and then setting them up at the proper location. If you still have the gall or urine bladders of animals you have killed, you can use the fluid to mask the human smell.
- Try to use older wood instead of fresh live vegetation. Live vegetation broken apart will bleed, and animals can smell this and become alerted that something is wrong. If you do have to use young wood or you have left damage that might make animals suspicious, rub dirt over your trap.
- Get familiar with your traps and snares before you really need to use them. Mastering building two or three types of primitive snares or traps is far superior to knowing five different snares or traps without having any practical experience setting them up. ? For traps and snares without bait, location is even more important. If you have a bait that the animal is unfamiliar with, you can add a few bits of it a small distance away from the trap or snare so that the animal can get familiar with it and develop a craving for it. Most animals will simply keep eating and overcome their inhibitions to approach the snare or trap.
- If you suspect another animal that you didn't expect to show up took your bait and your snare or trap didn't work, set up a different snare or trap that could catch this other animal at the same location.
- Use some parts, such as the intestines, of animals you caught to use a new bait.

If you do not have professional traps or snares with you, you can build your own.

Basic snare

You can make a snare from a simple rope—all you have to do is make a slipknot. In the best-case scenario, you have snare wire. The loop has to be as high as the animal's head.

Twitch up strangle snare

This is a more advanced snare that snaps upwards once the animal's head moves the wire or rope. The benefit of this type of snare is that the prey will be kept out of reach of most other predators, and the chances are smaller than the animal can escape (it might get strangled right away).

Figure 4 deadfall

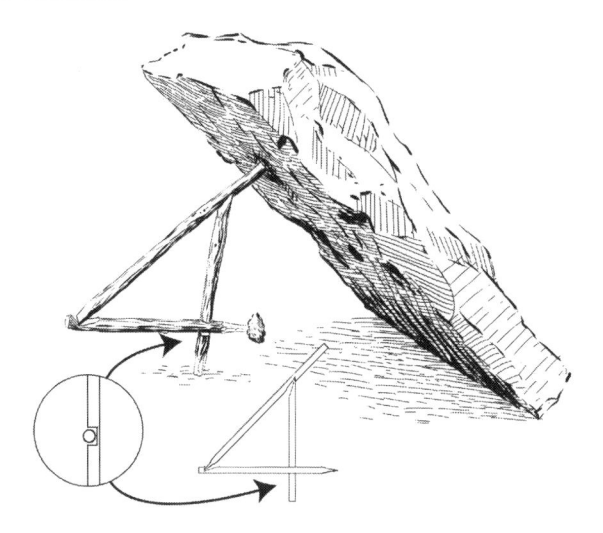

The deadfall is a trap that is used to kill small animals such as mice and squirrels. It is a mangling trap.

Hole trap

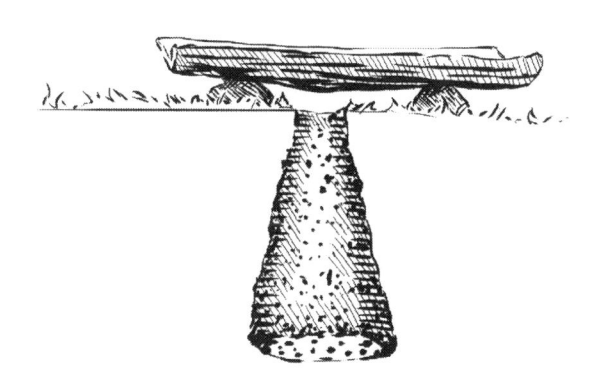

Bottle trap for fishing

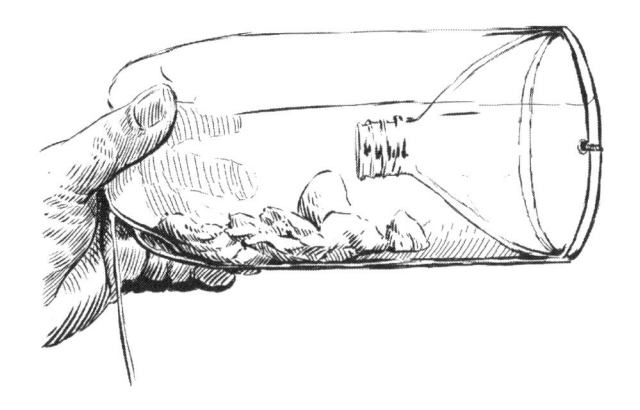

Box trap

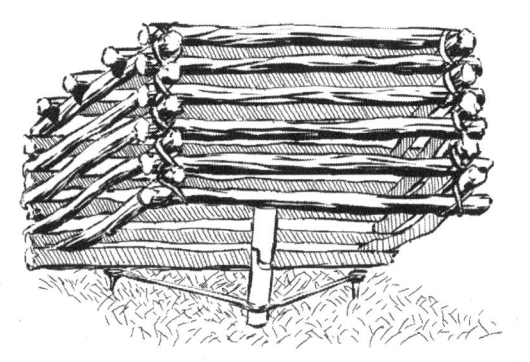

We make box traps using an L-shaped two-pin toggle trigger.

TOBY ON TRAPS

You need to check any traps or snares you set at least twice a day (ideally sunrise or sunset), approach traps with caution, and have the means available to you to dispatch any animals caught, but that maybe have not died.

Be aware that a trapped animal is one of THE most dangerous things you can deal with. Even small animals can cause significant damage to a person.

Building Weapons in the Wilderness

Bows and arrows

Crafting a usable bow and arrows is an art in itself. You have to know which trees have the best wood in your area and store the wood for some weeks before you can even start working on building your bow. That's why we do not cover building bows in this course. In survival situations, you will want weapons you can use right away that take little or no time to build.

Spears

To make a spear, find a straight, long sapling and sharpen one end to a barbed point.

To make the tip harder, hold it close to fire without burning it. You want to get all humidity out of the wood, so it becomes denser and, therefore, harder. You can also use sharp pieces of bone or stone and fasten them with rope onto the spear.

If you only have bigger bone pieces, smash them onto a hard surface and look for sharper, smaller pieces.

Use a knife to split the top of the stick to create an opening for the spearhead. You can carve out the insides of the split so the spearhead will fit more snugly into the opening. Use some rope to tie it securely into its position. Wrap rope around the thicker side of the spear just a few inches beneath the top.

Keep in mind that spears easily break if you miss the target or if it penetrates through the target into the ground.

A throwing spear should be between 5 and 6 feet long and strong enough to withstand the force of being driven several times, forcefully into the ground.

To throw the spear, hold it in your dominant hand and raise it above the shoulder so that it is parallel to the ground.

Your hand should hold the spear in the middle so that it is balanced and won't tip forward or backward. Mark this area with charcoal or whatever else you have at hand so that you can easily find this spot if you have to act fast. Twist your body so that your left leg is forward (if you hold the spear in your right hand) and extend your other arm to point towards the target. Thrust the arm that holds the spear forward and release. Aim for the chest.

Similar to a spear, an Atlatl uses a throwing stick to amplify the power of the darts it shoots.

Rocks and other throwing weapons

Hand-sized rocks can be great weapons to stun and kill animals. Throw them as if you were throwing a baseball and aim at the animal's head or shoulders. If you miss, you might still hit one of the legs and break it. Then move in for the kill.

A throwing stick (also called rabbit stick) works in a similar way. It is a two- to three-foot-long stick that is heavier on one side. You should fire harden the wood. The boomerang used by Australian aborigines is a modified version of a rabbit stick.

If you have a rope, you can tie several rocks together, wrapped in fabric, and create a bola. You swing the bola above your head until it reaches the desired speed and then releases it so that the stones hurl towards your prey and disable it until you can move in for the kill.

Slingshot

With a bit of practice, slingshots can be great for hunting small rodents and birds. You can make slingshots with pretty much any kind of elastic cord or surgical tubing. We recommend you buy latex tubing and carry it along. It is a great multipurpose item and works great for making a slingshot.

Weighted Clubs

Chapter 3: Wilderness Survival | 229

To make a weighted club, find a good solid stick (hardwood is best) and split the top in half. Find a rock that fits into the stick and lash it in place with some rope.

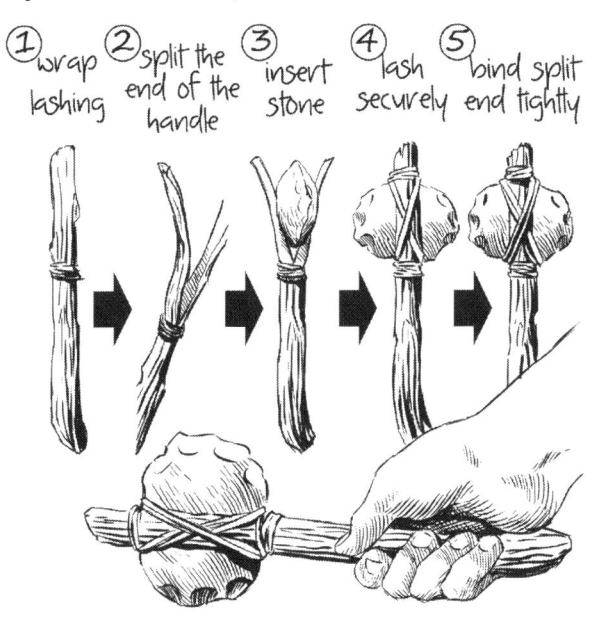

① wrap lashing ② split the end of the handle ③ insert stone ④ lash securely ⑤ bind split end tightly

Processing Meat

Processing Meat

So you made the kill and made sure the animal is dead. Now what?

To make animals edible you have to skin, gut, and butcher them. Do this far away from your camp so that when you process meat, you don't attract any predators.

In hot climates, meat spoils quickly, so your priority is to get the body heat out of the animal as soon as possible. Try to keep all meat cool and dry at all times. Get it out of the sun and into the shade. Another reason to start processing the animal as soon as possible is that the stomach and intestines quickly get bloated, and the gas that is released when you cut up the animal is rather unpleasant.

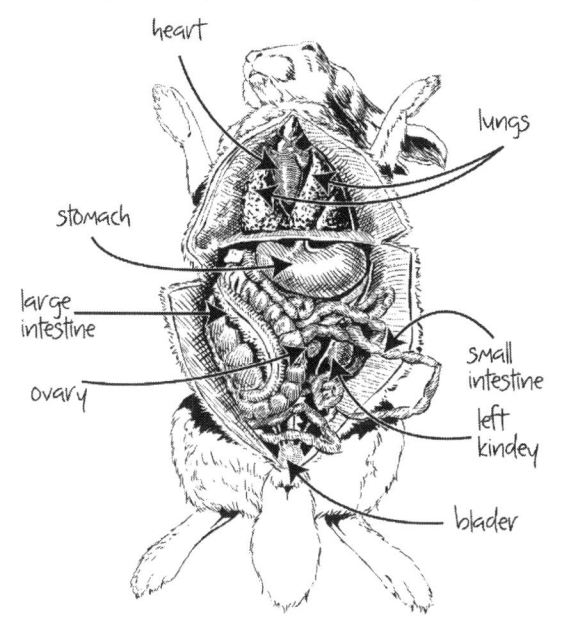

Labeled diagram of a rabbit's internal organs: heart, lungs, stomach, large intestine, ovary, small intestine, left kindey, blader.

Here are the steps to butchering an animal:

1. Start by cutting the animal's throat. If it is a bigger animal, collect the blood in a container for later use or don't bleed it out at all. The blood can stay in the animal to be cooked along with the meat. It is another great source of nutrition.
2. Turn the animal on its back and cut it open from above the anus around the male genitals (or start your cut above the vagina) all the way up to the breastbone (lower end of the rib cage). Insert the knife under the skin and turn the blade so only the hide gets cut, and you don't get the hair into the meat (and also so the fur doesn't dull your knife). Do not let the knife get in too deep to avoid damaging internal organs.
3. If any internal organ is punctured, make sure you wash the

meat with water immediately.
4. Reach inside underneath the organs and find where the organs are connected to the spine. Cut the connection. Cut the stomach lose from the esophagus and any connective tissue it is attached to. For bigger animals, you might have to reach all the way in and find the part where they are attached by touching. Pull out all the organs in one piece.
5. Take out the liver and kidneys. Be careful when cutting out the liver as the gallbladder is attached to it, and you do not want its contents all over your meat. Remove the gallbladder carefully from the liver. It breaks very easily.
6. If you are in a rush, someone else can start cooking the liver and kidney. Otherwise, just bag it or put the edible parts in a container to avoid flies getting to it.
7. Make sure you cut open all internal organs and search them for worms and other parasites. The liver should be smooth and deep red or purple. If it looks rotten, discard it. If the kidney is spotted, it is a sign of disease – discard all internal organs and cook the remaining muscle meat for at least an hour.
8. Next, remove the bladder. You can pinch the bladder shut before you cut it off. Then cut out the genitals and anus. Avoid pressing the lower intestines, so feces don't spill out. Now you can completely remove the intestines.
9. The next step is to cut through the diaphragm and split the chest open up to the throat. Reach into the chest cavity to take out the lungs and the heart. If you haven't already, cut off the head and take out the windpipe as well.
10. The liver, kidney, lungs, and heart are very nutritious and can be cooked in a stew (along with the blood).
11. Now cut off the legs and break the ribs so you can easily remove them from the backbone.
12. When you cut the meat into smaller pieces, pay attention to bones and sinews. There is a long sinew along the spine of many animals that can be used as a rope when dried. The Achilles sinew is shorter but can also be used in a similar

fashion.
13. Use the fat quickly as it spoils easily. Cut the fat off other parts of the meat. Cook what you can eat and cut thin strips of the meat to either smoke it or sun dry it.

Cooking times

Cook birds a minimum of 20 minutes to kill parasites. Cook internal organs of all animals for 20 minutes or more. Intestines and meat that is hard or rubber-like should be cooked for an hour to make it tender.

Preserving & Preparing Food

In the best-case scenario you can keep animals alive until you need the meat and then slaughter them.

If temperatures are below 40F (4C), you do not have to worry too much about your meat and can simply keep it as it is for a few days. If temperatures rise, try to cool the meat during the night by hanging it. Protect it during the day with insulation material such as sleeping bags, down jackets, or foliage.

If the weather permits, you can sun dry your meat. The best temperature is 85F (29C) or hotter. If the temperature drops below 20F (7C) degrees from the highest temperature, then you will have a problem with condensation and mold. If that's the case, try to move the meat to warmer places at night. You should only do this in areas with low humidity. Under very humid conditions, you have problems with mold in any case.

You will also want to have proper air circulation in the area where you are drying meat. Place the meat on strings or wire and hang it between two trees in full sunlight. Move the meat to a dry location if it starts to rain.

Sun-drying does not remove any bacteria, and the meat can spoil easily in the process if not all conditions are met. It takes one to multiple days until the meat is dark and brittle – this is how you know it is ready. Check on the meat daily and if conditions suddenly turn bad, finish the drying process next to a fire or hot coals.

You can create a tripod over the fire and spin wire or rope around it. Hang meat on the wire or rope and cover the tripod with a tarp or big piece of cloth. Make sure the cover is not in contact with the meat. The cover can have a small opening on top to let some of the smoke out.

If properly dried and stored, dried food can be kept for 6 to 12 months. Vegetables will expire more quickly than fruits because they do not have the high sugar content that fruits have. Store dried meat, vegetables, and fruits in dark, dry conditions. It is best if you can seal them in boxes so that pests can't get near the food.

Preparing Meat and Vegetables

The best way to make sure the meat is heated through and that bacteria and other nasties are gone are to boil the meat. To get all nutrients, you also have to drink the broth. Roasting meat is another option.

After grilling the meat over a flame, keep it hot next to the fire or hot coals, so it gets baked even more. This will ensure it is heated through, and bacteria get killed.

If you have sticky soil, you can also try mud baking. In this process, you wrap the meat or complete the animal in mud and bake it in the fire. The mud gets hard, which usually rips out the feathers of birds and the skin and fur of animals when you take the mud off.

You can also bake and cook in some plants. Bamboo can be filled with meat and placed into a fire. Bigger leaves from non-poisonous plants can also be used.

Underground baking is also a popular way to prepare food in many cultures. Dig a hole that is slightly larger than the food you want to cook. Line the insides with rocks (the rocks should be very dry, so they do not explode) and make a fire in the hole.

Place other stones in and around the fire—you'll need these later to put on top of the food. Once the fire has burned out, add some green grass and leaves on top of the hot coal and stones, and then add the food. Add another layer of green matter and cover it with the hot stones and then some soil to close the hole. Let your food cook for some time. Smaller animals can be done in two to three hours, while bigger animals such as deer can take 12 to 24 hours.

Boiling

Hopefully, you have a container you can place in a fire. If not, you still have some alternatives.

For instance, you can dig a hole and line it with some plastic, foil, clay, or a big leaf to keep water in it. Or, you can find a bowl-shaped hole in a tree stump or rock formation. Anything that can hold water will do. Then, heat up some stones in or next to a fire (watch out for stones that might contain humidity because they can explode) and put them into the hole filled with water. The hot stones release their heat into the water, and by adding several stones, you can get the water boiling.

SELCO ON FOOD

After some time, we all adopted habits of eating the food that tasted awful or, in better cases, did not have a taste at all. We get used to the fact that there was always something missing. For example, if we had wheat to make something, we did not have salt or the opposite. Also, we all developed some kind of mechanism of how we coped with unpleasant food. When we were very hungry and had something to eat that taste very bad, we add some stuff.

Usually, that were all kinds of plants that simply "kill" bad taste or add some of its own taste and smell. The sauce in small bottles from MREs was very good for it. I even used my imagination. For example, when I ate some pasta or rice that was infested worms or maggots. I simply did that in the dark without being able to see all the nasty details in a bowl, and I imagined that I am eating something nice. Sometimes it works, sometimes not.

Cannibalism

This is a very controversial topic with many different points of view. We cannot offer definitive advice because, at the end of the day, some people might prefer to die instead of eating fellow humans. Hunting other people to eat them is pretty much out of the question if you are still guided by any morals. However, if someone is already dead, the meat can be a good source of energy.

4. Chapter 4: Violence

Thanks to popular media, the use of violence for survival is romanticized. Unlike the picture of some movies and games paint, survival is not about having the most firepower or being the toughest fighter. It is about avoiding violent encounters, getting away from them if they can't be avoided, de-escalating them, and, only if that fails, fighting.

Two Main Types of Violence

The first, necessary violence, is violence that comes from the survival instinct, such as when you have to butcher an animal to eat it, or when you have to take water by force from a spring that is guarded by unfriendly people.

The second type, unnecessary violence, isn't as black and white. Unnecessary violence is motivated by emotion. Social violence fits into this category. This kind of violence is motivated by emotions such as anger, hatred, revenge, or the desire to affirm or gain social status.

Examples of social violence include domestic violence, road rage, gang violence, and bar fights.

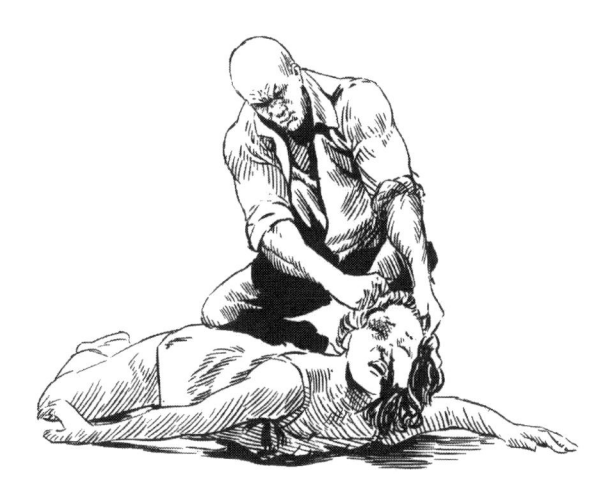

The good news is that, with social violence, you can often manipulate the one who is threatening you to get out of the situation. Let's have a look at some common social violence situations and what you can do.

Situation:

You are sitting in a bar, and you end up looking at some guy for a bit too long. He realizes you are looking at him and is offended. He gives you the classic: "What are you looking at?"

What Happened:

The guy feels you have challenged his status—even if he is a big guy, he may always feel like he has to prove he is tough. Drugs and alcohol just amplify this behavior.

Best Course of Action:

Apologize and let him know you didn't mean to stare at him. For example: "Oh, I didn't know I was staring at you. Sorry if that offended you." Say this with a confident but not arrogant or aggressive voice. Look sideways while saying this—if you look up, you seem arrogant, and if you look down, you seem weak.

You do not want to come across as weak or scared because that would show him that you are an easy target if he wants to fight, but you also don't want to seem as if you are challenging his social status. If you state what just happened and that you did not mean to challenge him, you can both walk away from the situation without either one of you having your pride injured.

SELCO ON USING VIOLENCE AS TOOL

Urban legend says that if you show your teeth to the aggressor, he will go away and leave you alone. Reality says that if you show your teeth in the wrong moment, you may lose it.

Pride and winning are usually two totally different things, so in real life, choose how you are gonna look and on what way you gonna act based on a given situation. Sometimes (many times) leaving the place and "turning your back" is actually winning, however wrong could look. On the other hand, forget about honor when involved in real-life violent situations.

So always choose when it is best for YOU to be violent, not for the enemy. If that means to wait for him to turn his back so you can attack him, or for you to play weak and sissy just to fool him, then play like that.

The best course is to avoid trouble, but if you are really involved in it, then play by YOUR rules (no rules) and win. In a real fight, there is no background music and "highlighted" epic scenes.

Problems:

The first problem is you. Your ego tells you not to back down. This is especially a problem if women or other people you know are around. You feel that your social status is challenged, and you have to defend it.

This is b#llsh!t.

First of all, women think differently about the use of violence than men do. If you do happen to be with a woman who enjoys seeing you fighting for her, it might not work out well for you in the end—you can't be sure that she will be there for you to push your wheelchair around after someone breaks your spine.

Engaging in social violence to keep your ego from being hurt is a bad deal. You risk broken bones and long-term injuries, along with punishments dished out by the government—all to avoid a bad feeling that would probably bother you for a few hours at the most.

The second problem might be that the threat is not happy with your answer and escalates the situation. This usually results in more verbal abuse or him coming over and touching/ pushing you.

If this happens, your best course of action is to say loudly and clearly that he should stay away from you (this helps if the fight escalates so that any bystanders and police know who the bad guy is). You still can't hit him first unless he attacks you. Try to leave. Walking away is hard on your ego, but if you have avoided harm, that is what matters.

Keep in mind that fights are more often won by someone giving up than by someone being so hurt that they can't keep fighting. Most fights are won by breaking the will of the enemy to continue, instead of making him unable to continue fighting.

You think this advice is wrong at a survival course and didn't expect such "coward" solutions? Read on.

Control Over Your Ego

The ability to control your ego goes a long way when it comes to dealing with everyday violence. To get the point across, let's have a look at another social violence situation, this time with group violence.

SELCO ON AVOIDING GROUP VIOLENCE

The main thing is always to stay out of trouble, and a big group of the people in SHTF time means trouble for you almost always.

It is usually a gang or mob, and they are having their own mind (group). The first choice, of course, is always to get out of there. For example, you and people rioting and looting are coming on their way is not a good option, even if they are just blocking the road without rioting. Very easy and "casually" change your direction and avoid them, run only as a last option.

If you cannot avoid them, then "join "them. For example, if a group of folks rioting and looting on your way, and you cannot avoid them, then just act like them until you are able to slowly go "through" them.

You need to follow a group dynamic if you cannot avoid them. If they were beating someone, you do not necessarily need to join them in that, but you can be angry too. You can yell, etc.

One of the last options if you need to go through them (for example, a group of "punks" blocking your only way to BOL, some passage or similar), then you can "scare" them or bluff them. For example, in the early stages of SHTF playing "authority" in some cases works ("OK guys, I am medic, need to go there immediately" or similar) it can work in some specific situations. During my SHTF, I worked in a situation on one road barricade when the man played "foreign reporter." It is a high risk, of course.

Social Group Violence

Groups often show their power by intimidating people around them. They block passages, make loud noises, or do other things that catch people's attention. Once a person challenges their power in any way, they go after him.

Situation:

You are out in your neighborhood and run into a group of people. The group is a loosely formed gang that just got together recently.

What Happened:

Wrong place, wrong time. The problem with groups is that everyone wants to prove how tough they are. In these kinds of groups, the strongest, cruelest person gets the most respect.

Best Course of Action:

Get out of this situation. You have nothing to gain fighting a group of people if you aren't sure you can win. Try to avoid the group without obviously fleeing. Fleeing is a sign of weakness, and that makes you an easy target.

Problems:

If you realize people are coming after you, just run. This is better than taking the beating, or something even worse. **Asocial Violence**

Another type of violence is asocial violence.

You have to understand that there are evil people who enjoy being extremely violent and sadistic. Many people do not want to acknowledge this reality. They think these sorts of evil people only appear in horror movies, but that's not the case. In order to be mentally prepared to deal with them and what they could potentially do to you, you have to acknowledge the existence of these asocial predators.

There are some common characteristics of asocial predators. One of these is that they are very impatient. They also tend to drop their masks from time to time because it is hard to keep up a nonstop façade of civility. If you can, speak to friends and family of the suspected asocial predator to see if the person has left a trail of destruction in their wake.

Predators can be roughly split into two groups. You have the resource predator, who is interested in something you have, and you have the process predator, for whom hurting or killing is the ultimate goal.

Robbers are typical resource predators, while people who enjoy seeing others suffer, such as rapists or violent psychopaths, are process predators. Of course, a predator can be both a resource predator and a process predator. Some robbers enjoy applying unnecessary violence, and some killers rob their victims afterward.

A group made up of predators is often not very stable and can fall apart violently because each individual is just out to satisfy his or her own needs. Process predators like to isolate their victims and avoid killing in a group because witnessing such an act gives the group leverage against the killer.

SELCO ON HIS EXPERIENCES WITH PROCESS PREDATORS

> *I was surprised when I saw how many people turn to sadistic violence. The point is that you can expect it from some people based on their "reputation" prior the SHTF (for example, your neighbor who beats his wife without reason, or some jailed rapist or similar), but the true danger comes from a lot of "normal decent" folks who finally find themselves "awaken" when SHTF, and start to do their sick dreams in reality.*
>
> *You cannot do too much today about those folks, you never know who is who (from those normal folks) before SHTF and they get some power. But you can be careful with your plans and preparing and with who do you talking about it.*
>
> *When SHTF, your best defense from those types of people is good preparation, a good group of people, and no remorse and mercy.*

Two common approaches by predators are charm attacks and surprise attacks. In a charm attack, the predator might ask you for help or encourage you to follow him to a quiet place where he can hurt you or threaten you until he gets what he wants.

Surprise attacks come out of nowhere and are a popular tactic because no predator wants a fair fight. They want to overwhelm you so they can get what they want. Asocial predators are encouraged when they hear their victims cry or beg.

A predator wants to be alone with you to unleash all their violence. This is why people often die at a so-called secondary crime scene. They get attacked at crime scene number one, and then the predator forces them or simply takes them to crime scene two where they are alone.

So keep in mind if an attacker wants to take you for a ride, it means bad news.

It is important to understand that the use of violence is usually connected to power or domination. Violence is just the tool of choice to exert power over others. This is the main motivation of most hostage-takers when they rape, murder, or torture other hostages in front of the remaining hostages.

Aggression in response to violence often makes little to no sense. When you train for violence, you will want to perfect your techniques and how to fight, move, and handle your weapons. When it comes to actual fighting, a technique often plays a much smaller role–your mental determination and clarity determine if you get out of the situation alive and/or as a winner.

The mindset of a Predator

What Enables People to Kill?

Do you have it in you to kill? You might say "no" right now, but if SHTF, your answer may change. Here are the reasons why people may kill:

1. **Killing to preserve yourself and/or your way of life.**

This one is self-explanatory. If your way of life is threatened, or those you love are threatened, you will do what you need to protect them.

2. **Killing because you feel you are better than your victim.**

This feeling of superiority may be there because you feel that your culture, ethnicity, and social class are all the better than those of your victim. It may also be a feeling of moral superiority–it is OK to kill because your cause is more important than your enemy's cause.

3. **Killing because you don't see your enemy as a human.**

This kind of killing can result from such a deep hatred of your victim that you don't even believe that they are human, which makes you feel like it is OK to kill them.

4. **Killing because someone told you to.**

The prime example of this reason to kill is soldiers in the military, who are trained to kill on command and without hesitation. They are put through the drills over and over again until killing becomes a reflex that is performed as soon as the order is given.

5. **Killing because it's what everybody else is doing.**

Lynch mobs and rioting are two examples of situations with this kind of killing. It doesn't accomplish anything, and there is no reason for it, but once the killing starts, many people in these groups will join in.

6. **Killing for revenge.**

Maybe you're getting revenge for murder, theft, or adultery—or maybe it's an offense that is all in your mind. Whatever the case, revenge can often be the impetus that propels people to pull the trigger.

7. **Killing because it doesn't seem real.**

If you have a rifle with a scope, night vision goggles, or other fancy gear that makes you feel invisible as you kill, then killing can seem very easy—like you're doing it in a video game instead of real life. It may seem like there are no real consequences to your actions.

8. **Killing just for the heck of it.**

Although it is only 2% of the population, you should still keep in mind that there are those who will kill without any reason to.

Some of these reasons for killing might sound extreme to you, but you have to keep in mind that you will have your reasons for killing, and others will have theirs. Survival means not only killing when you have a good reason to, such as when you need to protect your family but also being aware that others out there are capable of killing for far less important reasons.

Interview with a Killer

This is an interview with a guy who started his "career" during the war and continued to work in this field. It can give you some insight into the reasoning of people who do not value other people's lives much. He is working alone. He is something like a „muscle guy" for some politicians, tycoons, loan sharks, and similar.

How did you start getting into doing what you do/did?

Remember how life was simple in a way in the war? Yea, it was shitty, of course, no food, no anything, fear, dirtiness, and all that.

But it was simple if you want it to be simple. If you were ready to kill, then life could be good. Without parents (he was an orphaned, the state raised him), I learned to take care of myself. I know street rules, and I beat a lot of other folks, and they beat me too.

When the war started, I saw that the state is dead (society, police, laws...). I jump in. The state was constricting me. Without it, I was doing very well. I did what I wanted.

What do you think about other people in general? What's your picture of humans?

People are fools. I figured out quickly. When the war started. You just need to act in your favor, and that's it. Do whatever you want because you want to do (in terms of earning, stealing, and getting rich).

You take the group of people who is capable of surviving **** like war, and inside that group, there is a small group who are capable (physically) for doing real **** for survival and living (capable for killing), and then inside that small group, you have a very small group of folks who are really (mentally) capable of doing some real **** (kill) without problems.

I found myself inside that small group, and I am good at that.

Everyone outside that group is fools and idiots who are either believing that someone gonna protect them, or they believe if they do only good stuff, they will be good, or they will end up in paradise or some similar ****.

How did you pick your targets?

Man, you know how it was at that time. Stuff was everywhere (in terms of stuff for taking, robbing, he means opportunities were everywhere and targets). Targets picked me. Actually, those victims wanted that. You know how big numbers of fools were everywhere around us. You needed to just go out and take stuff from folks.

What makes a target a good target?

Fools were unprepared for folks like me. I was like a devil for them. They could not imagine there are people like me. A good target was a man who had his mind like living in normal times. He did not recognize that new times had come and that there are folks like me. I remember so much surprise by people when I was in action. People have no idea.

What makes a target a bad target?

Of course, there were people who are dangerous, and actually, I did not have too much business with tough guys simply because there are a lot of weak ones outside. Why should I attack some armed and dangerous guy if I had enough other targets?

How do you think about your targets?

I do not give **** too much about them. I do not think of them as men or women. I actually consider the level of threat that they are to me. I do not have any other interest in them.

When I get sent to do my job (to collect money, beat someone, today for a boss, loans, etc.) I do not look at them as people. I think of them as objects. It is easier to work like that.

How do you get new jobs?

Look at me. Today I do not need to talk too much. Other people talk about me instead of me. Folks know what I did to some people. They do not want to end up like that. I do not need to talk too much about my work. I am popular; that's it.

How do you feel about killing?

I do not feel anything for a long time ago, from my first time, and even then, I forgot what I was thinking. I remember that feeling back then was strong, and that's it. I do not feel anything for a long time. I just do a job.

Is there a fun side to hurting people?

No, it is not supposed to be fun. At the moment, when it becomes fun, then something is wrong with your actions, and you are just losing it (losing focus of job). It is fun when I beat someone, maybe, but the real stuff is not fun, and it is not supposed to be.

Did you ever feel regret afterward?

Yes, when I did something wrong, and it could be dangerous for me (when he was „sloppy").

How did you feel during your first kill?

It was fast, it was like someone else is doing it, and I am just watching it. It was so fast that I actually do not even remember details.

How did your feelings change over time doing what you do?

I am thinking much more now about my safety and security. I just learned a lot. I know how people usually react to different things.

What are the typical reactions of victims?

Beg or pray. Almost always beg or pray. Or both, first beg, then pray when they realize that's it.

What was one of the worst reactions you had to deal with?

Sometimes screams bothered me too much. It is like sometimes I just could not stand when they screamed too much. ****.

What reaction is the best (most hassle-free for you)?

It is easier when they do not know what is coming. I mean, it is easier for me. Sometimes I do not want to watch their face.

>How do you prepare before a job?

Simple. All that I have when I do a job is simple, and I can close quickly (all equipment and clothes get thrown away).

What are your tools of the trade? What is your preferred mode of operation? (How do you do things?)

He was not too in the mood for talking about weapon details and his tactic. I guess it is normal because he still works.

Self Defense & Fighting

There are several layers of self-defense—from avoiding violence altogether, to how to deal with it when it happens.

1. **Avoiding Violence**

The best way to survive violence is to avoid it altogether. There are some basic steps you can take to avoid ever getting into violent situations, and many of them have to do with paying attention to your surroundings and your own actions.

1.1. **Planning**
- Stay with people whenever you can.
- Avoid places where people are intoxicated.
- Avoid people who have a history of violence.
- Blend into groups, dress, and walk like others around you.
- If you are with a group of people who might be violent, leave. If you can't leave, act like the others in the group—just tone down your behavior. Speak a bit less than others, and have little eye contact with them.

- Do not expect that people will act just the way you think they might, or according to your preconceived ideas.
- Draw lines that no one can cross without consequences. For example, don't let strangers enter your personal space within punching range.
- Don't follow people you do not know or trust in places they suggest.

1.2. Target hardening
- Show confidence
- Walk with a goal in mind
- Do not hesitate when you do something
- Look threatening if you have to
- Give out as little information as possible when you speak to people you don't know.

2. Escaping Violence

If you do end up in a violent situation, there are steps you can take to get out of it as soon as possible, and in one piece.

2.1. Being aware and spotting intent
- Be more alert in fringe areas (secluded areas close to busy areas such as parking lots, parks, alleyways, or bathrooms).
- Be aware of your thoughts and feelings and how they influence your behavior to avoid making the wrong decisions.
- Have different levels of awareness (see the end of this article for awareness levels). Each level has different practices and modes of operation.
- Look out for people who don't take care of their hygiene. People who are addicts or mentally ill usually don't take care of themselves.
- Some people play crazy. Truly crazy people try to be normal but can't. If someone wears crazy clothes, it is a choice; if someone wears random clothes but acts crazy, it is more likely he is really crazy.

2.2. Interview

Threats usually use the same pattern of behavior to approach you so they can see how easily they can control you or how scared you are. Disrupt this pattern by controlling the situation and showing confidence.

• Do not become defensive or offensive. Show the threat that you do not want to fight, but if it happens, you are the wrong guy to screw with.

• Try to stay neutral when a predator looks for reasons to become violent.

• Treat questions as reasonable questions or act crazy/mad.

• Act like a high-energy person with a psychotic disorder. Do sharp twitching movements and show different facial expressions quickly before returning to a neutral expression (practice all of this in front of the mirror).

• Keep talking and filibuster the threat. This can give him a chance to cool down.

• No threat likes attention. Loudly state that a person should back off. The threat might give up on you as a victim simply because he thinks some people might have noticed this. Better to be a bit rude than to get assaulted.

• Do not show you are scared. Speak with a calm, low-pitched voice.

• Scan people from head to toe to show your readiness.

• Keep walking. Do not let yourself get distracted or caught up on conversations.

2.3. Positioning

Some threats come close to ask questions. Just say no and keep distance between you. Stay aware of your position within the space so you can use your environment to your advantage.

2.4. De-escalating the situation

• If someone is staring at you, look at his mouth instead of his eyes when you talk to him. ? Forget about saving face. If you are instructed to do something, do it unless you are dealing with antisocial predators who will make you suffer regardless.

- If you accidentally get into a group of possible predators, ask for help or directions. This flatters the ego and can explain why you are there.
- Do not judge ill people. They do not just think they hear voices. They actually hear them. Don't threaten them. Instead, show them that if they do something positive, they get rewarded for that.
- Match the energy level, speed of talking, and pitch of voice of the threat and then start to talk slower and more calmly. This often calms the threat down as well without him noticing it.
- Ask people who are worked up how this situation could be resolved.
- Understand and accept that the threat's brain doesn't work the way your brain works.

2.5. Escape
- Don't simply run away from a threat. Run towards safety.
- Learn different escape routes in areas you frequent often. Stay aware of these routes so that you can use the best way to escape in a problematic situation. We develop habits of walking in certain ways, but these ways are often not the best routes to escape.
- When you have to escape in a new environment you do not know, try to go where you came from.
- Just as when you try to inflict damage in a fight, don't do anything half-assed. If you decide to escape, run–don't just walk faster in a certain direction, even if your ego tells you not to run because it will show that you are scared.
- Focus on where you are going and not on the person chasing you to avoid panic and accidents while escaping.

2.6. Get help from others
- Try to get other people around you to notice you.
- Do not expect others to come to your help. Ask people for help.

3. Fighting

The adrenaline that rushes through your body will severely impact you're fine motor skills. If you are not used to fighting, you might shake and tremble. This is just one reason why it is a good idea to train for a fight beforehand.

3.1. Training for a fight

- Look for local martial arts training. Every training is better than no training, but if you can, look for combative training and self-defense courses instead of training common martial arts such as judo, taekwondo, or karate. If you cannot find self-defense or combative training in your area, mixed martial arts, boxing, or Muay Thai (Thai boxing) are good alternatives.
- Use operant conditioning to train for some common fight situations. That means you rehearse certain situations over and over until your response to this situation is almost instinctive.
- Train for general situations, such as attacks from the front, the side, or the back. It is not important that you know many ways to react but that you can react quickly and efficiently.
- A perfect move betters your position (to control the threat or apply force on him), worsens the attacker's position (so that he can't reach you), protects you from damage (by being able to block the next move of the threat), and damages the attacker. ? Get into the habit of doing unpleasant things quickly and without hesitation to condition yourself to simply act without always questioning everything.
- Practice recovering from failures quickly (this helps you to easily deal with situations, such as when a fight doesn't go your way).
- Imagine you have an alter ego, a fighter's persona in you. If you switch to this persona, you forget about all the things society has taught you, and you can just be violent. This helps if you struggle with any hesitation to apply violence.

3.2. First contact

- Action beats reaction. Depending on the situation and consequences you might have to face, it might make sense to hit first. If you start the fight, distract the threat with a weird question such as asking him what he had for breakfast. Follow this question right away with your first hit. It takes time for the threat to process what he just heard and change into fighting mode.

Your goal is not to teach the threat of a lesson. Your goal is to get out of this with the least amount of injury. Escape whenever you see a chance to or neutralize the threat if this makes more sense (don't forget the long-term consequences).

- Try to hit back right away before you take more damage. Learn a simple and efficient counter-attack move you can use to do some damage. Don't do this if you are facing an overwhelming force in a fight you cannot win. In this case, cover your head and neck and hope for the best.
- Try to control the fight by changing your position and attacks.
- A ***** slap can remind someone of when they were a child and being punished. This may make them submit more easily.
- Some people freeze because they are so overwhelmed. Don't be that person – train to react automatically and follow through with what you want to do.

3.3. During the fight

- Every action has to be 100%. If you hit the head, imagine punching through it. It is about clearly sending the message to the threat that he is messing with the wrong person.
- Do not get stuck in behavior loops. For example, you have your enemy pushed to the ground, and you try hitting his head, but you can't effectively strike it. Some people get stuck at this point and keep repeating the same move instead of thinking about what else to do.
- Expect tunnel vision, extreme focus, and lack of peripheral vision. It is easy to sneak up on people who are pumped up on adrenaline.
- Avoid getting lost in thoughts. Unrelated thoughts will pop up in your head. Stay focused on your next move.
- Take a break if you have the attacker safely under control and try to breathe a bit slower to get control of your survival stress response.

- Use all your senses to stay in the moment. Focus on your smell or other bodily sensations to be more present.
- Don't expect certain reactions from the threat even if all your training partners showed a certain kind of reaction. Expect to be surprised.
- Use your environment to help you. Use it for cover or as a weapon.
- Use everything you have to overwhelm the threat. Shout, act mad, laugh when you get hurt. Use everything you can to surprise the threat and put him in an uncomfortable position. Create situations the threat cannot cope with.

If you deal with social violence, leave a face-saving exit. Let them run away from something else and not you – for example, by announcing that reinforcements or law enforcement are arriving soon.

- Inform the threat of what you are going to do next if you have him under control. This can help to justify the force you applied and offers the threat to the possibility to comply and submit. Tell the threat of what he can do to give up.
- Order the threat to stay down or offer them other directions to submit.
- Make sure the threat is incapable of harming you once he submits.

3.4. Losing a fight

- Try playing dead/unconscious as a last resort.
- Introduce chaos into the fight. If you throw yourself and the threat down some stairs, the cards get shuffled anew. Your advantage in this situation is that you know that it's going to happen, but the threat is surprised.
- Accept defeat, and don't get hurt more because your ego tells you to get up and keep fighting.

4. After the Fight

You not only have to take care of yourself physically and mentally after a fight, but you also have to think about the next fight and what you can do better.

- Check yourself for injuries, look for blood, and see if anything doesn't feel right. Then check others.
- Check others for ABC (airway, breathing, circulation).
- Do not move injured people if you don't know what you are doing.
- If you get sweaty, cold, or agitated, you might have internal bleeding.
- Drink a lot of water in the hours after the fight to metabolize stress hormones. ? Be prepared that you might experience really weird sensations like shaking, collapsing, crying, and so on.
- Don't let people talk you into having problems – it's ok to be ok.
- Surviving violence will shake up your worldview, so be prepared for that. The problem with violence is that we are not used to it anymore. It takes away trust that you had in people and in safe environments. See the good side of this. It is a wake-up call on how quickly things can get nasty.

Do some sort of debriefing for yourself in which you go step by step through the whole situation again and think about the decisions you made and what you could have done better. This will help you to learn from any mistakes and will also help you to better process what happened. Do not be too hard on yourself.

- Did the attacker have a group, gang, or family that might come after you?
- If you talk with someone who has inflicted or experienced heavy violence, just listen and don't judge.
- The world is, luckily, secure enough that small things can become big problems in our life, but understand that nature hasn't always been like this. The horror of a survival scenario is just that we revert back to a more primal basic way of living and this change is scary. More is at stake, more can go wrong, and you lose your feeling of being immortal when you see people dying around you.
- Assess your tools, your weapons, your body... know what you can do with them.

Threats do not try to fight you. They try to overwhelm you. That's why stealth attacks or surprise attacks are often used in nature and in our society.

Levels of Awareness

Black (Oblivious):

This is when you are lost in thought, daydreaming, and not aware of your surroundings. If you get attacked, most likely, you are going to get hurt.

Green (Aware):

In this mode, you are alert but relaxed. You pay attention to how people approach you, what distance they keep, and how they move and act. You look for things that are out of place or unusual and possible places to hide or that provide cover. You exhibit confident body language **Yellow (Alert):**

You have detected a possible threat and evaluate it. You look for escape routes, possible weapons, and people who could help you nearby. You pay attention to the potential threat but don't completely forget about your surroundings. If you carry a weapon, you make sure you can access it quickly. This is also a good time to play through several scenarios of what might happen next and how you will react. This way, you are some steps ahead and can react more quickly if necessary.

Red (Engaged):

You are confronted with a real threat that either moves towards you or starts threatening you. If you didn't make a plan of how to react yet, now is the time. Try to position yourself so that you

Can fight or escape. If you have a weapon, get ready to pull it out and make the threat aware of it. You can launch a verbal attack and tell the threat to back off. This also alerts bystanders that something is wrong. Self-defense teachers also recommend you look out for pre-contact cues before the threat turns violent.

Common pre-contact cues are:

Spot these cues to be prepared to either fight or use your last chance to try to escape. ? Fiddling with their hair or face or using another movement to bring the hands up to the head area, ready to extend them to strike.

- Speaking in very short words instead of whole sentences such as "yeah," "so," or "OK."
- Looking left and right as if making sure they know in what environment they are going to fight.
- Clenching the teeth or setting the jaw.
- Moving in to come closer and be in striking distance.
- Repositioning the feet for the first strike.

Consequences of Violence

How Constant Exposure to a Violent Environment Takes Its Toll

After 60 days of constant combat, 98% of people become psychiatric casualties, meaning they come away with some kind of psychological problem. The remaining 2% show aggressive psychopathic character traits.

There are four factors that combine to form the "state of prolonged and great fatigue," also known as the Weight of Exhaustion.

These four factors are:

- Physiological arousal is caused by the stress of existing in what is commonly understood as a continual fight-or-flight arousal condition.
- The cumulative loss of sleep.
- Reduction in caloric intake.
- The toll of the elements, such as rain, cold, heat, and dark of night.

Fear, combined with exhaustion, hate, and the task of balancing these with the need to kill, eventually drives the soldier very deeply into a mire of guilt and horror.

Rape is another example of violence that results in a psychiatric casualty. In rape, psychological harm usually far exceeds the physical injury. The trauma of rape involves minimal fear of death or injury; far more damaging is the impotence, shock, and horror in being so hated and despised as to be debased and abused by a fellow human being.

Common symptoms of the weight of exhaustion are:

Battle or mental fatigue:

People get overly emotional, unsociable, and lazy, with certain bouts of intense feelings of terror or anxiety. Evacuation and rest is the only fix.

Confused states:

People experience psychotic dissociation from reality. They don't know who or where they are. Another type of confused state is Ganzer syndrome, in which someone tries to use humor in order to avoid reality.

Conversion hysteria:

A state in which people become paralyzed or begin to shake in a state of hysteria.

Anxiety:

The symptoms of this are sleeplessness, inability to concentrate, and constant tension. This can degrade into hysteria or post-traumatic stress disorder.

Obsessive and compulsive problems: Behavior loops or tics.

Fundamental altering of one's personality:

Whereas people without battle experience fear death, people with battle experience fear not living up to the expectations of others on the battlefield. The combination of fear for your life, fears of not meeting other's expectations, the resistance to open aggression, and guilt causes much of the suffering and resulting mental casualties.

SELCO ON HOW PEOPLE REACTED TO COMBAT EXHAUSTION

> *I experienced a feeling of being something like "invulnerable" or "numb" it happened very often to the guys who were*

involved in a constant fight. It manifested by "stopping to care" to the same degree of possibility of having shot or hurt simply because you stop to be afraid. My fear was "numbed" because I watched how people being killed, and I somehow keep going to survive. Of course, it was completely wrong and a very dangerous way of thinking, but in those moments, it made sense. You may be calling it "pushing the luck."

Also, a lot of people "managed" to act in a fight like in some kind of tunnel, in a way that "get your **** together" do the same dangerous job, fight, etc., and after that, you break down and cry, or just shiver for hours. We call that stage "living the death fear" or something like that.

Violence Hurts

The problem is that death, killing, and violence is not part of our everyday life anymore. We mostly know it from movies and games. That's why people are often shocked when someone attacks them.

In movies, everyone can take a beating, get up, and move on.

In real life, that's not the case. Even minor violence can have lifelong consequences. People have died from one hit in the face or from being pushed, falling, and knocking their heads against a hard object.

Do not get involved in other people's fights if you are not sure if you can control the situation and protect yourself or the group. Make sure you know who the bad guy is when you do get involved. You don't want to end up helping the bad guy just because he is losing the fight.

264 | Chapter 4: Violence

SELCO ON STAYING OUT OF TROUBLE

I choose more than once actually to stay out of trouble when I could try to help someone. After some time, I just learned to pay attention to myself. First, it is not nice, but it is survival. When you hear screams somewhere close, and you chose to stay put because there is a big chance to be hurt too. It is not fear. It is learning.

Weapons and Tools

Weapons and which weapons you should have are two of the most hotly discussed topics for survivalists.

Many people go a bit crazy about weapons and buy a lot of unnecessary stuff, but weapons are a very important part of being prepared. If you are not able to defend yourself, you may lose all those resources you gathered or even your life. You also have a better chance to get medicine for your sick kid if you head out armed with a rifle and not just with a smile.

What weapon you should get depends on a lot of factors, such as what weapons are available in your area, how proficient you and other members of the group are with certain weapons, and, of course, your budget.

Caliber, Size, Brand, etc.

"Have what everyone around you has" maybe boring advice, but it makes sense for a lot of reasons.

This will increase the availability of ammo, parts, and knowledge about how to maintain and repair the weapon. You do not stand out by carrying the same weapon others carry, and your weapon does not become an object of desire for others.

This gives you the ability to drop your weapon and pick up someone else's weapon without hesitation. This also means that you own the weapon, and the weapon does not own you. That is, you do not love your weapon so much that you hesitate when you have to leave it behind.

You are used to operating the same weapon like everyone else and can continue fighting efficiently if your weapon breaks, and you find another on the battlefield.

Also, keep in mind that you are the one that has to use the gun. Your hand might be too big or small for a certain gun, or the recoil might be too much for you. Try weapons at the local shooting range if you can. The best weapon is the weapon that works for you.

Having more firepower only makes sense if you can handle it well. Some people prefer, for example, an AK 47 and a 9 mm Glock, but these choices are very personal, and you should be used to handling whatever you have.

Here are some more thoughts on common calibers:

- The .22 caliber is used in a wide variety of rifles, is cheap to shoot, and is great for learning how to shoot. You can find many modifications for different rifles and hunt small game with it. It is not very powerful and not the best choice for self-defense.
- Twelve gauge shotguns are great and versatile rifles, but ammo is rather heavy to carry. You can use birdshot (many small pellets in one round) in close quarter fights if you want to avoid over-penetration. You can use 00 buckshot, which has fewer but bigger pellets than birdshot in one round, as great all-purpose self-defense ammunition. It is effective up to 60 yards. If you need a longer effective shooting range of 40 to 120 yards, you can use slugs. The Remington 870 is a popular shotgun you might want to check out.
- Hunting rifles such as the cheap Mosin Nagant with a scope is a good choice to keep attackers from getting too close.
- Consider having a revolver as well as a pistol because revolvers are easy to maintain and won't jam. They also have fewer moving parts, which means they are sturdy and require less

maintenance.

General advice when getting started with weapons:

- Keep in mind that you are buying a whole system and not just a gun or a rifle. Research modifications you might want to have in the future and make sure you get enough spare parts and magazines right away.
- Try different holsters and slings to find the ones that enable you to carry your weapons comfortably while giving you quick access to them.
- Learn to shoot at moving targets and to shoot and run, crouch, and crawl. You should also learn to shoot with both hands.
- Learn proper gun maintenance and get a full cleaning kit for each of your weapons. Clean your gun after every time you have fired it. Get gun manuals that help you to understand how your gun works and maybe even how to fix it when it's broken.
- Get as much ammunition as possible. Ammunition for common calibers will also become a great item for trading in long-term collapse scenarios.

Other Weapons

Forget about fancy ninja weapons and focus on something that works. **Learn knife fighting** in case you run out of ammunition or lose your firearm.

Unless you have a machete or kukri knife, forget about slashing attacks. To disable or kill a person, you will want to focus on thrusting attacks that injure organs. Your knife should penetrate at least 2 inches to do proper damage (or even deeper if you are stabbing someone who is overweight). Get fixed blade, full tang (the blade and handle are made from one piece of metal) knives with blades at least 5 inches long and a handle that won't get slippery when it's wet. You also might want to consider some guard on the handle so that your hands don't slip onto the blade while stabbing. Many good knives come with cheap sheaths. Consider getting a high-quality sheath such as one of the Kydex sheaths available. Just like with guns, learn how to maintain your knives. Get cleaning and sharpening equipment.

Get a **bow or crossbow** if you think you need a quieter way of hitting an attacker. While crossbows are usually smaller, they take longer to reload than bows.

Unless you are trained in other martial art weapons, forget about them. A bo (fighting stick) is much less effective in untrained hands than a baseball bat.

Pepper spray is great to have. It is easy to get, cheap and comes in many sizes. You can keep pepper spray stored at different locations throughout your house and take some along with you as well. Make sure you get real pepper spray or a mix of pepper and cs gas.

Cs gas takes some time to incapacitate the attacker, while pepper spray burns his eyes and lungs right away. Try to get a spray that either shoots a stream or gel instead of a fogger that creates small droplets that are easily blown away by the wind. Gel sprays have the advantage that people have to clean themselves to stop the effect.

Your goal is to get away as quickly as possible from the attacker or use your knife to harm them, so anything that incapacitates them for a longer time is good.

Tasers and stun guns are also effective, but we recommend you go for pepper spray as it has less chance to fail and has longer-lasting effects on attackers.

"Carrying" Weapons

Having a weapon and "carrying" it can be two completely different things. You need to have easy access to your weapon (and any other equipment that you carry too).

That means many things. Very often, people kill themselves with improper weapon handling. Once a guy one meter from me shot himself in the ass because he was clumsy while he was trying to pull his pistol out from the back from his belt. This was a case of him not being "connected" with his weapon.

Being "connected" means everything from being able to a reload rifle without thinking (or looking at it), to be able to draw a pistol from a holster (or pocket, belt, bag, etc.) in controlled movements.

Do not think too much about speed, think about movements (speed is the economy of movements and the proper order of movements) and think about control (control it at all times without panicking). Practice, practice, practice.

What, how much, when, and how to carry when it comes to SHTF is a matter of common sense. Just keep in mind that you have to stay highly mobile. There is no sense in carrying so much ammo that it slows you down.

Choosing other equipment connected to your weapon is like choosing your weapon–choose what is good for you. I had a backpack, boots, pants, and a jacket that most survivalists would call ridiculous today, but it all worked well for me at that time. My tactical equipment was a joke, but I survived, and I am here to write about it.

Today I have equipment that works for ME. My old assault vest may look funny to some. I use an old military gas mask bag as my small, quick access hip bag. It is perfect for me.

The "Written in Stone" Philosophy

Adopt a philosophy that nothing is written in stone. Be ready and willing to change things, such as your weapon and equipment, if the situation around you dictates it. Do not be stubborn. For example, I had (and still have) pistols in one caliber stored for SHTF time, but over the years, other things have become popular, so I have adapted to using them.

Do not find yourself in the middle of SHTF, realizing that you have the wrong things because you were too stubborn to get new items.

5. Chapter 5: First Aid & Hygiene

First aid and hygiene go hand in hand. The biggest problem is that we live in such a comfortable society in which waste is managed for us and taken care of that hygiene is an often-overlooked factor for many people. An untreated fungus can cripple you, and this happens faster than most people think.

First aid is equally important. The good first treatment can make the recovery process much faster and with fewer complications. Even with little equipment, there are many ways how you can help and at least stop a condition from getting worse.

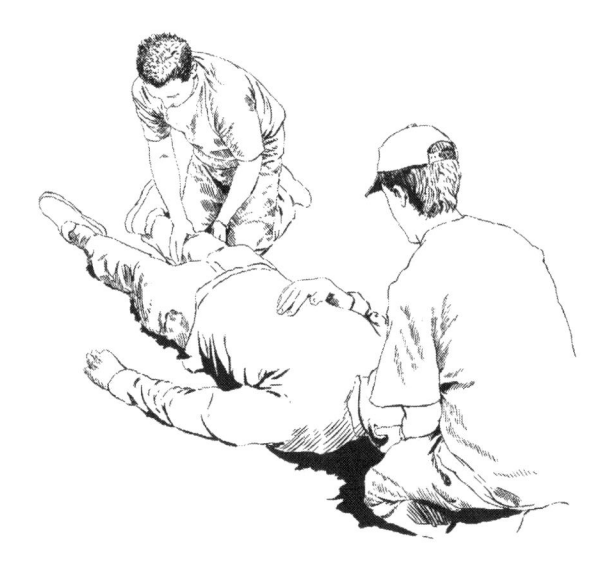

Hygiene Basics

SELCO ON COMMON HYGIENE RELATED PROBLEMS

Very soon after we realized that water needs to be rationed, we started to see hygiene problems because of a lack of water. Remember, it was a situation when we needed to go out look for things, to be active, it was not about lying at home and waiting for the situation to be better. We needed to live, we needed to be very active, and that adds more to hygiene complications.

If you are forced to go through the destroyed house in order to find anything usable, you get dirtier then working your regular job prior to SHTF, and you have less water.

Rashes, diarrhea, fungal problems, lice were the most common and maybe most mentioned problems, but all kinds of other diseases also were there because of lack of hygiene. Simple not washing hands add much to the risks of all kind of diseases, and that situation lasts for months.

If you have never been in a survival situation, you probably do not realize how healthy we are because of modern advances. The water that comes out of the tap has been cleaned by a complex mix of chemical and industrial treatments, making it safe to drink.

Our garbage is taken away the same morning each week by a garbage truck, and our human waste conveniently disappears when we flush the toilet. When SHTF, the system that provides all of this for us, can be brought to its knees – the rules are changed, and you need to learn how to play a new game.

This first part of the chapter will provide essential information about personal hygiene, food and water, keeping your space clean, waste management, and hygiene and sanitation in first aid. See our chapter on Preparedness for items that you need to take with you or store to stay healthy and hygienic in survival situations.

Why Hygiene and Sanitation Are Important

You might not think that cleanliness as a part of survivalism is not a particularly important topic. You might think it would be much more useful to learn about what to stash in your bug out bag, or how to get an enemy off your tail.

However, when SHTF, it is highly likely that a lack of hygiene and sanitation will kill more folks then violence. Cleanliness is of great importance in the prevention of many kinds of infections–infections of the gut, the skin, the eyes, the lungs, and the entire body.

Personal cleanliness (or hygiene) and public cleanliness (or sanitation) are both important. Without high standards of hygiene and sanitation, you can die from dirty water, bad food, improperly treated minor cuts, or even just from the bacteria on your hands. You could be sick for days and unable to stand or walk. If an infection is not prevented, the consequences will be grave.

You need to stop thinking that hygiene is a minor issue, and take it seriously. Staying as clean as possible after SHTF will not only prevent you from getting sick or dying but can also make the difference between staying human and becoming an animal.

How Hygiene and Sanitation Can Affect Your Health

Many common infections of the gut are spread from one person to another because of poor hygiene and poor sanitation. Germs and worms (or their eggs) are passed by the thousands in the stool of infected persons. These are carried from the feces of one person to the mouth of another by dirty fingers or contaminated food or water.

Diseases that are spread or transmitted from feces-to-mouth in this way include:
- Diarrhea and dysentery (caused by amoebas and bacteria)
- Intestinal worms (several types)
- Hepatitis, typhoid fever, and cholera

You might find the idea repulsive, but it is not difficult to see how germs can travel quickly from one person's feces to another's mouth.

For example A child who has worms and who forgot to wash his hands after his last bowel movement offers his friend a biscuit.

His fingers, which have a trace of feces on them, are covered with hundreds of tiny worm eggs (so small they cannot be seen). Some of these worm eggs stick to the biscuit.

When his friend eats the biscuit, he swallows the worm eggs, too. Soon the friend also has worms.

Animals such as pigs, dogs, and chickens also spread intestinal disease and worm eggs.

For example:

1. A man with an intestinal bug defecates behind his house.
2. A pig eats his stool, dirtying its nose and feet, then the pig goes into the house.
3. In the house, a child is playing on the floor. The child gets some of the man's feces on her hands and arms.
4. Later the mother picks up her child and also gets some feces on her hands.
5. Then the mother prepares food, forgetting to wash her hands after handling the child.
6. The family eats the food.
7. Soon they all have the intestinal bug.

Many kinds of infections, as well as worm eggs, are passed from one person to another in the way just shown.

The spread of the sickness could have been prevented:
- If the man had used a toilet, out-house, or a separated area for human waste.
- If the family had not let the pig come into the house.
- If they had not let the child play where the pig had been.
- If the mother had washed her hands after touching the child and before preparing food.

Personal Hygiene

Keeping Yourself Clean

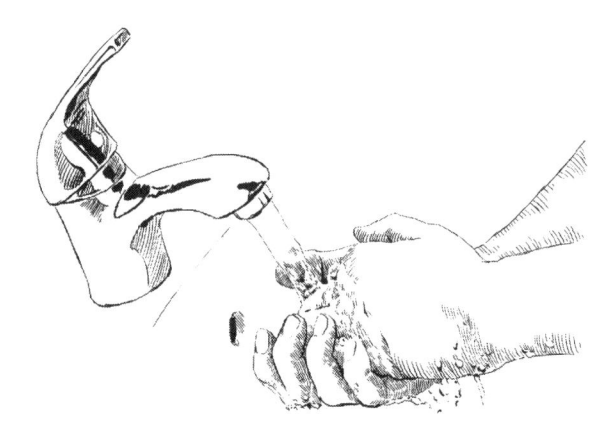

Especially when you are on your own, you need to pay extra attention to keep yourself clean. A few days with heavy diarrhea and nobody who can look after you can mean you are too weak to carry on and simply die.

Your Hands

The best advice that we can give you when it comes to basic sanitation is: **keep your hands clean!** If you have a continuous water source, then wash them as often as possible.

Otherwise, carry a small container of hand sanitizer, Betadine, or rubbing alcohol. Antibacterial wipes are also an excellent idea. Always wash your hands with a soap product when you get up in the morning, after having a bowel movement, and before cooking or eating.

Be careful what you touch. Avoid using your hands to touch things when possible. Try using your elbow instead, for example, because your fingers and hands are the most likely parts to come in contact with your mouth, nose, and eyes, where bacteria can enter into your system.

Use disposable latex gloves if you need to rummage through something or treat a sick or injured person. Believe it or not, people can die from biting their nails. There is a huge amount of bacteria in the mouth, and it is not uncommon for the bacteria to travel from the mouth into breaks in the skin around the nails, causing a potentially deadly infection that, without medical treatment, will travel from the fingers up the arms and into the internal organs.

Always keep in mind, in a survival situation, small problems can quickly escalate and become huge problems.

Your Body

Frequent bathing or showering helps prevent skin infections, dandruff, pimples, itching, and rashes.

Whatever the scenario, it is likely that there will be a time in a survival situation where you cannot bathe or shower like in normal times – usually because you lack a sufficient amount of water. We recommend trying the following options:

1. The "wet rag bath."

I used this type of "bath" very often to keep myself clean. It is a very simple way to clean yourself in a very fast way. It is not a smart procedure. If you have means and time, then it is very good to use hot water (as hot as you can stand) and a towel. If that is not possible, then just use cold water and any kind of rag and brush yourself vigorously. If you are doing it in some bad condition (cold water, no time, etc.), then use common sense and start with parts of the body that are less dirty.

2. The "chemical bath."

The most used way of "quick" cleaning in my SHTF time was alcohol, we had it a lot, and we use it for wiping the dirtiest areas of the body when we did not have any better means of cleaning ourselves. It was also easy to carry small bottles.

What you can do is store a lot of hand sanitizers, baby wipes, alcohol pads, and similar.

Bathe, shower, or clean yourself every day and always after working hard or sweating. This is especially important for sick people. It is easy to forget about this because surviving is so stressful, but keeping yourself clean prevents major problems down the road.

If you do not have access to regular soap, consider using:

• Soapwort (found in disturbed soil, on riverbanks, and in streambeds). Rub the leaves together brusquely until you have created a green lather or use dried roots. ? Yucca leaves and roots. Dip them in water and beat them with a stick alternately to create good washing suds.

• Do NOT use agaves, because the sap is acidic and will not only give you a burning rash, as well as burn holes in your clothes.

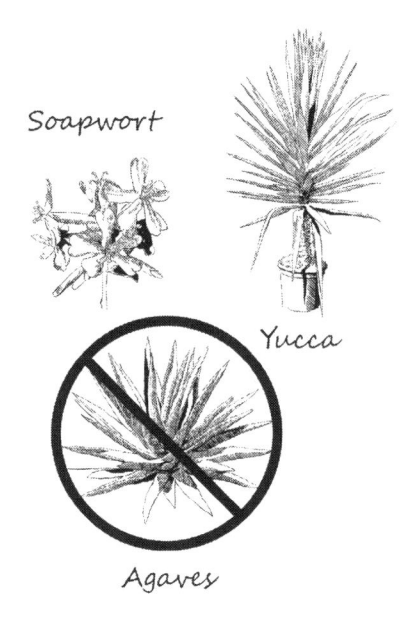

Other alternatives are:
• Chlorogalum (soap plant)

278 | Chapter 5: First Aid & Hygiene

- Red campion root and leaves
- Atriplex root
- Guaiac leaves
- Papaya leaves
- Quillaia bark
- Sapindus fruit
- Passiflora foetida
- Alphitonia excelsa
- Acacia concinna (and other soap pod fruits)
- Hesperoyucca whipplei root (Our Lord's Candle)

Your Hair

If you have running water, then try washing your hair with clay, or even better, mud from a hot spring. Mix the clay with water until it is liquid, apply it to your hair and scalp, massage it in, leave it for five or 10 minutes, and then rinse thoroughly.

You may need to wash it again afterward with a deodorizing soap such as soapwort or ground herbs.

Delouse the whole family often – lice and fleas carry many diseases. If your dirty hair or scalp becomes itchy or problematic, cut it off.

Your Teeth

Brush your teeth every day, and after each time you eat something sweet. If you do not have a toothbrush and toothpaste, rub your teeth with salt and baking soda.

There are also various twigs that can be chewed so that one end is frayed and used as a toothbrush. Oak and black birch are particularly useful for this purpose. Oak also acts as a kind of toothpaste, helping to kill bacteria and reduce the risk of cavities.

Your Feet

In areas where hookworm is common, do not go barefoot. These worms enter the body through the soles of the feet and can cause severe anemia. Change socks often and keep your feet dry as much as possible to avoid fungal infection.

Defecation

SELCO ON DEFECATING

After the water was gone, the bathrooms stop to "work," or they needed too much water. People simply start to solve this problem by "taking it out" from the house. So any area close to the house but still reasonable far from it was good for that. Green areas, or ruins close to the house, anything.

We used a primitive latrine close to the house on a small green area, squatting position, and clean rug work for us.

Anyone who's been on a long camping trip will be familiar with the idea of defecating in the woods.

The standard recommendation is to dig a six-inch hole, do your business, then fill it in and cover it up. Make sure you defecate in a squatting position to minimize the need to wipe. Roll up your pants to your knees and pull down your pants to your knees, so they are out of the way. You can hold onto a tree or similar for a more stable position if you have problems squatting comfortably.

The big question is: how do you wipe? Fortunately, nature has provided you with many options, no matter what terrain you are in. Try one of the following, or mix and match.

• Snow – cold, but effective. ? Sand – also very effective by the handful and not as uncomfortable as you might think. Use several handfuls.

• Stones – rounded and slightly rough ones are effective, but make sure they are not too hot or too cold.

• Pinecones – check first for pitch. If any is found, discard it. If not, wipe from the stem to the tip. Pinecones are comfortable to use and are effective.

• Sticks – a bit tricky, more of a backup option.

• Leaves – okay, if doubled up, but don't press too hard or your fingers might "pop" through! Use the ribbed side of the leaf. Do NOT use poison oak, poison ivy, or stinging nettle leaves.

• Grass and moss – an excellent option. Wad them up into a clump like a little green scrubbing brush.

• Water – great but best used in combination with one of the above. If water is to be used, carry it in a container away from the

water source to avoid contamination. You can use cheap plastic bottles with a hole in them, so squeeze water out and use it as a primitive bidet.
- Grass
- Bark

Your Clothes

SELCO ON TAKING CARE OF HIS CLOTHES

We wash it in the yard, by soaking it in a big washbowl of hot water, leave it there for a while, then wash it by the hands by "scrubbing it." Sometimes with soap, sometimes without it.

More important from that was that we tried to have clothes that we used for outside dirty jobs, and we tried to clean it in the yard before entering the house, then leave it and not wear it in the house.

Be sure to own clothes that are difficult to get dirty and easy to get clean. Try to keep a set of clothes for outside and a set of clothes for inside only.

You need a lot of water for laundry. If you have enough water, one effective way of cleaning clothes without detergent or electricity is to use baking soda (sodium bicarbonate) in the water

in a large metal tub with the clothes in it and heat it over a fire. If water is scarce, use disinfecting liquids such as bleach, tincture of iodine, hydrogen peroxide, or colloidal silver.

If in the wilderness, you can use yucca or soapwort but again, do NOT use agaves – they will burn holes in your clothes. If no other options are available to you, consider "sunbathing" your clothes – exposing them to ultraviolet rays. Note that sand and stones are great washboards for scrubbing out clothes (as well as for scouring hands).

Change the bedclothes of a sick person daily, and each time they become dirty. Soiled or bloodstained clothes, bedding, and towels of a person with an infectious disease should be handled with care. To kill any viruses or germs, wash these in hot soapy water or add some chlorine bleach.

Food and Your Space

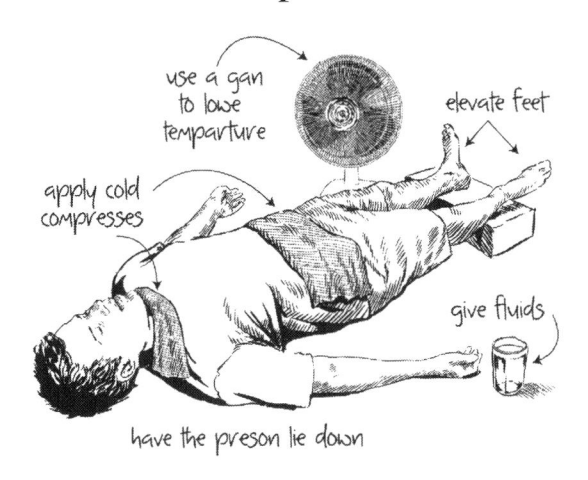

- use a fan to lower temparture
- elevate feet
- apply cold compresses
- give fluids
- have the preson lie down

Food and Water

Sometimes it will be impossible to eat food and drink water that is totally hygienic, but remember, it is better to eat or drink something a bit dirty than to starve or die of dehydration. Keep your food and water as clean as possible. One of the most common causes of sickness (diarrhea, typhoid, hepatitis, or cholera) and death is drinking bad water – see our chapter on Water for information about how to purify your water, as well as our chapter on Food for information about avoiding eating spoiled foods.

Below are some extra tips about keeping your eating habits as clean and hygienic as possible:
- One huge help will be storing your food in separate containers. Protect food by keeping it covered or in boxes, jars, etc.
- Do not eat fruit that has fallen to the ground before washing it well.
- Do not let flies and other insects land or crawl on food. These insects carry germs and spread disease.

- Do not leave food scraps or dirty dishes lying around, as these attract flies and breed germs.
- Do not eat food that is old or smells bad or has mold on it – it may be poisonous.
- Do not eat canned food if the can is swollen or gas comes out when opened.

Chickens carry germs that can cause food poisoning. Wash your hands after preparing chicken before you touch other foods. Also, be careful with chicken that has been sitting out for several hours after it has been cooked.

If possible, only eat meats and fish that are well cooked. Do not eat meat with any raw parts – especially pork as it carries a risk of disease.

If possible, eat only food that has been freshly prepared. This is important, especially for the sick, the very young, and the old.

Before eating left-over cooked foods, reheat them to a very high temperature.

Sick people should eat separately from others, and their plates and utensils should be especially well cleaned before being used by others, or not used by others at all.

Keep Your Space Clean

SELCO ON KEEPING YOUR SPACE CLEAN

When trying to build a protective space, cleanliness is your first line of defense.

When SHTF in my time, we simply use the method of „cleaning zone. " Actually we use one place in the yard to take off dirty clothes, clean ourselves there, leave dirty boots, etc.

It does not sound like something special. At that time, usually, it means that I would simply take off dirty (or bloody) clothes, use a bucket of water (rain) to clean myself.

But the point was to keep ourselves as clean as possible and to minimize getting our house contaminated.

You can take this method and advance it as more as you can, or as more money as you have to make it very good.

As well as a cleaning zone, we recommend:

1. Pay extra attention to those wells, and water sources stay clean. Do not let animals go near where people get drinking water. Ideally, put a fence around the place to keep animals out.

2. Do not defecate or throw garbage near the water hole. Take special care to keep rivers and streams clean upstream from any place where drinking water is taken.

3. Burn all garbage that can be burned. Garbage that cannot be burned should be buried in a special pit or a place far away from where you stay and the places where people get drinking water.

4. Build toilets and latrines so that pigs and other animals cannot reach human waste.

Your Home

Stock your storage space well with products that can keep your house clean (see our chapter on Preparedness for specific items that are useful).

Improve general cleanliness:
- Stop wearing shoes in the house.
- Encourage everyone to pick up after themselves.
- Keep your food preparation area completely free of crumbs at all times to avoid pest infestation.
- Do not let animals into the house, including dogs – fleas on animals carry diseases.
- If children or animals have a bowel movement near the house, clean it up at once. Teach children to use a toilet or at least to go farther from the house.
- Hang or spreadsheets and blankets in the sun often. If there are bedbugs, pour boiling water on the beds and wash the linens.
- Watch out where you spit. The spit can spread disease. When you cough or sneeze, always cover your mouth with your hand or cloth or handkerchief.
- Clean the house often. Sweep and wash the floors, walls, and beneath the furniture. Fill in cracks and holes in the floor or walls where roaches, bedbugs, and scorpions can hide.

Human Waste

Sewerage

Nature can cope easily with urine. In fact, it is a useful fertilizer. However, concentrations of human waste can contaminate local water supplies and create breeding grounds for disease, which is why a sewerage system is required. Before proper human waste disposal systems existed, there were vast epidemics of cholera, wiping out many human lives.

Your sewerage system will usually need both an open sewerage line and lots of water to flush the waste down. If either is missing or if you are in the wilderness, you will need an alternative. If it is just water, you are short of, collect it from any local water source such as a well, dam, sea, or river, or put containers out to collect rainwater (the wider the container, the more water you will catch). If you cannot access water, your sewerage line is blocked, your septic system is not working, or you are hiding out in a bunker or the basement of your house where there is no toilet, you will have to construct one.

Long drop toilet

This method involves simply digging a large hole in the ground, placing a seat over it if possible (or constructing one by, for example, cutting a toilet seat-sized circular hole in a flat piece of wood) and using it until it is almost full, then filling it and digging another one. The downside of this method is that it smells disgusting and attracts many flies, which can spread disease. For this reason, you would want to construct it at least 20 meters from where you are sleeping and eating, which could expose you to danger when traveling to and from the toilet. Also, remember to construct this type of toilet at least 60 meters from any watercourses, as it can contaminate your precious water supply. A shallow pit will promote rapid decomposition.

Waste Bucket Toilet

Another way to deal with your waste is to compost it directly. If you have a toilet seat, put it over a bucket and after use, throw in a handful of soak (e.g., sawdust, ashes, or straw). When it's full, tip it onto a compost heap and add a straw, hay, garden waste, and kitchen waste.

Although this system is cheap, easy, and convenient, you should remember that human waste contains pathogens, and having to handle the waste in the bucket when transporting it to the compost heap could lead to illness or disease. If using this method, always try to wear gloves when handling the waste bucket and ensure that nobody comes into contact with the compost heap.

Wheelie bin toilet

A more hygienic long-term solution would be to use a large container such as a wheelie bin. Place it above or underground, construct a seat on top, cover it with a soak after each use, and when the container is full, bury it and leave it to decompose for a year while you use another one. This method has the benefits of being reusable as compost to fertilize your garden and not posing any risk to your water supply.

Whichever option you choose, add powdered lime, limestone, or bleach regularly if possible to suppress the smell.

Hygiene and Sanitation in First Aid

SELCO ON WHY HYGIENE IS A MATTER OF LIFE AND DEATH

Just like with most of the stuff most vulnerable will be those who are very young and those very old. A friend calls me to go and check his old relative, who had a small cut on his stomach. The old guy cut himself while he was working on some homemade tools for grinding. When I saw that wound for the first time, it was badly infected with a very bad smell coming from it.

When a man cut himself, he washes it with water (probably dirty) and put some tobacco on it.

And he did not pay too much attention to it until it was too late. The man died from the infection. Everything would probably be different if he just used alcohol for cleaning the wound or soap with water and regular cleaning and bandaging.

When it comes to cleanliness and first aid, it is more obvious that prevention is better than cure. If we all took more care to eat well, to keep ourselves, our homes, and our villages clean, and to be sure that our children are vaccinated, we could stop most illnesses before they start.

Basic Cleanliness and Protection

In our chapter on First Aid, we pointed out the importance of keeping wounds clean and using good hygiene to prevent small infections from turning into serious medical conditions. In addition, remember when you are treating a sick or injured person:

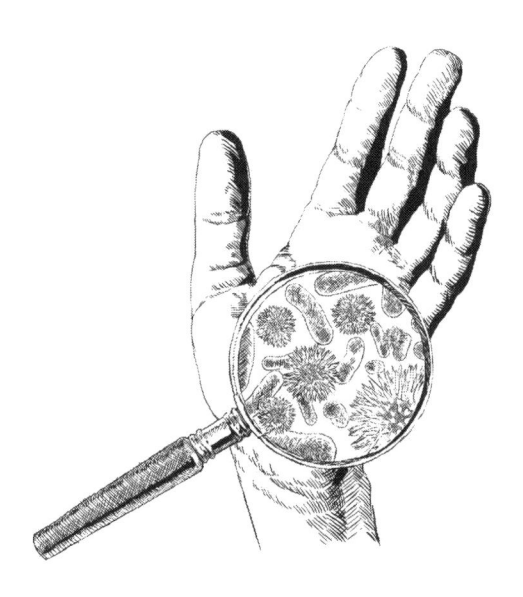

If possible, show the injured person how to stop the bleeding themselves, by applying direct pressure on the wound.

If they cannot do this, wash your hands and keep the blood off yourself by wearing gloves or a clean plastic bag on your hands, and placing a clean, thick cloth directly over the wound before applying pressure.

Avoid objects soiled with blood. Be careful not to prick yourself with needles or other sharp objects around the person you are helping. Cover cuts or other wounds with dry, clean bandages to protect them.

Be especially careful when you have to provide first aid where there are many people wounded from an accident or fighting.

If you do get blood or other body fluids on you, wash your hands with soap and water as soon as possible. If body fluids touched other parts of your body (especially your eyes), wash thoroughly with lots of water.

Sterilize any instruments that you are using.

How to Sterilize Instruments

First, always clean any obvious debris off your instruments. Clean with soap and water or alcohol. Use a cloth or brush if needed.

A couple of quick methods for sterilization are:

1. **Heat the instrument**

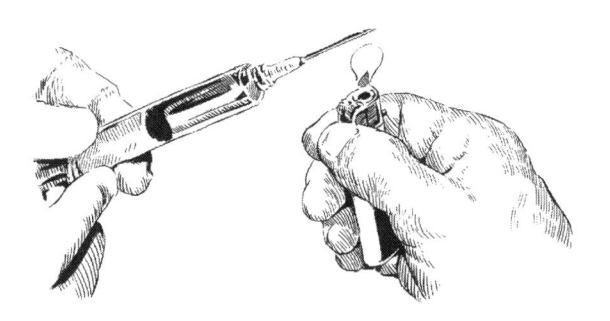

Hold the part that's going to touch the injury over an open flame. If the handle is also metal, find something to hold the instrument with so you do not burn your fingers. When the part over the flame is red, that's enough. Let it cool, and then it is ready to be used.

Alternatively, let the instrument soak in boiling water for twenty minutes. This is a good method for larger instruments or those that might melt under the flame.

If you have alcohol, dip it in that as well for additional protection.

2. **Using a disinfectant**

If you don't have fire and you're in a hurry, you can wipe the instrument off with a clean cloth soaked in iodine or alcohol. If you don't have a clean cloth, dip the instrument in the solution and stir it around for ten seconds. If you are not in a hurry, let the instrument soak for twenty minutes.

The Importance of First Aid

Why First Aid Is Important

I will keep this section brief because I'm sure anyone reading this has enough common sense to realize that first aid can mean the difference between life and death when SHTF. You may be hiking and get bitten by a dangerous animal, lost in extreme weather conditions, or stranded in a remote area after your vehicle has crashed.

You might simply be taking a leisurely stroll with your family when someone collapses or has or a bad fall.

Whether you are close to medical facilities or there is little chance of help arriving, the first few minutes are critical. Someone's survival may depend on any immediate treatment you can provide.

First aid can help you to treat injured and sick people, but I want to say that you should not expect miracles. I speak from experience when I say that in some situations, there may be nothing more you can do than offer a few words of comfort.

On the other hand, if you prepare and master the first aid skills I have set out below, you can save someone's life in a whole range of scenarios involving major and minor injuries, not just by resuscitation, but more importantly, by providing proper treatment that will prevent minor injuries from becoming more serious and complicated ones.

I have worked my whole life in the medical field, and I have watched too many people die of simple diseases and injuries that became major problems, although they could have easily been contained with basic first aid. I am writing this guide because I do not want this to happen to you or your family and friends.

SELCO ON WHAT A SMALL INJURY CAN MEAN DURING SURVIVAL

"Small cut can kill" may sound boring because many people in the "survival world" mention it all the time, but not always explaining it in the correct way.

It can kill you in a few ways. SHTF means that you gonna be forced to pull maximum from your body (and mind) all the time in order to survive.

So, for example, let's say that you have strained ankle or back pain because you lift something heavy, what you were gonna do today in a normal world, probably take some pills or physical therapy and take few days off from your job, not a big deal, just a few days or week watching TV at home and taking it easy.

When SHTF, there is no "take it easy," so strained ankle or back pain means that you cannot give 100% of yourself, for example, during the shootout in your street or running from an attacker. You are dead.

"Small cut can kill you" also mean those small problems WILL lead to bigger and bigger problems, and then you are dead-or some of yours family members are dead because you cut yourself during the scavenging, forget to clean small cut, it led to infection, then to sepsa, then you are dead.

Preparation
What to Expect

As in all survival situations, mental strength and preparation are just as important as physical strength. When it comes to medical emergencies, it is very important to understand and accept the fact that bad things not only can happen, they do happen.

At some time in your life, you are likely to encounter an accident or a medical emergency, and if you're an outdoor enthusiast, your chances of being involved in such an emergency increase exponentially. When you are readying yourself for an intrepid trip, or if you find yourself in a conflict zone, it helps to mentally prepare for the inevitability of sickness or injury.

The sooner you accept this fact, the sooner you will be ready to deal with a medical emergency. If you're not ready, people can die in the time that you spend mentally processing the fact that something has gone seriously wrong. The good news is you don't need to be a brain surgeon to save a life.

You can give lifesaving first aid if you have some basic supplies and know, for example, how to stop bleeding, perform CPR, immobilize broken bones, prevent an infection from spreading, etc.

Humans often like to think that problems solve themselves somehow. In survival situations, this is not going to be the case. You might find yourself in a situation where you and only you are the difference between life and death.

Anyone who is serious about survival techniques will tell you that situations are common where you have to save somebody or treat them, and at times this can mean putting yourself in grave danger. Do not forget that the point of survival is to survive, not to be a hero.

Getting Help

SELCO ON GETTING HELP

> *I always advocate that you need to know how to use stuff that you have stored. You can have the most expensive first aid kit, but still, without knowledge, you cannot use it. But also if you have means, then you need to have that stuff, you can also trade something for men who have knowledge or trades with other things.*

Even if you become an expert in first aid, there will be many medical emergencies that you are helpless to fix without access to medical personnel and facilities. This is why having access to the outside world is crucial.

Do your research and consider carrying:

- A fully charged cell phone.
- A portable VHF or HF amateur radio for trips that are a few hours from the trailhead.
- Satellite phones for longer treks.
- When it comes to your radio, learn how to use it and practice.
- Make sure it has two-way communication.
- Make sure more than one person in the crew can use it, in case the knowledgeable or licensed operator is injured.
- Someone must be listening on the other end.
- Radio wave propagation must fit the terrain.

Medication

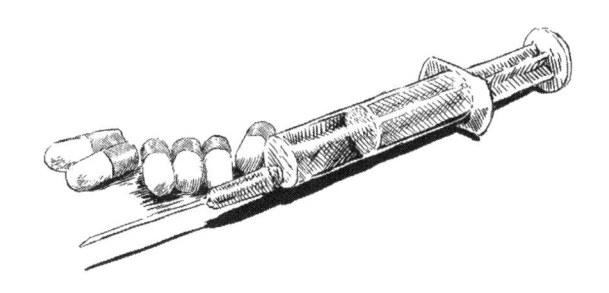

SELCO ON HOW VALUABLE MEDICATION WAS

> It was very valuable, and it is common sense if you were having a sick kid, and if you are aware that kid is gonna die unless you find somewhere therapy for him, then you realize that nothing has value except that medication.

The black market was alive, and you could try to find wanted medications in that way, but many times it was dangerous to even try to contact those folks, not to mention to make some kind of deal with them.

A guy who I know gave all his gold for several antibiotics treatments for his wife, and it was in the beginning period when gold had a higher value, other people I knew did not have any way of finding medication for them, so at the end, they died because of that.

Junkies were especially dangerous, simply because certain folks could make them do whatever they wanted, promising them stuff and that things were almost always violence.

You can significantly increase your first aid skills and your abilities as a survival medic if you know your stuff when it comes to medication. The most important thing to remember is that if you or someone in your group requires regular use of prescription medication, stock up on it! Also vital to survival is ensuring that anyone with known adverse reactions to insect stings, drugs, or particular foods or plants has the appropriate anti-anaphylaxis medication, such as an EpiPen®. Teach the others in your group how to administer your medication if necessary.

If you have children, it is very important to be sure what kind of antibiotics your child responds to best. Some people react really bad to certain antibiotics, make sure you know what works for you and members of your group or family.

Get a drug reference book that features different medications and their uses, side effects, and interactions.

It is critical to research the area where you are traveling, if possible, or visit a specialized travel doctor before you leave. The medications you should take with you will vary depending on what region of the world you are in. In some cases, such as when traveling to areas prone to malaria, yellow fever, typhoid, cholera, or rabies, you will need to get vaccinated or start taking medication before you arrive there.

For malnutrition and exhaustion (the most common combination of ailments in a survival situation), administer a mix of 250 mL normal saline, 3 concentrated glucose ampules, and various vitamin injections. You mix all of that in 250 mL infusion and give the person one each day for five days to get them back on their feet.

Print out or write down all details on when and how to use each medicine you keep in your storage. You can also lookup drugs that are not in your drug reference book on WebMD, Drugs.com, or PDR.net.

A list of miscellaneous "must-have" medications is as follows:

- **Ibuprofen (e.g., Motrin)** – pain reliever and fever reducer. Good for cases of mild to moderate pain from trauma, sprains, etc. It can also help against fever.
- **Anti-diarrheal (e.g., Loperamide)** – you can be sure that sooner or later, you will need it in an SHTF scenario, especially when retention of fluids becomes vital.
- **Hydrocortisone cream (e.g., Cortizone)** – for rashes, itching, allergic dermatitis, etc.
- **Ivermectin (e.g., Heartgard)** is a broad-spectrum antiparasitic drug that can kill many worm infections, along with scabies and head lice.
- **Diphenhydramine (e.g., Benadryl)** for allergic reactions and can also be used as sleeping aid.

Antibiotics:

- Amoxicillin and Ampicillin have a broad spectrum of activity. They are both members of the aminopenicillin family. Some infections have become already resistant to penicillin-based antibiotics, so it is often necessary to combine them with other antibiotics.
- Cefalexin is used to treat a number of infections, including otitis media, streptococcal pharyngitis, bone, and joint infections, pneumonia, cellulitis, and urinary tract infections.

- **Ciprofloxacin** treats most strains of bacterial pathogens responsible for respiratory, urinary tract, gastrointestinal, and abdominal infections.
- **Doxycycline** is an effective treatment for chlamydia, chronic prostatitis, and a variety of other infections. It is also used as a prophylaxis for malaria and to treat cholera, two conditions that are often observed in the aftermaths of disasters.
- **Azithromycin** is used to treat or prevent certain bacterial infections, most often those causing middle ear infections, strep throat, pneumonia, typhoid, gastroenteritis, bronchitis, and sinusitis.
- **Sulfamethoxazole** is one of the few antibiotics that treat the "superbug" MRSA (methicillin-resistant Staphylococcus aureus).

Background Information

Many antibiotics are available for your pets without seeing a doctor. Many people get fish antibiotics, and yes, they do have the same active ingredients as human antibiotics but are often even cheaper.

Below is a more comprehensive list of useful medications in survival situations, together with their uses. I keep all of these at my bug out location to be prepared for the most common problems. Remember, these are not only useful to use on yourself and others, but also very valuable trading items in long term survival scenarios.

- Normal saline (IV solution, or for wound irrigation, also used in eye washing)
- 5% glucose (IV solution)
- Antibiotic creams (cuts/wound treatment)
- Anti-fungal creams (Miconazole, Tineacide)
- Iodine (wound treatment)
- Rivanol (wound / inflammation treatment)
- Hydrogen peroxide (wound treatment and mouth antiseptic, needs to be 3% for that)
- Hexetidine (to treat mouth infections)
- Gentamicin (antibiotic)
- Lincocin (antibiotic)

- Antitetanus treatments (important is to have regularly updated shots, and boosters)
- Snake venom kits (injection drugs for snake venom, we have only two types of dangerous snakes)
- Apaurin/Diazepam (sedative, muscle relaxant)
- Analgin/Metamizole (analgesic, for fever)
- Reglan/Metoclopramide (stomach problems, nausea)
- Ranitidine (Zantac, stomach problems)
- Oral glucose gel (hypoglycemia treatment)
- Aminophylline (bronchodilator, helps with breathing problems, asthma, bronchitis...)
- Urbason/Solu-Medrol (breathing problems and conditions, allergic reactions)
- Synopen (allergic reactions)
- Spasmex (antispasmodic)
- Adrenaline (allergic reactions, cardiac arrest)
- Dexasone/Dexamethasone (different inflammations processes, corticosteroid)
- Voltaren gel (pain)
- Lasix (high blood pressure drug, edema) furosemide
- Glycerol suppositories
- Bisolvon solutions (Bromhexine, solution for inhalation via nebulizer to clear mucus from the respiratory tract, for bronchitis, asthma, pneumonia...)
- Tylenol (cold or flu symptomatic treatment, pain, fever)
- Aspirin (headache, pain, fever)
- Voltaren suppositories (Diclofenac Suppository Rectal, pain, fever)
- Sulfadiazine creams (SSD, Flamazine, for burns treatment)
- Multivitamin pills
- Paracetamol / acetaminophen (pain, fever)

Of course, you will not always have access to the ideal medication for a medical emergency, and sometimes you will not have any medication at all. Do not forget that your natural environment can provide many natural remedies.

I would also recommend getting herbal medicine reference books that detail effective natural medicines and herbal remedies, such as Medical Herbalism: The Science and Practice of Herbal Medicine and Encyclopedia of Herbal Medicine.

Medical Equipment

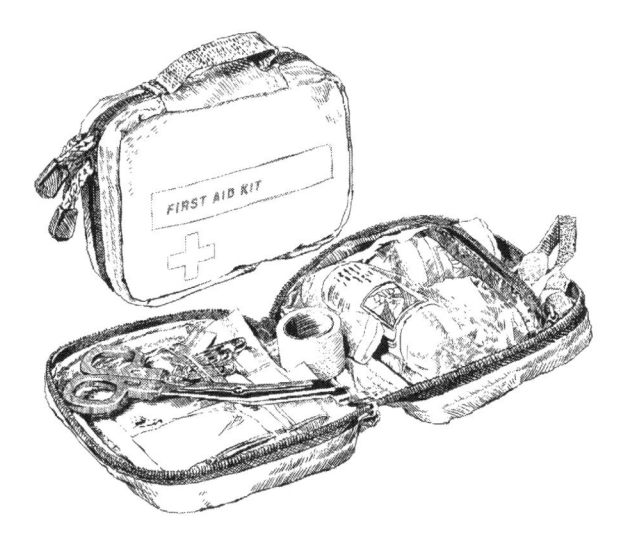

Having basic medical supplies, especially things like sterile dressings, can prevent one of the biggest killers in the outdoors – infection. They can also vastly reduce pain and increase mobility in the case of broken bones and other musculoskeletal injuries.

It is not only important to have medical supplies for treatment, but you should also think about the gear that will protect you when you are dealing with casualties, particularly when it comes to wounds and infectious diseases. Diseases are caused by pathogenic organisms, such as bacteria and viruses.

Pathogens can spread through the air or can be transferred through blood or other bodily fluids. In other words, the afflicted person can infect you through breath, saliva, blood, or any other bodily fluid, especially when the fluid has come into contact with your eyes, nose, mouth, or damaged skin. Even minor breaks of your skin, like tears around the fingernails, can be enough for pathogens to enter your body.

Using Protective Equipment

SELCO ON HOW MESSY THINGS CAN GET

> *It is a messy job. For example, when a man gets hit with several bullets or stabbed with a knife, you can expect lots of blood.*
>
> *I witnessed a situation when people were helping a guy who had several wounds. He bled very seriously from the wounds on the thigh and stomach. A few minutes later, people who were helping him looked like they were wounded too like they were bleeding too.*

Expect to be very dirty, and I am not talking about blood only, but also other body fluids. Keep in mind that your first mission is to protect and save YOU, "so having gloves, masks, goggles" and similar equipment ready make sense.

When you deal with real casualties in real situations, there can be a lot of spraying and splashing of all kinds of fluids. Do some tests at home to figure out what might happen in a real medical emergency – for example, put on your gloves, mask, and goggles, then put plenty of red paint on your hands.

Now try to do some tasks rapidly, like fetching items from another room, taking objects out of a sealed bag, rummaging through another bag to locate a pair of scissors, etc. You will see that you are probably going to have red paint all over you and everything else. This not only puts you at risk of contracting an infection, but it also means you might have to waste precious water to clean up all the fluids.

You will not always have the items below on you in an emergency, but if you have access to them or can improvise them with the materials around you (e.g., use sunglasses instead of medical eye protection), I highly recommend the following:

1. *Gloves*

If possible, use gloves whenever there is the chance for contact with blood and other body fluids.

Whenever possible, put the gloves on before you start to treat the casualty, whether we are talking about bleeding, CPR, resuscitation, or anything else.

Make sure you take the gloves off properly after treating the casualty, i.e., without making any contact with the outside of them.

2. *Eye protection*

If possible, wear eye protection when dealing with casualties, as the mucous membrane around human eyes is capable of absorbing fluids.

Eye protection should ideally cover your eyes from the front and the sides.

3. *Mask*

Whenever possible, use a mask if there is a chance of bleeding or splashing of fluids, preferably a surgical mask.

You can also put a mask on casualties while you are treating them if you suspect that they have an infectious disease.

If you happen to have access to one, it is good to use a face shield together with a surgical mask for maximum protection.

Remember, you can make an improvised mask by putting a scarf or piece of clothing over your mouth and nose.

4. Shoe covers

Remember, it is going be much easier to throw away your dirty shoe covers than to clean your shoes.

Must-Have Medical Supplies

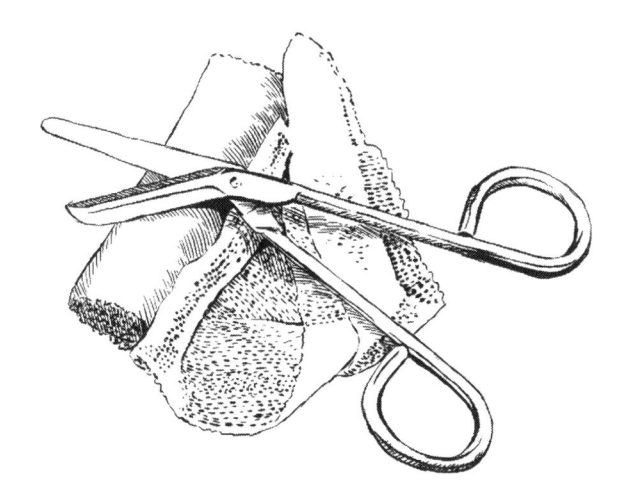

Make sure these "must-have" medical supplies are in your first aid kit:
- Absorbent compress dressings
- Adhesive bandages
- Adhesive cloth tape
- Antibiotic ointment packets (approximately 1 gram)
- Antiseptic wipe packets
- 1 blanket (space blanket)

- 1 breathing barrier (with one-way valve)
- 1 instant cold compress
- Pair of non-latex gloves (size: large)
- Hydrocortisone ointment packets (approximately 1 gram each)
- Scissors
- Roller bandages
- Sterile gauze pads
- Oral thermometer (non-mercury/non-glass)
- Triangular bandages
- Tweezers

Also, consider a suture kit (see below).

A more comprehensive list of medical supplies is listed below. These are the items I keep at my bug out location so that I am prepared and well equipped to administer first aid in case conflict breaks out.

- Sterile gauze compresses
- Elastic bandages
- Medical alcohol
- Burn dressings (sterile water gel soaked dressings, used as a first-aid treatment for burns, in order to cool and keep the affected areas sterile)
- EMT shears (heavy-duty scissors, very good for cutting different stuff, with good quality EMT scissors you can cut wire)
- CPR masks (disposable)
- Suture and surgical kit (tweezers, needle, needle holders, scalpel blades, blade holder)
- Disposable suture removal kits (trays, scissors, metal forceps, gauze, bandages, and compresses)
- IV catheters (different sizes)
- Syringes (different sizes)
- Needles
- IV sets (also can be used for setting up a wound irrigation system)

- Iodine scrubs (used for surgical handwashing in normal times, can be perfect for wound treatment)
- Large tubes of non-sterile gauze
- Stainless steel drums for sterilizing things (like the gauze from those large tubes)
- Small oxygen tanks (5 kg) to deliver oxygen to casualties, or to deliver drugs via inhalation
- Oxygen regulator
- Humidifier (to humidify breathing oxygen, use sterile or boiled water, change the water regularly)
- Oxygen masks (non-re-breather)
- Nebulizers (to administer drugs in the form of aerosol inhalation)
- Powered respirator (for resuscitation use)
- O2 powered suction unit (the tool used to suction secretion from a casualty's airway, for example, during reanimation or in a semiconscious casualty who is vomiting)
- Laryngoscope sets (used to intubate non-breathing casualties)
- Sets of ET tubes (endotracheal tubes), in all sizes, for people who stop breathing
- BVM masks, pediatric and adult (bag valve masks to keep casualties breathing with your help)
- Sets of comb tube (easier to intubate with these, some restrictions, laryngoscope not needed)
- Sets of the airway, nasal, and oral boxes of tube holders to keep the airways of unconscious people open
- Urinal catheter sets (very important if you have a sick person who is laying down for a long time, in order to prevent further hygienic complications and infections)
- Disposable masks (to use for dealing with casualties, scavenging, cheap low protection masks)
- Disposable medical gloves (nonsterile)
- Pairs of sterile gloves (for treating wounds)
- Sterile fields (for small surgical treatments)

- Respirator masks (to use in more "dangerous" medical situations, such as disease outbreaks or pandemics)

Primary Assessment

SELCO ON PROBLEMS WITH PRIMARY ASSESSMENT

> I was helping the man who had a piece of wall stuck in his leg after the explosion. I did not know that at that moment, I only hear him scream very loud and yelling at me, "help me, I am gonna die." I need a few minutes to remove dirt from him and

to see that his wound is the only minor. Other people at that moment had much larger and more dangerous wounds.

I knew before that for saying "those who scream need to be treated last," but knowing something and using that in a real-life situation is different things.

When you find yourself in a situation where you need to help injured people, stop for the moment and check and think what you were gonna do, do not let to panic lead you.

Surveying the scene and doing an initial assessment of the casualties are critical steps in the first aid process. You will make most of your mistakes at this moment – you might forget a step like radioing for help, failing to see an important symptom of the casualty, or you could get killed or injured because you wanted to help someone and you did not pay attention to the possible dangers in your surroundings.

There is a simple, easy to remember sequence to ensure that you do not mess up at this pivotal moment: DR ABC.

- **D** – danger
- **R** – resuscitation
- **A** – airway
- **B** – breathing
- **C** – circulation/CPR

The sequence of these steps is essential, and you should not underestimate how easy it is to forget them when you're in a real-life medical emergency.

For example, you might discover your friend collapsed on a trail and run to his aid without checking for dangers, only to realize too late that he was bitten by a deadly snake nearby, which now has the chance to bite you as well. Or you might find a loved one bleeding from a serious wound and run back to camp to get supplies without checking his vital signs first, only to return and discover that he is dead because his airways were blocked, and you could have saved him simply by putting him in the recovery position.

Maybe there will be distressed, screaming people on the scene, and you will panic or become confused and not know what to do.

To avoid this, get used to following the steps to recognize and treat injuries and to distinguish between priorities and distractions. Never forget "Doctor A.B.C." to ensure that you give your loved ones the best chance of survival.

Dangers

Survival situations involve all kinds of dangers, from nature – storms, floods, fires, avalanches, mudslides, dangerous animals – and from mankind – violence, weapons, intoxication.

You always need to minimize risk to yourself. If it is someone else in a medical emergency and you want to assist them, don't do it if it means endangering yourself – you will be no good to them dead. Learn to recognize dangers. Use three words: plan, observe, and react.

Plan

Wear safe and practical clothing. Try to wear clothing that can carry necessary equipment on your body without restricting you or attracting unwanted attention. Always think about mobility and keeping a low profile.

A photographer's vest is useful because it has many pockets. If you are traveling to an area with mosquito-borne diseases, take lightweight, long-sleeved shirts and pants.

Prepare all your equipment and ensure that it is not too heavy or bulky. Consider purchasing a bad that is easy to identify as a first aid bag to store all your first aid supplies and make them easily accessible in an emergency.

Observe
- Always take a few moments to observe a scene before entering or starting treatment.
- Look for external causes of injury – is there a dangerous animal in the area, has a weapon been used, is there a cable that may be an electrical hazard, is there a risk of fire or flooding, etc.?
- Call out to the casualty first, to see if you can ascertain anything about their condition before approaching.
- Look for signs of violent tendencies and alcohol and drug abuse. Even family members can become dangerous in their altered emotional, mental, or physical state.
- Watch out for injuries or illnesses that can cause a person to become violent, e.g., head injuries, a low glucose level, and seizures.
- Keep a close eye on them for changes in their emotional state, particularly confusion or disorientation – remember the person may not recognize you even if it's a member of your family.
- Continue to observe casualties for signs of hostility after treatment is administered. For example, I have seen casualties who are unconscious and with low glucose levels become aggressive after glucose is administered.

React
- First of all, if you or the casualty is in danger, do what it takes to get some help. Scream, call, or signal for help.
- Remember, it is entirely justified to retreat from any situation that endangers your life.
- If you observe a danger, get far enough away so you can have enough time to consider your next move before it is too late.

- If the danger is a human, such as enemy forces, the basic rule is to have two big obstacles between you and them. If they move through one obstacle, you should move through another one, too. Conceal yourself and take the position behind a large object, for example, a boulder or a large tree, in order to both hide and to protect yourself from projectiles.
- If you are outnumbered, and your chances of fleeing them are small, consider climbing a tree until the danger has passed – humans rarely look above eye level. Once you reach safe ground, do not return to the scene.
- If the danger is due to aggression from the injured or sick person, always allow yourself space and be ready to move away from them, or be prepared to restrain them if you're in an enclosed space.
- If the danger is presented by nature, take time to look for a way around it. For example, if a person is in treacherous water, look for a stick to extend to them or a floatable object to throw to them before you decide to jump in.

Response

SELCO ON RESPONSIVE AND UNRESPONSIVE CASUALTIES

> *Do not mix an unresponsive man with a man in shock. You can expect that after a traumatic situation, a lot of people are in shock. They can look to you like they are unresponsive, but they are in shock. Persons who are unresponsive are at that moment your priority over them because their life could be in danger.*

use a gan to lowe temparture

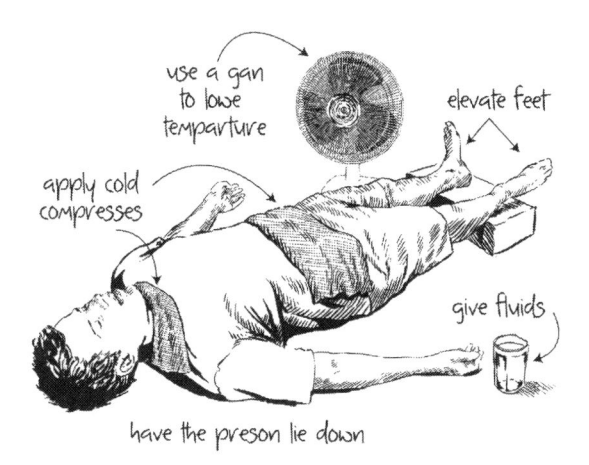

elevate feet

apply cold compresses

give fluids

have the preson lie down

Once you have ascertained that it is safe to approach the casualty, the next thing you have to work out is the state of their condition, and in particular, whether or not they are conscious.

Ask if they can hear you, if they can tell you their name and where they are and, if they are responsive, ask what has happened to them. Often the casualty might not know what has happened to him or her because of either head injury or shock.

In this case, ask: Can they move? Where does it hurt? Can they feel all of their limbs and appendages? What is the last thing they remember?

For conscious casualties, use this information as well as your observations to determine how critical their condition is and what immediate treatment is required. Consider and weigh your priorities. For example, is the possibility of harm caused by leaving the casualty alone greater than the possibility that you will be able to find help if you leave them? Do they appear to be unconscious with a low risk of infectious disease, and therefore, should you check if resuscitation is required before fetching your medical supplies?

For unconscious or unresponsive casualties, continue with "ABC."

Airways

Your first priority with an unconscious casualty should always be to ensure that the airways are clear and that they remain open so that the casualty does not asphyxiate by choking on vomit or bodily fluid. To clear the airways:

1. With the casualty supported on the side, tilt the head backward and slightly down.

2. Open the mouth and clear any foreign objects. Only remove dentures if loose or broken.

Recovery Position

Unless you think the casualty has a spinal injury (see below), you should put them into a recovery position to keep the airways open.

To place someone in the recovery position:

- Put the arm that is closest to you at a right angle to their body, with the palm facing upwards.
- Put the palm of their other hand against their chest.
- Lift the knee that is furthest from you so that their leg is bent at a 90-degree angle, and their foot is flat on the floor. Placing your hands on the hip and shoulder of the person's far side, gently roll the body onto its side so that it is facing you.
- Put the top hand under the head, so that the palm is on the floor, and the person's cheek is on the back of the hand.
- Point the mouth towards the floor so that any vomit or blood can drain out. ? Push the chin (away from the chest, not away from the floor) to keep the epiglottis open.
- Ensure that the knee of the top leg stays bent at a right angle to their body to prevent them from rolling onto the stomach.

In the end, the knee stops the body from rolling onto the stomach, and the hand supports the head.
Spinal Injury

SELCO ON SPINAL INJURIES

It happens more than you think, people, trying to help and do more damage with "wrong" helping.

When you are helping a man who just had some serious trauma, let's say part of the wall collapsed on him, or he had a car accident, always suspect a spinal injury, and treat it like that. More than once, people had a car accident and were pulled out from the car from the people who are not trained for that, later it was realized that serious injuries were made with that "pulling." If it is possible, treat it like spinal injuries.

If you think a person may have a spinal injury, only move them into the recovery position if they have obstructed airways or are vomiting, are choking, or are in danger of further injury, and if possible, only do so with the help of another person.

One person should be at the head and another along the side of the injured person. Work together to keep the person's head, neck, and back aligned while gently rolling the person onto one side.

Otherwise, if it is necessary to open their airway, place your hands on either side of their face and gently lift their jaw with your fingertips. Take care not to move their neck.

You should suspect a spinal injury if the person:

- has a head injury, especially one where there has been a large blow on the back of the head, and is or has been unconscious
- complains of severe pain in their neck or back
- won't move their neck
- feels weak, numb, or paralyzed
- has lost control of their limbs, bladder, or bowels
- has a twisted neck or back

The Recovery Position for Babies

For babies less than a year old, a different recovery position is needed. Cradle the infant in your arms with their head tilted downwards to make sure they do not choke on their tongue or vomit.

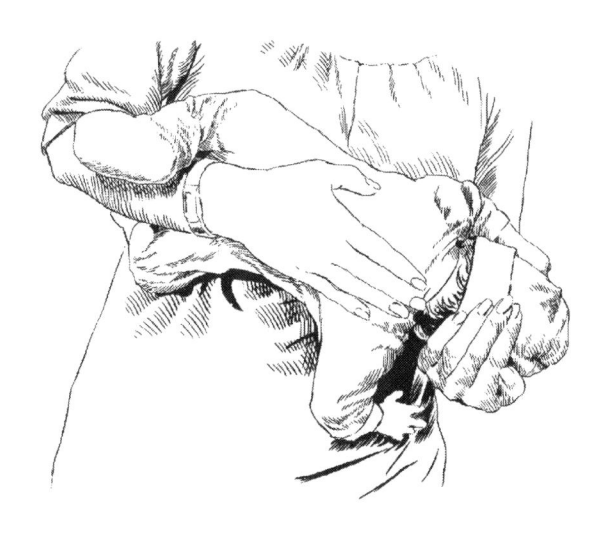

Breathing
- When the casualty is in a recovery position with the airways clear, you need to establish if your casualty is breathing normally. Place your ear by their nose and mouth and feel and listen for breath, while watching their chest to see if it is rising and falling.
- If your casualty is unconscious but breathing normally, they should remain in the recovery position where you can start treating any obvious injuries such as bleeding, or otherwise wait for them to regain consciousness.
- If your casualty is not breathing, return the casualty onto their back, and commence resuscitation (see "CPR and Resuscitation," below).
- If the casualty recommences breathing, return them to the recovery position and go back to "R" (Response). Once breathing has stabilized, commence treating any other injuries.

The 'C' in DR ABC used to stand for circulation, but according to current medical practices, you are no longer required to check for a pulse when managing an unconscious patient who is not breathing. Instead, you should commence rescue breathing and CPR.

Basic Treatment: CPR and Bleeding Wounds

Diagnoses and Treatment: CPR and Resuscitation

SELCO ON SETTING PRIORITIES WHO TO HELP FIRST

> CPR needs to be started as soon as possible, the sooner you start it, more chance you have to restore vital functions.
>
> Now, in reality, if we are talking about multiple casualties, then you need to do triage and help injured people that have the chance to live.
>
> That means if you have, for example, seven injured people after some incident, explosion, for example, and you have a man without breading and pulse, and on the other side man with massive bleeding, you gonna choose to help the guy with bleeding. When you have more injured people, you are simply given help where you can really help. Never forget to think about your own safety first.

If the heart stops pumping, it is known as a cardiac arrest. During cardiac arrest, the heart is starved of oxygen and cannot pump blood around the body.

When blood stops circulating the body, the brain is also starved of oxygen, and the person rapidly becomes unconscious and stops breathing. Without treatment, the person will die. Cardiopulmonary resuscitation (CPR) is a combination of mouth-to-mouth resuscitation and chest compressions that delivers oxygen and artificial blood circulation to save the life of someone during cardiac arrest.

The proper way of administering CPR

Your chances of saving someone with CPR when SHTF is low. Even if you restore life functions of the casualty, they will still need a high level of medical care post – CPR to remain alive. CPR is ordinarily used in an effort to manually preserve intact brain function until further measures can be taken to restore spontaneous blood circulation and breathing in a person – i.e., until trained medical personal arrive. Always make calls, sending, or signaling for help a priority when performing CPR.

CPR – Chest Compressions

- ADULT – Position the heel of one hand on the center of the lower half of the breastbone (sternum) and put your other hand on top of the first with your fingers interlaced.
- CHILD – Position the heel of one hand on the center of the lower half of the breastbone (sternum).
- BABY – Position two fingers in the center of the breastbone (sternum) just between the nipples.

1. Compress the chest about 1/3 of its depth (at least 2 inches or 4-5 cm or for adults).
2. Allow the chest to completely recoil before the next compression.
3. Aim for at least 100 compressions per minute.
4. Give two breaths to every 30 compressions (around every 18 seconds).

If the casualty's pulse returns, but the person is still not breathing, continue to rescue breathing without CPR. Check for a pulse regularly by putting two fingers on a vein in their wrist. Straighten the casualty's arm with the underside facing upwards. Place your index and middle fingers on their wrist, on the inside of the outer wrist bone just under the thumb.

Resuscitation – Rescue Breathing

Open the airway by tilting the casualty's head back and lifting their chin, then commence rescue breathing as follows:

- ADULT – pinch the patient's nostrils and seal your mouth over the patient's mouth and give two full breaths two seconds apart
- CHILD – use two smaller breaths for a child two seconds apart
- BABY – seal your mouth over the baby's mouth and nose and give two quick puffs two seconds apart

Ensure that the chest is rising and falling with each breath. If the chest doesn't rise on the first breath, reposition the head and try again.

If you are untrained and not confident, you can perform compressions at 100 per minute without doing rescue breaths. Remember that even if you are worried that your skills or knowledge aren't up to scratch, it is far better to do something than to do nothing at all. The difference between your doing something and doing nothing could be someone's life.

Bleeding

SELCO ON BLEEDING OUT

The man was wounded from the shrapnel's (?) from tank shell, and as folks tried to help him, there were five people trying to help him and to make some sense, he had multiple wounds, bigger and smaller, and partially his guts were out. They all make a lot of effort trying to cover that wound and make some sense. The wounded man screamed and kicked around in delirium. They managed to get him to the field doctor, but he died, he lost a lot of blood.

There they figured that he had a big wound on the leg, and he bled from there very bad.

> *The point is that when they start to help him, the priority was to STOP arterial bleeding from his leg. His stomach wound was (in that moment) less important, however bad was.*
>
> *It is not gonna be a clean case almost never. It is going to be dirty, smelly, and confusing, but in case of a wound, your first priority to found the most serious bleeding and control it.*

Unlike cardiac arrest, bleeding is one of the most preventable causes of death. Remember that your task when it comes to treating a life-threatening bleed is primarily to STOP it, and secondly, to keep the area clean.

There are a lot of different classifications of bleeding and many different schools of thought when it comes to how to treat wounds – protocols are changing all of the time. We will focus first and foremost on the essential task of stopping the bleeding. First, we need to determine what type of bleeding we are talking about.

Types of Bleeding

1. Capillary bleeding

Insignificant bleeding where the smallest blood vessels are injured, there is no danger caused by blood loss, and the body will stop the bleeding on its own.

2. Venous bleeding

The wound is deep, and larger blood vessels are damaged, bleeding is more severe, and the blood has a dark red color. The wound is bleeding slowly but continuously.

3. Arterial bleeding

Although someone can die from even the smallest wound, for example, if an infection is contracted, the most serious danger when it comes to bleeds is arterial bleeding. People can die in just a few minutes in the case of arterial bleeding, or in extreme cases, even faster. Blood will have a bright red color, stream out of the body fast and in large amounts, and follow the rhythm of the heart.

Ways to Stop Bleeding

To stop bleeding, you need to use common sense and to combine speed and hygiene. Some real-life examples might be:

You have a casualty who is wounded from an explosive device, and he is bleeding severely from a wound on his leg. Your priority here is to "plug the hole" – to stop the bleeding by any means available – or he will die. You do not have time to check the wound, or fetch your iodine, or even to open your sterile gauze. You are just going to have to use whatever you can to stop the bleeding, and later you can clean it – if he's still alive.

In another example, say you cut yourself with a knife. The wound is long, not too deep, and you are bleeding slowly. Clean it first, check for debris in the wound, apply iodine, and use sterile gauze to bandage it.

1. Pressure

The most simple and effective way to stop bleeding is to apply pressure to the wound. Use your clothes, bandages, gauze, even your hands if necessary – whatever you have to stop the bleeding. Continue to use pressure until the bleeding stops.

Once you have applied pressure to the wound, do not remove it. You can put more gauze or bandages on it if the fabric becomes blood-soaked, but remember it is not important how it looks. It is important only to stop the bleeding.

2. Elevation and positioning of casualty

If the casualty is conscious, lay him down. You want to try to keep the casualty conscious, but this way, if he does lose consciousness, he is not at risk of injuring himself further in a fall.

More importantly, you want to keep the injured part of the body above the level of his heart, if possible, to reduce blood loss with the help of gravity. If the bleeding is in a limb, for example, prop the limb upon another object, so it is above chest height.

3. Digital pressure points

In addition, you can use pressure points on the human body to lower the blood flow and reduce the bleeding, as described in the image below.

4. Tourniquet

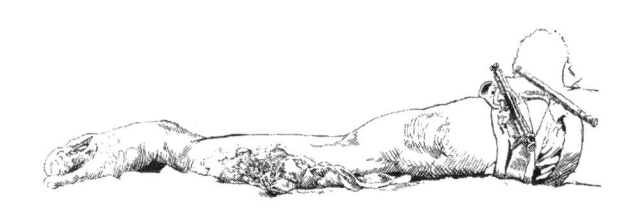

A tourniquet is essentially any device for stopping or slowing bleeding by forcibly compressing on blood vessels to cut off blood supply to the wounded area. As a last resort, when everything else has failed to stop the bleeding, you can use a tourniquet. Unless you are a trained medic, a tourniquet can cause significant damage, and therefore should only be used if blood loss reaches a critical level and the casualty's life is in danger.

Obviously, there are military-style tourniquets, but more often than not, when SHTF, you will be using a bandage or a torn strip of cloth. There is a lot of conflicting opinion about the proper use of tourniquets. From my experience, I would recommend:

• The tourniquet should be applied on the skin surface, 2-3 inches above the wound.

• Apply it tightly, so tightly that it hurts. If applied properly, the tourniquet should eliminate the distal pulse in the affected limb.

Once applied, the tourniquet should be left in place on a severe, ongoing bleed until medical facilities are reached. This might cause significant pain to the casualty and even increase the chance of a later amputation, but in my opinion, there is a more serious risk of death from the additional blood loss caused by repeated removals of the tourniquet.

Always leave a tourniquet visible on the casualty, or mark some sign that you used tourniquet on him.

Treating Wounds – Cleaning and Suturing

SELCO ON THE CONSEQUENCES OF NOT CLEANING WOUNDS

As life gets harder when SHTF, it was almost normal to get scrapes and cuts in everyday life. So an infected wound was very often a thing.

My relative had an injury from the hammer, nothing too big, but his nail must go out, he did some disinfecting with alcohol, but I guess not on time.

That finger went infected very fast. We cleaned it every day or two, using alcohol and homemade paste. It went better and worst in a period of some three months and eventually healed, but after all that, hi simply lost almost all functions of that finger.

If you are dealing with a serious wound and the chances of reaching medical facilities any time soon are slim to none, you may have to make a decision about whether or not to suture the wound.

In its most basic form, a suture is simply a series of knots tied over an open wound to enable and aid the skin to close properly. Understanding the mechanics of suturing and applying them correctly can mean the difference between life and death. The best treatment of a wound is conservative treatment – that is, keeping it clean, bandaging it, and allowing it to heal on its own.

If the laceration can be closed using steri-strips or another technique available to you, you should use that method, as suturing can cause more harm than good. However, if the skin on either side of the wound will not stay together, and it continues to bleed, suturing may be the best option.

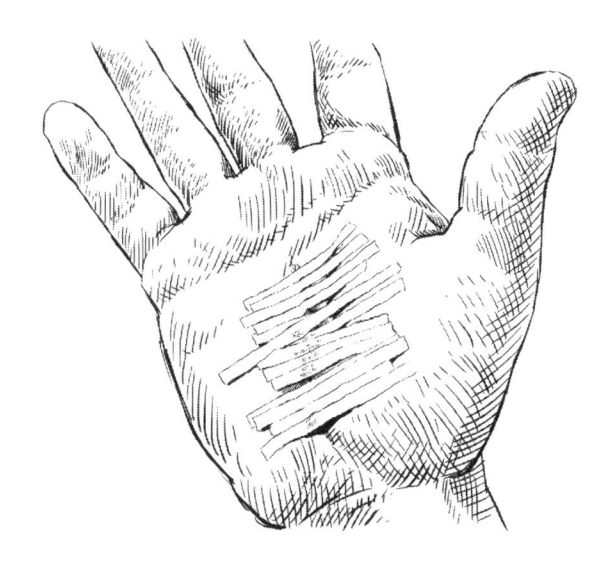

Materials

You should only consider suturing a wound if you have suitable medical supplies. Consider getting a suture kit and only go ahead with suturing if you have:
- Clean water
- Betadine
- A needle driver
- An irrigating syringe
- Suture material (needle and thread)
- Gloves

Appropriate suturing material will depend on the location of the wound. Ideally, your suture kit will come with a variety of needle shapes and types and suture threads. Most wounds can be closed with thin, curved needles. Common muscle tissue, arm, and leg wounds can usually be closed with suture thread size 4 or 5. For more delicate areas like the mouth, suture size 2 or 3 is preferred.

Cleaning the Wound

After stopping or slowing the bleeding, cleaning the wound is critical to avoiding infection and optimizing chances of survival. If the wound is not cleaned, the infection will undoubtedly set in, causing more severe complications.

In most cases, simple, clean water can be used. If clean water is not available or if a wound shows evidence of debris, diluted Betadine should be used (a few drops of Betadine to one cup of water).

Fill the irrigating syringe with your clean water or Betadine solution and cleanse the wound. It is imperative you keep the injured area as clean and sterile as possible before, during, and after suturing – be sure to wear gloves if possible and keep the area where you are treating the wound as clear of foreign objects as possible.

Method

The basic steps of suturing are as follows:
- Move the casualty so that the wound is parallel to your body.
- Put gloves on to minimize potential infection.
- Clean and irrigate the wound, removing any foreign matter or debris.
- Thread the curved needle, or open your suture kit and grasp the needle with your needle driver.
- Start at the center of the laceration and work outwards.
- Leave approximately 1/8 inch between each stitch.
- Bandage the wound to minimize later infection.

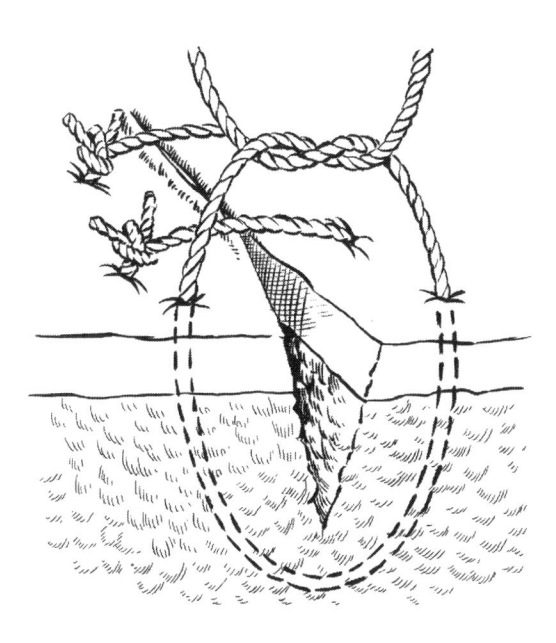

Aftercare

Remember that your primary focus when dealing with wounds is to avoid infection. To do this, ensure that the bandages are regularly changed, and the wound is checked for signs of infection (at least twice a day).

If the wound does not appear to be healing, or if there is any sign of infection (such as yellow or greenish fluid, or if the skin around the wound becomes red, warm, swollen, or increasingly painful), it may be necessary to reopen the wound and determine if any foreign debris is inside.

Give the casualty antibiotics if they are at your disposal and keep track of infections by marking the skin where the redness stops and monitoring it to see if it is traveling upwards (a sign that the infection is spreading and IV antibiotics are required).

Basic Treatment: Burns, Heat and Cold Related Injuries
Burns

SELCO ON TREATING BURN VICTIMS

> *When you were helping someone who is suffered burns, do not forget to remove everything from him. People did make mistakes by not doing that, so I saw how things like necklaces or rings and clothes continued to burn and injure people when they were put "out of the fire."*

Burns can be one of the most painful and untreatable injuries. Not including sunburn, any burns to the face, hands, and feet should be treated as a significant injury.

For major burns (second and third degree), follow these steps:

- Remove the victim from the burning area, remembering not to put yourself in danger.
- Remove any burning material from the casualty.
- Call or send for help.
- Once the victim is in a safe place, keep them warm and still. Try to wrap the injured areas in a clean sheet if available. DO NOT use cold water on the victim; this may drop the body temperature and cause hypothermia.

For minor burns (first-degree burns or second-degree burns involving a small area of the body):

- Gently clean the wound with room temperature water.
- Rings, bracelets, and other potentially constricting articles should be removed (edema or swelling from inflammation could occur, and the item might cut into the skin).
- Dress the burn with a topical antibiotic ointment like Sulfadiazine.
- Apply a sterile water gel soaked dressing. **Other Heat-related Injuries**

As for many injuries and illnesses, prevention is key. In the case of head injuries, that means:

- Consuming adequate amounts of water
- Not overexerting yourself with physical activity
- Avoiding overexposure to direct sunlight

- Wearing proper clothing

In short, when heat builds up faster than we can cool ourselves down, we have problems. It can happen for many different reasons and over varying periods of time – in hours or over the course of several days. Below are various types of heat-related injuries and how to treat them.

Heat exhaustion

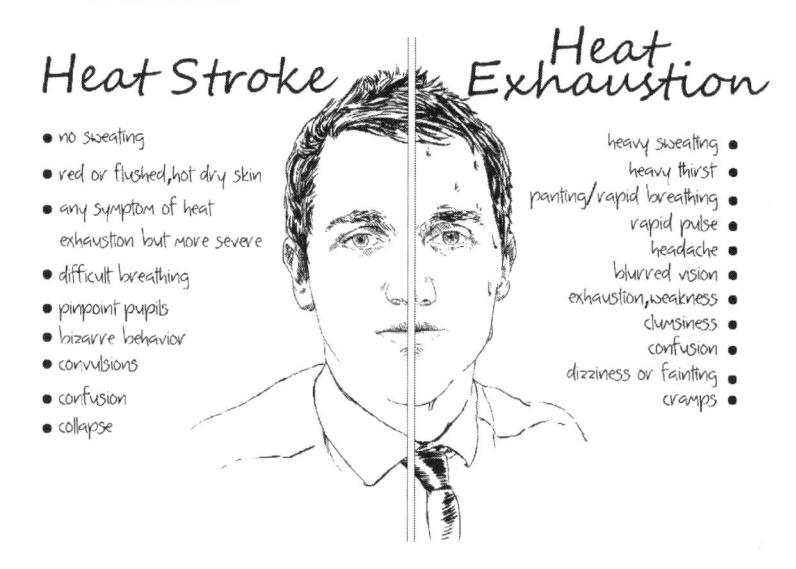

Heat Stroke
- no sweating
- red or flushed, hot dry skin
- any symptom of heat exhaustion but more severe
- difficult breathing
- pinpoint pupils
- bizarre behavior
- convulsions
- confusion
- collapse

Heat Exhaustion
- heavy sweating
- heavy thirst
- panting/rapid breathing
- rapid pulse
- headache
- blurred vision
- exhaustion, weakness
- clumsiness
- confusion
- dizziness or fainting
- cramps

Heat exhaustion occurs when the body loses too much fluid and electrolytes because of sweating and a lack of adequate fluid intake. This can often happen if you are doing a high level of physical activity in a hot environment. Some of the signs and symptoms are headache, nausea, fatigue, apathy, cool and clammy skin, and light-headedness. Body temperature can be normal or slightly elevated.

You need to get the casualty out of the hot environment, lay them down, make them comfortable, and remove excessive clothing

Rehydrate them, ideally with IV fluids, or otherwise with oral fluids, slowly and in small amounts. To avoid nausea, limit fluids to around 100 to 150 mL every half hour.

Heat cramps

Heat cramps will happen together with heat exhaustion in about 50% of cases. A lot of time, heat cramps will be confused with cramps from heavy physical activity. It happens when the balance between water and electrolytes is lost. Symptoms are typically muscle cramps in the lower extremities, abdomen, arms, or back.

- Immediately remove the casualty from the hot environment.
- Gently stretch the affected muscles.
- Give the casualty fluids, if possible, with an electrolyte solution (salt tablets are not recommended in this case because they can induce vomiting and cause further damage).

Heatstroke

Heatstroke is a serious, life-threatening condition. It can occur with a combination of high temperatures, high humidity, and physical activity. This combination elevates the body's production of heat and minimizes its ability to regulate it. Signs and symptoms can include confusion, disorientation, loss of consciousness, and hot and flushed skin.

Act immediately – the higher the temperature, and the longer the casualty remains in that state, the more deadly it becomes

Cool the person down rapidly by any possible means. Pour ice directly on the casualty, put them in cool water, use ice packs, fan them, and remove all clothing.

Cold Related Injuries

SELCO ON COLD RELATED INJURIES

> *I experienced personally beginning of "white death." It was not a painful experience, but very close to death for sure. After long walking through the snow, in inadequate shoes and clothes, wet and cold, I simply stop to care what is happening around me. I did not feel bad; actually, luckily, I survived.*

Prepare for cold weather before it starts and also thinks about things that you are gonna see more often in cold weather when SHTF, for example, think about facts that very young and very old are sensitive to hypothermia. If you have older folks in your family or group, check them more often since they are more prone to hypothermia.

Cold weather-related injuries are not as dramatic as heat trauma, as far as the rate of onset or visible clues and symptoms. The main factor in cold-related injuries is prolonged exposure. These injuries usually happen to more exposed parts of the body, like feet, face, fingers, toes, etc.

Frostbite

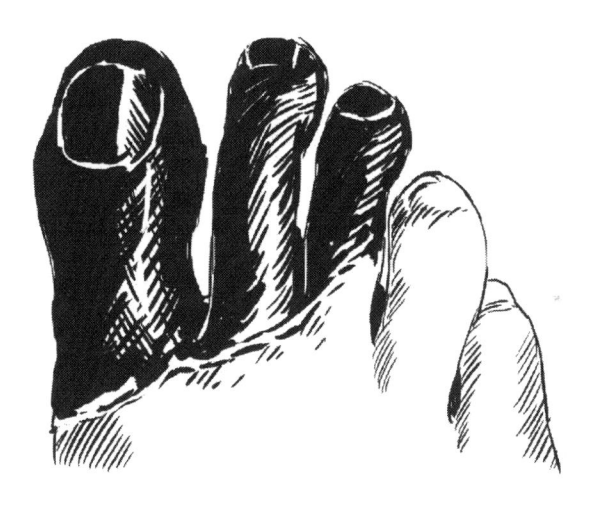

Frostbite is the freezing of the water in the body due to exposure to freezing temperatures. In short, when outside temperatures are too low for the body, the response of the body is to heat its core more than its extremities. This is the reason why the more distant parts of the body, such as fingers and toes, are the first ones at risk.

There are two main types of frostbite.

Superficial Frostbite

The casualty will have a burning sensation or some level of pain or discomfort in the affected area. The skin will be yellow or grey and feels soft like normal tissue.

- Remove the casualty from the cold environment.
- Heat them up with appropriate shelter, clothes, fire, or body heat. Reheat the affected area, for example, by heating ears with warm hands or placing affected fingers under the armpits.
- Remember that superficial frostbite only needs to be reheated to normal temperature. ? Do not use cigarettes or alcohol because they may cause vasoconstriction (the narrowing or constriction of blood vessels by small muscles in their walls).

Deep Frostbite

The casualty does not recognize or react to sensation in the extremity. If freezing continues, the affected area will become "shiny," and the skin will be hard. When the nerve endings become frozen, the numbness and pain will stop.

- Remove casualty from the cold environment.
- Heat them up with heated shelter, clothes, fire, body heat, or ideally immersion in hot water (39 degrees).
- Consider pain management as the process of reheating deep frostbite is extremely painful.
- Once reheating has begun, do not allow the casualty to refreeze again because gangrene can occur, leading to probable amputation.
- During reheating, keep affected parts elevated to reduce swelling.
- Separate digits with pieces of gauze, if possible, to prevent them from sticking together.
- Do not puncture blisters (if formed).
- Never run snow or ice on frostbitten or frozen areas.

Hypothermia

You are much more likely to encounter hypothermia than to see deep frostbite. Hypothermia is common in the wilderness and in urban areas, and can quickly become deadly. Signs include muscular shivering (in early stages – in late stages, shivering will stop), altered level of consciousness, confusion, slurred speech, diminished pulse, and slow reacting pupils.

• Stop further heat loss, first by moving the casualty to a warm area, then reheating them by any available means.

• Remove any wet clothes from the casualty and cover them with warm and dry blankets if possible. If they are awake and alert, give them sweet and warm fluids. Do not give them cigarettes, alcohol, or caffeine.

• If the casualty is not conscious, you should give him warm fluids intravenously (if trained).

• Do not try to reheat extremities first, or you will increase peripheral circulation before central warming can occur, causing complications. Focus on heating up the core.

• Casualties with severe hypothermia can be unresponsive. Do not confuse that state with death – always check the pulse and look, listen, and feel carefully for breath.

Only as a last resort, you can use "bathtub reheating" by placing the casualty in a tub of warm water (40 degrees C). Remember to keep his extremities out of the water.

Basic Treatment: Musculoskeletal Injuries / Broken Bones

SELCO ON TREATING MUSCULOSKELETAL INJURIES

> After peace came, there number of people with weird-looking fingers or hands, or limping, etc. When they get injured during the SHTF, broken arm, for example, there was no X-ray or mostly no doctor. So people fix it as they could, sometimes id did not work well, so they have problems for the rest of their life. In some situations, old ladies who knew some primitive ways of fixing this did that instead of doctors.
>
> Learn how to properly treat musculoskeletal injury. It will save you a lot of pain, it can save that part of body function, and it can save your life.

Musculoskeletal injury refers to the damage of muscular or skeletal systems, including sprains, strains, tears, dislocations, and fractures of muscles, ligaments, tendons, joints, and bones.

These injuries are usually due to a fall or strenuous activity. In most cases, musculoskeletal injuries are not life-threatening but can lead to serious complications such as bleeding if not properly treated.

In World War I, the mortality rate from a closed femur (thigh bone) fracture was reported at 80%. After the splint was invented, the reported mortality rate fell to 20% (and today it's much lower), demonstrating the importance of conservative management of this type of injury. Be sure to splint any swollen, painful, or deformed extremity.

In terms of first aid, you do not need to know for sure that it is broken – treat for the worst-case scenario and splint it.

Some injuries will be obvious, others not. Use your common sense and skills of observation when examining a casualty for injury. If possible, it is desirable to remove all clothing from problem areas when you inspect the casualty.

Symptoms and Signs of Musculoskeletal Injury

- **Swelling:** Broken bones and damaged muscles, tendons, and ligaments lead to internal bleeding and swelling. Swelling can increase proportions, resulting in lasting deformity.
- **Pain and tenderness:** The casualty will experience pain when the injured body part is touched or moved. In most cases, on the first inspection, the casualty will hold the injured part gently, in order to protect it and minimize movement and pain.

Immobility: Often, people with musculoskeletal injury will not be able to move the affected area or appendages on the affected limb. The more immobile the casualty is, the more serious the injury.

Crepitus: Crepitus is sound or feeling when broken ends of bone rub against each other. Do not try to provoke crepitus.

Bruising: Black or bluish discoloration of skin signifies possible musculoskeletal injury.

The exposed bone ends: In compound fractures, bones can protrude through the skin.

- **Deformity:** You may be able to see that a bone is broken by its appearance under the skin. Always look at the uninjured side and compare it with the injured side to determine the injury.
- **Joint lock:** Dislocated joints can lock in an abnormal anatomical position.

Realignment and Splinting

Always remember, if there is any other life-threatening injury present, then splinting is secondary.

All painful, deformed, or swollen extremities must be splinted. An effective splint will both stabilize the area and protect it from further harm. The basic rule in splinting is to immobilize adjacent joints and bones.

The purpose of splinting is to minimize the movement of affected joints or bone ends, decrease the casualty's pain, and increase their mobility if you need to keep on the move. By doing proper splinting, you are also preventing further injury to surrounding tissue and blood vessels and stopping closed fractures from becoming open ones.

Realignment

If the chances of reaching medical facilities any time soon are slim, then in order to restore effective circulation to a deformed (i.e., dislocated or seriously broken) extremity and before applying a splint, you will have to realign it. This maneuver can appear dangerous, but it is important:

Without realignment, the splint would be ineffective and will actually cause more damage to the surrounding tissue and much more pain.

Without realignment, circulation can be compromised, and tissue around the injury can die. Effective splinting after proper realignment greatly reduces pain.

To realign a deformed extremity, follow these steps:

• Apply manual traction while another person supports the extremity above the site of injury. Traction is applied in the direction of the long axis of the extremity.

• If resistance is felt, or if it looks like bones might break the skin, then stop the action and splint in the position in which you found it.

If no resistance is felt, then maintain gentle traction until the extremity appears normally aligned.

Do not push protruding bones back unless they fall back under gentle traction (and do not forget to treat it as a wound).

Splinting

sam spling folded in half and edges bent

sam splint applied to a fractured leg or ankle

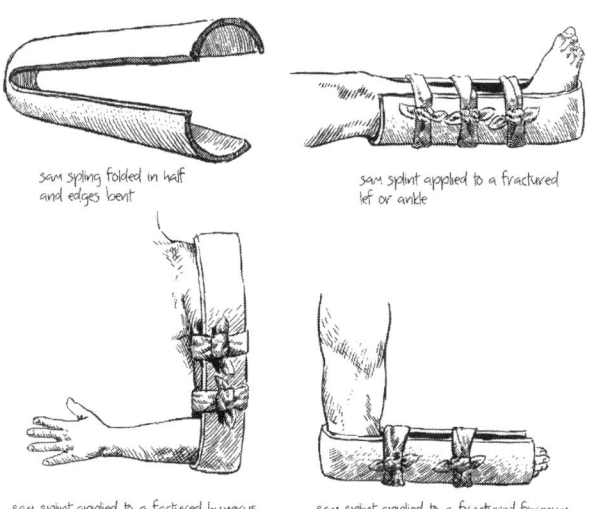

sam splint applied to a factured humerus

sam splint applied to a fractured forearm

Splinting is one of the most common and useful medical treatments, particularly in the outdoors. The beauty of splinting is that it's 99% common sense, and once you learn the rules for splinting, you can use whatever is available to splint. You can improvise with cardboard, plywood, pillows, or rolled blankets, whatever is available.

Whatever method you use, there are some important general rules:

Examine the whole area of injury to check and control any bleeding before moving and splinting the extremity.

Rings, bracelets, and other potentially constricting articles should be removed (edema or swelling from inflammation could occur, and the item might cut into the skin).

Align the bone to its anatomical position with gentle traction before splinting.

• With splinting, you need to immobilize the injury site and adjacent joints.

- If possible, always first immobilize serious musculoskeletal injuries before moving the casualty. If you need to move the casualty quickly because of some danger, try to at least temporarily immobilize the injured site, then move to a safer place and immobilize it properly.
- When you are securing the splint, make sure that it's tight enough to stay in place but not so tight that it cuts off circulation to the injured area.

Components

To make a splint, you need three essential components: a rigid material for support, padded material for comfort, and fabric that can keep the splint in place.

Instead of panicking when you need to splint an injury when SHTF, look at the gear you're carrying and at the items in your surroundings and get creative.

For the rigid component of an improvised splint, you could use:
- Wood, i.e., driftwood, a stick, a branch
- A tent pole
- A trekking pole
- A section of a camping chair
- Rolled up newspaper
- A blunt knife

For padded material, you could use:
- Clothing (wrapped around the injured area and around the finished splint for additional padding)
- Grasses and leaves
- Gauze, bandages, tissue, etc.

For the fabric to fix the splint in place, you could use:
- Clothing

Strips of tent material

- Bandanas tied together
- Socks
- Bandages

- Belts
- Neckties
- Duct tape
- Straps
- Shoelaces

Instructions

1. Take the rigid component of your splint and place it along the injured area.
2. Extend the splint beyond the injured area in order to keep it from moving. In general, try to include the joint above and below the injury in the splint.
3. Secure the splint by tying fabric or tape it above and below the injury (make sure the knots are not pressing on the injury). Avoid over-tightening, which can cut off the circulation.
4. Note an injured body part can also be taped to an uninjured body part in order to prevent it from moving. For example, you can tape an injured finger to the finger next to it to keep it immobile.

Basic Treatment: Shock and Fever

Shock

Shock is a serious condition that can result in death. It is caused by a lack of oxygen in the brain as a result of decreased circulation. To help someone with shock means to fix the underlying cause. A variety of conditions can cause shocks, such as external and internal bleeding, burns, pain, hypothermia, allergic reactions (anaphylactic shock), overwhelming stress, dehydration, or heart problems.

Stages of Shock

Be aware of the four stages of shock: initial, compensatory, progressive, and refractory.

- **Initial**

During this stage, the state of hypoperfusion causes hypoxia. The first stage of shock is reversible, but there aren't any signs to indicate shock at this stage.

- **Compensatory**

In this stage, the body tries to fix the lack of oxygen by increasing its activity. The heartbeat increases, and the arteries restrict to maintain the blood pressure. In this stage, the casualty has a very shallow but rapid pulse. Most likely, you can only detect it on the neck. The person may hyperventilate or suffer from vasoconstriction (the narrowing or constriction of blood vessels by small muscles in their walls).

- **Progressive**

When the compensatory mechanisms begin to fail, the body cannot maintain its normal level of blood pressure, and it quickly drops. Damage to the body is more severe and may even be irreversible. Cellular function deteriorates, and organs start to be damaged by a lack of oxygen.

- **Refractory** the final stage of shock. Treatment is futile. At this stage, the organs completely fail and lead to death. It is important to understand the stages of shock in order to recognize them and prevent the progression to this final stage.

What to Do

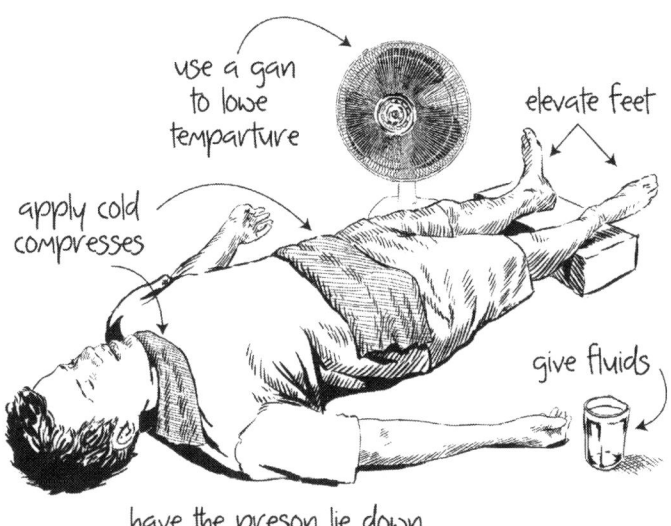

Illustration labels: use a gan to lowe temparture; elevate feet; apply cold compresses; give fluids; have the preson lie down

- Make sure the casualty lies down flat with his legs elevated to make it easier for the blood pressure to stabilize. If the casualty has a severe head injury, do not raise the legs and keep the casualty flat.
- Isolate the casualty and make them feel comfortable. If they have problems breathing, elevate the upper body slightly with one or two pillows or similar things.
- Do not scare the casualty by telling them to calm down or that they might die. This just causes more stress. Loosen any tight clothing and make the casualty as comfortable and relaxed as possible. Talk to them as casually as is appropriate. Gently encourage deep breathing and inhaling and exhaling through the nose.
- Do not give the person food or liquids to prevent the inhalation of vomit.

Fever

SELCO ON HOW THEY TREATED FEVER

> *Natural remedies were used, stuff like clothes soaked in apple vinegar and wrapped around body parts did actually good job in high temperatures (fever).*

Fever is caused by the body trying to fight something. The body increases its production of white blood cells, and they start to attack whatever threat they identify. Fever is not a cause but rather a symptom of another underlying condition.

The regular body temperature of humans is 98.6 Fahrenheit (or 37 degrees Celsius). It is hard to determine if someone has a fever without a thermometer. The best indication is if you ask the casualty if he feels feverish and also considers the external circumstances such as ambient temperature and humidity.

- If your temperature is between 98 – 100 degrees Fahrenheit (or 37 – 38 degrees Celsius), you have a low-grade fever, and if the situation doesn't get worse, you should be fine.
- If your temperature is between 101 – 103 degrees Fahrenheit (or 38 – 39 degrees Celsius), you have a mid-grade fever and if you have access to medication that can help you, such as antibiotics or aspirin, take them.
- If your temperature is between 104 – 106 degrees Fahrenheit (or 40 – 41 degrees Celsius), you have a high-grade fever and besides taking medication, if available, try to cool your body externally. Strip naked and submerge your legs in cold water if possible or wrap wet cloths around your shins and knees, under your armpits, and on the neck or groin area. A cold wrap on the head adds additional comfort.

Basic Treatment: Poisoning

Poisons Bites

Once again, doing your research might get you out of serious trouble when it comes to poisonous bites. What poisonous creatures are you likely to encounter where you are heading? Are you going to Australia, for example, where you might come across a blue-ringed octopus, a funnel-web spider, or any number of deadly breeds of a snake. If so, make sure you learn pressure immobilization first aid.

Pressure Immobilization First Aid

The purpose of the pressure-immobilization technique is to slow down the movement of venom from the bite site into circulation, thus "buying time" for the patient to reach medical care. Research with snake venom has shown that very little venom reaches the bloodstream if firm pressure is applied over the bitten area, and the limb is immobilized. Pressure-immobilization was initially developed to treat snakebite, but it is also applicable to bites and stings by some other venomous creatures.

Bites to the Lower Limbs

1. Apply a broad pressure bandage over the bite site as soon as possible. Crepe bandages are ideal, but any flexible material may be used. Clothing, towels, etc., may be torn into strips. Pantyhose has been successfully used.
2. Do not remove clothing. Keep the casualty (and the bitten or stung limb) still.
3. Bandage upwards from the lower portion of the bitten or stung limb. Even though a little venom may be squeezed upwards, the bandage will be more comfortable, and therefore can be left in place for longer if required.
4. The bandage should be as tight as the one you would apply to a sprained ankle.
5. Extend the bandage as high as possible up the limb.
6. Apply a splint to the leg.
7. Bind it firmly to as much of the leg as possible.
8. Keep the patient still. Lie the patient down to prevent walking or moving around. Have the patient taken immediately by ambulance to the emergency department of the nearest hospital.

Bites to the hand or forearm

1. Bandage as much of the arm as possible, starting at the fingers.
2. Use a splint to the elbow.
3. Use a sling to immobilize the arm.
4. Keep the patient still. Lie the patient down to prevent walking or moving around. **Bites to the Trunk**
5. If possible, apply firm pressure over the bitten or stung area.
6. Do not restrict chest movement.

7. Keep the patient still.
8. Have the patient taken immediately by ambulance to the emergency department of the nearest hospital.

Bites to the Head or Neck

- No first aid for bitten or stung area.
- Keep the patient still.
- Have the patient taken immediately by ambulance to the emergency department of the nearest hospital.

Remember these tips:

- Have the patient taken immediately by ambulance to the emergency department of the nearest hospital.
- Research stresses the importance of keeping the patient still. This includes all the limbs.
- Do NOT cut or excise the bitten or stung area.
- Do NOT apply a tourniquet.
- Do NOT wash the bitten or stung area. The type of snake involved may be identified by the detection of venom on the skin.
- Even if the bitten or stung person is ill when first seen, the application of pressure immobilization first aid may prevent further absorption of venom from the bite or sting site during transport to the hospital.
- If the bandages and splint have been applied correctly, they will be comfortable and maybe left on for several hours. They should not be taken off until the patient has reached medical care.
- The treating doctor will decide when to remove the bandages. If a significant amount of venom has been injected, it may move into the bloodstream very quickly when the bandages are removed. They should be left in position until appropriate antivenom and resuscitation equipment has been assembled.

- Bandages may be quickly reapplied if clinical deterioration occurs, and left on until antivenom therapy has been effective.

Anaphylaxis

Anaphylaxis is a severe allergic reaction that occurs in sensitive individuals as a result of exposure to certain chemicals foreign to the body, including bites and stings, plants, or medications.

Parts of the body, for example, the face or throat, can swell up so much that the casualty can't breathe. In severe cases, the patient may go into shock within a few minutes, and the heart can stop beating.

- If the casualty has an EpiPen, inject epinephrine immediately. The shot is given into the outer thigh and can be administered through light fabric. Rub the site to improve the absorption of the drug.
- Place a conscious person lying down and elevate the feet if possible.
- Stay with the person until help arrives.
- If trained, begin CPR if the person stops breathing or doesn't have a pulse.
- After 10 to 15 minutes, if the symptoms are still significant, you can inject another dose of epinephrine if available.
- Even after the reaction subsides, you need to go to an emergency department immediately.
- Steroids and antihistamines may be given, but these are often not helpful initially and do not take the place of epinephrine. However, they may be more useful in preventing a recurrent delayed reaction.
- Note that epinephrine makes you feel shaky and causes a rapid, pounding pulse. These are normal side effects and are not dangerous except for those with severe heart problems.

Plants

Depending on the region of the world that you are in, consuming certain plants can have significant consequences, including death. Again, do your research and learn about edible flora wherever you go.

Symptoms of poisoning from plants can include:

- Nausea and vomiting
- Stomach cramps
- Irregular heartbeat
- Burning to the mouth
- Convulsions (fits)
- Diarrhea
- Impaired consciousness

Take the following steps if you think you have ingested a poisonous plant:

- Remove any remaining portion of the plant, berry, or mushroom.
- Save a piece of the plant or mushroom in a dry container for identification.
- Wash out your mouth with water.
- Check for any irritation, swelling, or discoloration.
- Seek immediate medical attention if symptoms persist.

Minor Poisons

For minor stings and bites, including most spider bites, jellyfish stings, stonefish, and other fish stings, bee, wasp, and ant stings (in non-allergic individuals), bites by scorpions, centipedes, beetles, etc., as well as external exposure to poisonous plants, etc., follow these steps:

1. Remove contaminated clothing.
2. Wash with soap and water and apply an antiseptic if available.
3. Apply an ice-pack to reduce local pain and swelling.
4. If eyes are affected, rinse eyes with water (ideally lukewarm) for 10-15 minutes.
5. Administer pain relief if required, e.g., paracetamol or an antihistamine (to reduce swelling, redness, and itching).

Refer the casualty for further treatment if they develop any other symptoms or signs of infection.

6. Chapter 6: Preparedness

This is a basic introduction to preparedness. Preparedness has many topics, such as preserving food or living off the grid that can be very useful, and one can spend years studying them. Especially if you are older or handicapped, it makes sense that you focus more on preparing to overcome some of the physical disadvantages you have.

Introduction to Preparedness

Introduction

We talked earlier about the difference between survivalists and preppers, and how acquiring the skills needed for survival as well as general preparation is essential. Preparedness is about getting ready both mentally and materially for emergencies, by planning and by stockpiling.

Although having skills to grow food or light fires will help you in a survival situation, they will be useless to you if you have not thought ahead about what equipment is needed and where and how it should be stored. If you don't have an evacuation plan and disaster strikes, you may never even reach the safety of your storage space. In this section of the course, you will learn how to be both mentally prepared and fully equipped for a whole range of potential crises.

Kids and Prepping

When prepping, you want to make sure that your kids understand that everything should be kept secret. Make sure you explain to your children that they should not mention how much rice or canned food the family stores. They shouldn't mention it to anyone outside your circle of family members. If you practice some outdoor survival skills, just tell them you are going camping. Children aren't good at keeping secrets.

When your children are old enough, explain to them the whole philosophy of preparing and learning about survival. At this point, they will be able to understand why this should be kept private. Another reason to keep it all "fun and games" is that it can be very stressful and scary for a small child to learn about the possible dangers they face. Try to explain to them why you do certain things a bit differently compared to the people around you.

Make sure you listen to their concerns and worries. Children have vivid imaginations, and you do not want them to grow up feeling anxious about the world. Learning about survival is something that should make them more confident to face obstacles on their journey through life.

Teach them how to react in emergency situations. A 5-year-old cannot beat up a grown-up attacker, so screaming for help while trying to get away from the threat is their only choice. Make sure they know this and that it is perfectly fine to call for help.

Establish certain routines and practice them, so they happen almost automatically. Make practicing the routines playful and offer them some rewards for playing the game. For example, make a game out of successfully evacuating the house without forgetting anything. This way, your children learn what to do, which means there is a better chance they won't freeze up in critical situations. Also, these practice sessions will help you to identify any possible problems so you can modify the routines if necessary.

Give your children ways to contact you. There are mobile phones made for children or elderly people that are very easy to use. Get to know the staff that works at places your children frequently visit. Introduce yourself, so people know who the child belongs to. Include all important phone numbers into your communication plan.

Part One: Stockpiling
General tips for your storage space

- Before you pack for a trip or start preparing your home survival storage space, make lists! This is the easiest way to ensure you do not forget anything.
- Store things in more than one place inside your home.
- There should be one person responsible for storage. This person can devise a system to keep track of the expiration dates of items in storage and what items are going in and out of storage.
- Consider the amount of the goods that you will store outside of your home in hidden locations, for example, a first aid kit, items for trade or weapons, and ammunition. You might want to bury them underground in buckets or PVC piping. Remember to keep a tracking system of where the items are buried, e.g., a marked map or directions written in a code you've worked out with your family members.
- Do not show your storage location to anyone outside your immediate family. You may be tempted to show it to a good friend or neighbor, but do not forget that you are calculating your supplies to keep you and your family alive, and you may not have enough for your neighbors and friends, who will inevitably come knocking when SHTF. Keep it absolutely secret.
- Consider having a decoy storage location, in case you are robbed.

- Keep some cash at home in a place you can easily access in case of an emergency evacuation. Keep it in small banknotes and also consider storing small valuable mineral items such as gold.

- Divide your items in storage into sections (hygiene, food, tools, etc.). Make sure the most important things are the most easily accessible.

- Keep important family documents like passports, etc. in a waterproof and fireproof place. It is also good to scan your documents and wallet cards into an electronic document, like a pdf file, and then password protects it and stores it in an online e-mail account that you can access from any computer.

- Do not forget about storing valuable information and knowledge, such as books. In a long-term survival situation, you will need to learn a lot of new things, such as growing and preserving food, hygiene, medicine, self-schooling, etc. and Google might not be available to you!

- Store items not just for immediate use, but to help you get more when they run out – for example, seeds means hunting, fishing, trapping, caustic soda for making soap, etc. ? When packing or storing items, think about and research the possible value of some things when SHTF, not just for use but for trading. Periodically check and test your equipment in storage.

- Pack or store as many multi-use items as possible.

What to Store

SELCO ON HOW HE CHOOSES WHAT TO STORE

You need to make some plan about what to store in meaning to clearly divide items for your use and item for trade (if you are planning to trade)

While items stored for your use are easier to plan, you need to take many more thoughts on items that you are gonna have for trade.

or example, you find out that zippo lighter (or several Zippo lighters) are great for you when SHTF, you may find out that having 500 cheap disposable Chinese lighters are great things to have for trade.

So it is not about what you find out to be good for you. It also may be what have more sense too.

Few basic rules could be:
- *Have stuff that you know how to use.*
- *Have stuff that is "usual" (to have "rare" items can only attract attention).*
- *Have things that "make" or repair other things (tools, mills, techniques, and skills...).*
- *Do not blindly trust in everything that you read on the web- use your head and common sense ("with gold and silver you gonna solve all problems when SHTF"- it may work in some situations, but I would always choose things of more "real" value (food, weapon...)*

Even though surviving at home is much easier than surviving outdoors, you still need to put considerable thought and resources into it. You should list on paper all that you intend to use and eat during a survival situation, and make sure you have all of the equipment needed for it.

Preparedness Categories

The most important areas that need preparation are First Aid (see our chapter on First Aid), food, water, and power (following topics). As for the rest, break them down into various topics to make the job more manageable and less prone to error. Check our detailed supply list for a comprehensive inventory, but topics should include, for example:

Sanitation

If you are faced with a situation where you have to survive in your home for an extended period of time, particularly if you live in urban areas, then sooner or later, sanitation will become an issue. At first, it may just be the smell of stinky clothes or a malfunctioning sewerage system, but in no time, this will lead to illness and disease.

The deterioration of sanitation can cause the rapid spread of viruses and become more deadly even than the disaster itself. You need to learn about basic survival sanitation in order to properly prepare for a disaster. See our chapter on Hygiene and Sanitation for information on things such as how to cope with no sewerage system, and below for relevant items, you should remember to store.

Be sure to include in your survival supplies:
- Sanitation and personal hygiene items
- Cleaning supplies and disinfectants
- Alcohol-based disinfectant
- Gloves
- Respirators
- Goggles
- Powdered lime, straw, or sawdust for your toilet
- Buckets
- Garbage bags
- Disposable face masks

Communication

Having communication with the outside world is crucial to survival in a disaster situation. With communication, you can summon medical help, warn or be warned of danger, be notified of rescue opportunities, co-ordinate action, keep apprised of the current situation, and so on.

Technology is constantly changing, and the most suitable communication options for you will depend on your circumstances

and location. At a minimum, be sure to include in your storage space:
• Cell phone with chargers, preferably also two-way radio/satellite/GPS equipment
• Battery-operated AM radio
• Family and emergency contact information
• Whistle
• Flares and fire signal making material (e.g., rubber)

Also, consider using certain signs or markings amongst your family or group members (for example, a code phrase that means danger, or if you are returning home and you see a certain plant on the windowsill, you know that something is wrong).

Personal Items
• Originals and copies of personal documents (medication list and pertinent medical information, proof of address, deed/lease to home, passports, birth certificates, insurance policies)
• Bedding, particularly good quality blankets or sleeping bags
• Extra cash
• Maps of the area
• Towels
• Plastic sheeting
• Scissors
• Durable, earth-colored clothing (including hat, rain gear, and sturdy shoes)
• Sunscreen
• Insect repellent
• Books to read and games to play **Security**
• Supplies for securing your home – Locks, intrusion detection/alarm systems, material for exterior obstacles (fences, gates, razor wire, etc.)
• Smoke detectors
• Fire extinguishers
• Blackout screens/opaque curtains for your windows
• Corks (useful to burn and use for skin camouflage)
• Night vision gear

- Aluminum foil (see the section on EMP, below)

Sustainable living
- Hunting and/or fishing gear (depending on where you are)
- Seeds of edible and medicinal plants and garden supplies
- Animal husbandry supplies
- Fire-making equipment, including firewood, coals, etc. (see the chapter on Fire) ? Tools and spare parts, including an ax, shovel, bolt cutters, grinding wheel, tools for gardening, auto mechanics, welding, woodworking – preferably hand-powered tools. ? Duct tape, Wire, chain, nails, nuts and bolts, abrasives, twine, glue, etc.
- Work gloves

Food

In order to be prepared at home, you should have a minimum of three days worth of food in the house, but serious survivalists will have much more. Some foods have storage spans of 10 years or more, so it is important to be smart about which foods you keep in your storage space. As well as having long-lasting foods, it is important to have foods that you enjoy and normally eat – a survival situation can be unpleasant enough without having to eat foods you dislike and having digestive problems because of sudden changes to your diet.

Ideal foods are long life (not requiring refrigeration), low in salt, and do not require cooking.

If your water supply is limited, avoid foods that are high in fat and protein (since they require more water to process) and avoid salty food. Most canned foods can safely be stored for at least 18 months.

Low acid foods like meat products, fruits, or vegetables will normally last at least two years. Use dry products, like boxed cereal, crackers, cookies, dried milk, or dried fruit within six months. Mark a rotation date on any food container that does not already have an expiration date on the package.

Also, make sure that you include baby food and formula or other diet items for infants or seniors. Remember, it is not just what food you store that it is important. It is also how to store it. We recommend storing food in small quantities in airtight, pest-resistant containers in a cool, dark place.

What Foods to Store

For the ultimate long term survival pantry, stock up on the following items:

- Salt: Salt is useful not only for cooking but for preserving food and as a practical means to attract wild game. It will also be a valuable trade commodity.
- Rice: Storage life is approximately eight years.
- Wheat: grains will be one of the first items to be snapped up and become scarce in a disaster situation. The storage life can be 30+ years, they hold their nutritional value well, and they can be used not only to make a range of foods for you, such as breakfast cereal, pasta, and bread but also as food for your livestock. Buy whole grains and a hand wheat grinder.
- Flour: good for missing with wheats to make bread and other baked goods, storage life 2-3 years. Note it can also be used to clean steel and copper and to make glue (by mixing it with water, salt, and alcohol).
- Corn: The storage life of whole corn is 8 to 12 years, but cracked or ground corn stores only 18 to 36 months.
- Oats: The storage life of oats is 3 to 7 years, depending on the variety and packing method.
- Canned Fruit, vegetable, and meats: You should keep a one to two year supply and rotate continuously.
- Fats and Oils: We recommend storing primarily olive oil (frozen, in plastic bottles), mayonnaise, canned butter, and peanut butter. The canned products must be continuously rotated, or else donated to charity bi-annually. The frozen oil should be rotated or else donated to charity at least once every four years.
- Sugars: Sugar, honey, maple syrup, molasses, various jams, and jellies.

- Fat-free Powdered Milk: If possible, buy nitrogen packed dry milk from a storage food vendor, as it has a 5+ year shelf life.
- Spices
- Baking soda
- Yeast
- Vinegar
- Sulfur (for drying fruit)
- Seeds

What Equipment to Store
- Plates, utensils, and other eating supplies
- Tupperware containers
- Freezer and vacuum bags
- Aluminum foil (can also be used for improvised solar ovens!)
- Large pots, pans, and skillets
- Water/liquid vessels
- Good knives, including a skinning knife
- Canning lids and rings
- Jars for sprouting
- Manual can opener

Storing Food

If a local disaster strikes and you don't have anything to eat, you don't have to worry too much, as long as you have enough clean drinking water. You can expect to get out of the affected area before you starve to death. You can go for up to 3 weeks without food while being physically active, and eight weeks if you are not.

In the best-case scenario, you would have a box with fresh vegetables, fruits, and meat for every day, but of course, that's not possible.

When it comes to storing food, the variety of food, the nutritional benefits of the storage method, and the packaging are the major things you have to think about.

You can either buy food from preparedness companies that comes already packaged, or you can assemble your own food supply, package it, and have it ready when disaster strikes.

The later solution will take more time, but it will save you a lot of money. Grocery stores also have some products that keep well for a long time. Every preservation method has some impact on food quality, taste, and texture.

Most people have limited space to store food, so the food you are looking for should probably meet the following criteria.

It should be easy to store

You might have to move your food supplies or hide them, so having them all packaged nicely and in a space-saving way is a must. They also have to be packaged properly to resist moisture, oxygen, heat, mold, and pests. Store food on shelves for easy access. This also makes it easy to rotate food—just add the new stuff you bought behind the items you already have.

It should be healthy and enable you to eat a balanced diet

For many centuries the distance that ships could travel was limited by the inability to take properly perservered fruits and vegetables along. The diet of a sailor a few hundred years ago consisted of salted meat and other salted food and grains. This resulted in scurvy, which resulted in the death of many sailors. If you don't want this or similar problems to happen to you, you have to consider your long-term nutritional needs when you plan the food you are storing.

It should be something you enjoy eating (even today)

Getting all the food you need for three months, six months, a year, or even longer is expensive. You don't want to regularly throw food away, so include the foods you use in your daily meals. This has several benefits. First of all, you only store what you enjoy eating, even in good times. When things turn bad, you will still be able to eat the food you like and do not have to switch to something you really don't like. You will also save a lot of money by buying in bulk. If you take advantage of coupons and special offers, you can save even more.

It should have a long shelf life

Even though you are rotating your stored food, a long shelf life makes sense. First of all, you do not know what your survival scenario will look like, so you should be prepared.

Even if you have some fresh food available in the beginning because you were the first guy at the supermarket, once you realized that things were about to fall apart, you can simply eat what you have stored later.

When you package food yourself use vacuum packaging and oxygen absorbers to kill pests and keep food fresh for a longer time, heat sealers are better than zip lock bags, and most vacuum packaging machines can also heat seal your food.

You can also do dry ice fumigation. Add blocks of dry ice (frozen carbon dioxide) to the containers in which you store food. As it melts, it becomes gas that is heavier than air, so the oxygen gets replaced with carbon dioxide, and your container becomes an environment that is uninhabitable by bugs and other creepy crawlers.

It should be easy to prepare

Everyday life in a post-collapse society can be very demanding. It is unlikely that you feel like cooking something fancy at the end of the day, so make sure that you store food that is easy to prepare without the help of any fancy tools. If it can't be prepared with fire, water, and a pan or pot, then it is not worth the effort.

How to Plan Your Food

A great way to assess how much food you need is to simply monitor what you eat in a week. Write everything down and then simply replace any products that are hard to store with alternatives. Make sure you also track the calories throughout the week. Adults should have about 2,500 calories every day.

This gets much harder if you mostly eat fresh produce (which is great because it is healthy, but eating it gets tricky once there is no more fresh supply.

Here is a list of foods and the quantities you should plan on saving. The amounts are for an average adult male for one year.

- **Grains–375 pounds.**

Grains are cheap and readily available. Grains may include barley, rice, corn, oats, pasta, and whole wheat. They can also be sprouted, which converts proteins into different essential amino acids and dramatically increases their vitamin content. The problem with storing most whole grains (such as brown rice) is that unless they are kept cool, they can go rancid within six months because of the oils they contain. White rice can be stored much longer. Wheat is even better and can be stored for up to 10 years or even longer. If you plan on storing grains, make sure you also get a hand-cranked grain mill to easily process the grains to flour.

- **Legumes–60 pounds dry.**

There are many different kinds of legumes, including seeds, lentils, peas, and beans. Legumes can also be sprouted for maximum nutritional value. For example, sprouted soybeans have 700% more vitamin C than the dry beans.

- **Milk and other dairy, eggs–60 pounds dry.**

Non-fat dried milk will last for much longer than dried whole milk. Don't forget about dehydrated eggs and powdered milk, which will add some variety to your diet. You can even make some kinds of cheese from powdered milk.

- **Fruits and vegetables–10 to 30 pounds dry.**

Dehydrated fruits and vegetables are much cheaper than the freeze-dried variety. Sweeteners–65 pounds. You'll want sweeteners such as sugar and syrups. Honey is also a good sweetener to have–it is nutritious and has some antibiotic properties.

- **Fats, oils, and shortening–22 pounds.**

Foods in this category include butter, margarine, cooking oil, etc. These may not provide

a lot of nutrition, but they will last for a long time. It is a good idea to have a variety of these hydrogenated processed oils, and also some cold-pressed oils (such as olive oil), which do provide essential fatty acids but don't last as long.

- **Sprouting seeds – 20 to 50 pounds.**

These include whole grains, beans, and seeds, such as alfalfa seeds, mung beans, and soybeans. Growing these means you'll have live food to eat, and they will also supply essential vitamins.

- **Leavening**

This includes one pound baking powder and one box of baking soda, which will keep indefinitely. It also includes ¾ pound dry active yeast, which will only keep for 1½ to three years.

- **Multivitamins – Enough for one per day.**

Seasonings and other foods–This includes 8 pounds of salt, spices, and condiments.

Here is a general guide to how long foods last:

- Supplies with the **longest shelf life** are foods such as black pepper, apple cider vinegar, honey, sugar, salt, Worcestershire, and soy sauces. These will still be good after decades.
- Foods that last **five to ten years** include dried legumes, whole grains, powdered eggs, frozen butter, dehydrated cheese, instant coffee, vacuum-packed coffee, and baking powder.
- Foods that last **up to five years** include liquid vegetable oil, non-fat powdered milk, cornmeal, and cornflour.
- Foods that will only last **two to three years** include sprouting seeds, bouillon cubes, white rice, cornstarch, powdered gelatin, white wheat flour, dried white flour pasta, tapioca, dried fruits, canned foods (except for some canned meats, fish, and fruits), textured vegetable protein, hydrogenated peanut butter, catsup, and canned salmon and sardines.
- Foods that will only last for **up to a year** and a half include canned meats, canned seafood, unshelled raw nuts, sauerkraut,

pickles, cranberry sauce, active dry yeast, chips, cake mixes, dry puddings, herb and black teas, canned noncitric fruits, jams and jellies, most seasonings, and bottled juice.

- Foods that will only **last a year** include natural nut butters, canned citrus fruits, candy bars, natural liquid vegetable oils, mayonnaise, bottle dressings, rolled oats, canned nuts, and dry breakfast cereals.
- Foods that will only last **six months** include fresh potatoes, granola, shelled raw nuts, unshelled roasted nuts, most store-packaged food that comes in boxes, some fish, some fruits, and sprouting seeds.

You have different options to preserve your food at home.

Canning

Canned food can have a lot of flavors. Make sure you only use only the freshest produce for canning.

There are a few methods of canning, but the easiest is probably water bath canning. With this method, you fill clean jars with acidic food such as tomatoes and add some vinegar. Then it is as simple as putting the lids on the jars and boiling them in an open pan of water until a seal forms under the lid, creating a vacuum to keep out bacteria. Pressure canning, another canning method, takes special equipment and some skill.

Freeze-Dried Food

Freeze-dried food is more expensive than most other food, but it is a great addition to your storage. You can quickly rehydrate the food, and almost no nutritional value (just 5%) gets lost in the freeze-drying process.

Check to see what fresh products you can replace with freeze-dried products. A wide variety of vegetables and fruits are available. Before you buy freeze-dried products in bulk, buy just one package and try it.

Dehydrated Food

Low-heat dehydration causes only a loss of 10% of the food's nutritional value. A pound of dehydrated vegetables is equivalent to about 12 pounds of fresh vegetables. If you can't find some of the ingredients you like to use as freeze-dried products, you can either find them as dried products or dry them yourself. Just get a cheap food dehydrator and start dehydrating.

Your Storage

Try storing your supplies in low-temperature environments. Ideally, this would be something around 40F (4C), but in any case, try to keep them under 70F (21C). Opt for medium-sized plastic, wood, or steel containers for organizing your supplies and carrying them around. If some pest has somehow entered one container, then only a small part of your supplies are affected.

Paper packaging and other less solid packaged goods should be repackaged for long-term storage. If dirty pests such as mice, rats, cockroaches, or beetles get into your food, the food should be discarded. The little bugs that are sometimes found in packaged flour and rice can be eaten or picked out. The food is still edible.

Get some mousetraps and poison for pests. If possible, test what traps and what poison works best. Traps are favored by most people because poison often kills slowly, and the pests might die in hard to reach places. If you cook rats and mice well, they can also add some variety to your menu in case you run out of stored food.

Some Thoughts About Shelf Life

Freeze-dried foods, white rice, wheat, beans, potato flakes, dried apples, and oats, if they are packaged to remove oxygen, can be edible for 20 to 30 years. Baking powder can be stored for many years as well, and baking soda will keep indefinitely.

Food can be eaten well after it has lost its visual appeal. Mold can be cut out of cheese, apples, and meats, but moldy fruits, vegetables, or fats should be thrown out completely. If food smells rotten, foul gas is emitted when you open the containers, or cans are bulging, then get rid of it. "When in doubt, throw it out."

SELCO ON EATING EXPIRED FOOD

> I ate cookies that were 30 years old. They came in 5-7 kg steel containers with the date of production on it. We call it "Vietnam war cookies," different meat cans with some suspicious-looking meat inside without production dates on it, and some cans that were clearly expired. Not to mention all kinds of homemade meals that were more like experiments on how to make something edible from grass water and fire. And I survived everything.
>
> But I also need to say that many times I had bad cases of diarrhea that literally made me weak like a baby for days. And I know folks who died because of bad food. We eat all kinds of stuff simply because we had to. You need to understand that careful planning and preparing your food storage is the difference between life and death when SHTF.
>
> It is not a survival show. There is no emergency crew to help you if you eat something bad. You are alone with what you got and prepared. Do not take chances.

Giving Your Recipes a Survival Makeover

Try to substitute ingredients in your favorite recipes with the long shelf life version. A lot of vegetable-based dishes like stews, soups, chilies, and casseroles are easy and delicious to cook with long shelf life ingredients.

Meat is harder to replace, but with a food dehydrator, you can also explore this and get into the amazingly yummy world of making your own jerky.

Keep in mind that the food in your food storage supply is not meant for you to keep on living as if nothing happened. If you love eating fresh cheese, a lot of meat, or fresh vegetables, then you should be aware that you will not have most of this at hand once the food supply stops (unless you take steps to store these foods yourself).

If you cannot cook what you like with long shelf life ingredients, you should find some soups, chilis, and casseroles that you like that use the long shelf-life products. Make them as diverse as possible to cover all nutritional needs and yummy enough that you eat them on a regular basis, even if society still works.

If you are vegetarian, be aware that you will need a good source of vitamin B, such as spirulina, to meet all of your nutritional needs. Also, consider options that can help you stretch meals out, such as other dried supplies like rice and pasta. A hearty soup with some rice or pasta is much more filling and provides more energy than just the soup.

Growing Your Own Food

SELCO ON GROWING FOOD DURING SHTF

The important thing is to start before SHTF. It does not have to be a real garden, in "full scale." Consider it like "learning to grow." You need to know all about the garden before SHTF, what is best for your garden? What kind of soil you have? What you gonna need etc.

When SHTF, it may be too late to go with trials and mistakes. By the time you have something usable from your garden, you may already be starved to death.

This topic also goes your knowledge about edible plants in your surroundings. It may be your main source of food in the worst days.

Before SHTF, I did not have a clue that edible plants are around me, even in urban areas.

Sometimes it was usable only for tea, or soup, sometimes for something more, but it made a difference.

No matter how much food you have in storage, the day will come when it has run out. In long term survival situations, food is likely to become a scarce commodity, and it is likely that you will have to grow it for yourself.

It is not difficult – all you really need is seeds, soil, sun, and water. For all vegetable gardens, you will need to consider how much sunlight does it get? Is the soil rich and humus, with good drainage that will hold moisture during the hot months? Is it away from trees and large shrubs, as their roots will compete with your vegetable roots? Is it near a water supply? If need, does it have a windbreak?

However, methods of growing vegetables will vary greatly depending on what type of vegetable it is and what the soil and climate are like where you are growing them.

Sprouting

One particularly useful method of growing food is sprouting.

Sprouts are the germinated seeds of vegetables, grains, legumes, and nuts. Sprouting requires only warmth, moisture, and ventilation and can be done all year round and in the dark. Not only will they kick start your vegetable garden if you can sprout them first and then transplant them outside, but sprouts can be eaten raw or cooked, with other foods or by themselves.

Sprouts are a good source of vitamin C and the B vitamins, particularly riboflavin and niacin. Almost any whole seed can be used, although taking note that tomato and potato sprouts are poisonous. Sprouting techniques will vary depending on the type of seed, but the basic methodology is:

1. Place a small number of whole seeds into a wide-mouth jar. Add approximately double to triple times that amount of lukewarm water and soak overnight.

2. Cover the jar with any material having small enough holes the seeds can't go through (gauze, cloth, mesh, plastic, lids of cans, etc.). Secure the covering with a canning ring, rubber band, or string.

3. Pour off the water, rinse thoroughly, and then drain completely.

4. Shake the jar thoroughly in order to evenly distribute the seeds.

5. Lay the jar on its side out of direct sunlight.

6. Rinse and drain the seeds well with lukewarm water two to six times each day to keep them moist and prevent mold.

7. Harvest when they reach sprout length.

Water Storage

Without water, a person will soon suffer exhaustion, dehydration, cramps, heatstroke, illness, and, within a few days, death. Water is also necessary for food preparation and minimal sanitation needs.

In a whole range of disasters, your water supply can easily be cut off or become contaminated. To be prepared for any type of disaster, it is absolutely essential that you have stored sufficient water reserves, and you have the means to purify additional water.

Water Storage

SELCO ON HOW HE PREPARES FOR STORING WATER

The basic advice is to be sure that you do not store it all in one place, and the best way is to have it in small packages (2 l bottles or similar).

If you have all water in few big barrels, then if the barrel gets contaminated (or spilled), you are losing huge amounts of water at once.

Equally important is to know sources of water around you: rivers, springs, fountains, or sources like tanks and similar.

Be sure that you know what water is for drinking and whatnot.

Seek alternative ways of cleaning yourself and your stuff in order to be ready to save water when SHTF. We collected water from the roof of our house with drainpipes into the barrel, then filtrate it and boil it. We "invented" that system on the fly because we needed it.

Store a minimum of half a gallon (two liters) of drinking water per person, per day in regular climates and up to double that for hotter climates. In a regular climate, three gallons (10 liters) per person per day will give you enough to drink and for limited cooking and personal hygiene.

Minimize the amount of water you need by reducing activity and staying cool.

If you store tap water:

- Tap water from a municipal water system can usually be safely stored without additional treatment. But depending on where you are, and to be on the safe side, consider purifying the water anyway.
- Store water in BPA free containers.
- Label your containers and store them in a cool, dark place.
- Replace water at least once every six months.

If you buy commercially bottled water:

- Keep water in its original container, and don't re-store a bottle once it's been opened.
- Store in a cool, dark place.
- If bottles are not marked with the manufacturer's expiration date, label with the date and replace bottles at least once per year.

Water Treatment

See our specific section on the water for information about purifying it. Here are some more notes for residential water filtration and purification.

Note that these methods (straining, boiling, using bleach, iodine, or UV rays) will kill microbes so that the water is safer to drink, but they will not remove other contaminants unless you use a mechanical filter – another essential item in your storage space.

There are many filters to choose from that can filter out the contaminants. The two main types are activated carbon or microfiltration systems, and we would recommend getting one of each.

Activated carbon filters remove:
- Chlorine
- Chloroform
- Hydrogen sulfide
- Trihalomethanes and other hydrocarbons
- Many organic chemicals, including pesticides and herbicides
- Industrial chemicals and compounds like PCB, PBB, and TCE
- Dissolved organics, heavy metals, and some trace minerals.

However, note that bacteria and viruses are only partially removed by activated carbon filters, and fluoride, nitrates, salts, and asbestos fibers are not removed at all.

The other type, Microfilters, has two subcategories: ceramic and fiber. Ceramic filters are more effective than fiber and are used to filter out:
- Cysts
- Bacteria
- Viruses
- Parasites

- Fungi
- Radioactive solids
- Asbestos and fiberglass fibers

However, note that dissolved minerals, many toxic chemicals, and salts are not removed by microfiltration systems and nor will microfilters purify brackish or saltwater.

Hidden Water Sources

Suppose you run out of stored drinking water, strain, and treat water from other sources in your home, such as ? Hot water tank. Ensure that the electricity or gas is off, and then open the drain at the bottom of the tank. Start the water flowing by turning off the tank's water intake valve and turning on a hot water faucet. Do not turn the gas or electricity back on when the tank is empty.

- Water pipes. Let air into the plumbing by turning on the highest faucet in your house and draining the water from the lowest one and drain the water in your pipes.
- Fridges with ice cube makers.
- Toilet reservoir tank (not the bowl water). Only use as a last resort, and not if you use toilet tank cleaners.
- Swimming pool or spa water should not be consumed, but you can use it for flushing toilets or washing.

Living Off the Grid

SELCO ON LIVING WITHOUT POWER

> *It was about the difference between what we wanted and what we could have had.*
>
> *The first couple of days without electricity was not a big deal because we coped with many more important things, things like our security, etc.*

Later it got us on a full scale, but eventually, we managed to live without electricity. After some time, we even did not notice some things.

How we kept our food fresh? Mostly we did not have enough food to become spoiled. I mean, it did not stay enough to get spoiled. During cold days it was not a problem.

How we cooked and heated ourselves? We used wood stoves for both. We "upgrade" it to give more heat, to cook faster, etc.

Things in the yard and in the house were done during the light-day. The light of the candles and improvised lamps was too weak to do anything real and too value.

The point is that we were not prepared. Now we can prepare, so it is cool to think about things like batteries, candles, lamps, torches, stoves. Be very prepared in these things.

But the most important thing is to understand that when SHTF, you cannot make it like in normal time with your preparation. Just do what you need to do.

How long do you think could survive without power? If you know what you are doing and are well prepared, the answer is forever. Around 200,000 people in the U.S. currently live off the grid. This number is much higher throughout the rest of the world, due to the fact that many countries don't even have a reliable grid from which to disconnect.

Nonetheless, energy is a serious concern in the aftermath of a disaster, particularly if you live in a cold climate. How would you keep warm? How would you keep your food fresh, and how would you cook it? How would you see it at night?

There are many different approaches to preparing for living off the grid, depending on your needs and how serious you are about survival. For people planning for short term survival situations, a camping stove and a small supply of fuel may suffice, whereas others may want to build a completely energy self-sufficient home equipped with a wind-powered generator and/or solar panels.

Remember, the more renewable your energy source, the greater your chances of long term survival. We highly recommend installing a solar energy system and a solar-powered water system.

If you live in a windy area, we also recommend building or purchasing a wind-powered generator. Alternatively, if you want to have a power that relies on no fuel other than the energy in your own body, you could build a bicycle-powered generator.

In addition, we would suggest ensuring that your survival storage space has the following:

- Matches, lighters, and candles
- Solar-powered cooker (ideally one that also removes indoor pollution and toxins, such as Sol Source)
- Kerosene lamps (alternatively propane lamps, if you don't have kerosene) ? Flashlights (ideally including powerful ones as well as subdued ones and penlights

Batteries and battery rechargers (note solar chargers are available)

- Generator – If your home has propane appliances, get a "tri-fuel" generator, with a carburetor that can run on gasoline, propane, or natural gas. If you heat your home with home heating oil, then get a diesel-burning generator (and note if you have a diesel-burning pickup and/or tractor, you will be able to run your diesel generator and diesel vehicles on home heating oil).
- Fuels – kerosene, propane, home heating oil, gas, or diesel (stored in secured drums ideally underground if it will not affect the water table, or otherwise away from your living quarters and not visible from the road), wood, coals. The more fuel you can supply. Stock as much fuel as humanly possible – the more fuel you have, the longer and more comfortable you will be able to survive.
- An airtight wood/coal stove for heating yourselves and water as well as cooking. To heat larger spaces, a multi-fuel furnace (these can use gas/oil /propane combined with wood/coal). Alternatives, if no fossil fuels are available, include a wood/coal forced-air furnace or a boiler furnace for hot water and steam heating.

• A fuel-powered refrigerator and freezer operated by kerosene, LP, butane, or natural gas, depending on your fuel supplies.

Improvised Fuel

If you run out of fuel, there are many common household items that can be used to make it. You can burn papers, peat, corncobs, straw, grains, manure, old motor oil, small pieces of rubber tires. Digesters can create methane that can be used in place of propane and natural gas in lanterns, heaters, water heaters, ranges, refrigerators, and furnaces.

Alcohol stills can be created and fed with wood products, excess grains, and agricultural wastes. See the Fire section for information on using household items to create fire starters.

Living off the Grid and Food

Spoiled food can cause major health upsets. Below are some tips about how to best manage food following a power outage.

• Open the refrigerator door as infrequently as possible to keep food cold longer. Put a list of items inside them on the door to minimize the need to open it.

• Cover the freezer with a blanket to increase insulation.

• Refrigerated food should generally be consumed within 4 hours.

• Food in the freezer will normally remain safe for 2 to 3 days.

• Food that still has ice crystals in the middle is usually still safe to eat.

• If frozen meat or dairy is kept at room temperature (above 4 C or 39 F) for longer than 4 hours, it should be thrown away and not cooked or eaten.

• After power has been restored, do not re-freeze thawed food.

• Spoiled food can cause major health upsets.

Renewable & Back-Up Systems

Make your first choice as renewable as possible since your supplies will replenish themselves continually, and this will keep you alive for the longest. Also, increase your chances of survival by trying to always have a back-up system in place, in case your first choice fails.

For example, it is wise to set your house up with solar energy since when the electricity supplies cut out, you should still have power as long as there is the sun – BUT keep a generator and fuel on standby in case your solar power system is destroyed.

Grow a garden and raise animals, but have food supplies in storage in case you can't go outside or the garden and animals are killed or exposed to the disease.

Staying Fit and Healthy

SELCO ON THE IMPORTANCE OF FITNESS DURING SHTF

You do not have to be Rambo in order to survive but be prepared to push your body to the limits. Pushing those limits further is a very good thing. Survival is mainly a mental thing, but if you are weak as a baby, you are doomed no matter what is in your head.

I was pushed to the limits many times. I was hungry and wet and still pushing myself to live.

Put yourself into the "program" of exercise. Be ready for SHTF, because when that day comes, it can grind you from one survival situation to another for a long time without giving you a chance to "catch a breath" if you are not physically prepared for that, it can be very bad.

I know people who pulled their teeth out with mechanical tools because they did not have any other option or folks who died simply because they could not cope with the shock of hard new life.

You might have heard the phrases "survival of the fittest" or "only the strong survive" – well, they happen to be true. Preparing is not just about stockpiling goods, planning, and having certain skills. It is also about you being mentally and physically prepared.

Increase your chances of survival by staying in the good physical condition and avoiding disease. Establish a routine of eating well, exercising, and having regular medical check-ups. Sit with your family and work out what physical activities you like doing and how you can support and encourage each other. We recommend keeping an exercise calendar where each family member's exercise plan is set out, and regular medical check-ups are scheduled.

Preparing for Specific Disasters

Specific Scenarios

Part of being prepared involves learning what to do when specific crises occur. As well as taking the preparatory measures outlined above, learn these protocols and keep them accessible in your home.

Flood

Floods are a natural process influenced largely by the weather and driven by the amount of rainfall and length of time it falls. Floods are unpredictable and destructive, and they can happen anywhere, at any time – even in regions that have never seen rain.

They can cause death and injuries, isolate communities, major damage infrastructure, cut essential services, destroy property and livelihoods. Wherever you live, you need to prepare for the possibility of a flood endangering you and your family, impacting your property, and potentially isolating you from the community and essential services.

Apart from the physical damage to property, experiencing a flood can be an extremely emotional time. If you are not prepared for the possibility of a flood, recovery can be slow, stressful, and costly. A few hours spent making your home secure, as well as preparing your emergency supplies and evacuation plan, can help you to survive a serious flood.

To prepare your home for a flood:
- Secure hazardous items
- Roll up rugs, raise furniture, clothing, and valuables onto beds, tables, and into roof space place electrical items in the highest place ? Place important personal documents, valuables, and vital medical supplies into a waterproof case in an accessible location
- Empty freezers and refrigerators, leaving doors open to avoid damage or loss if they float
- Turn off the power, water, and gas and take your mobile phone
- Put sandbags in the toilet bowl and over all laundry/bathroom drain holes to prevent sewage backflow

Fire

You should devise an evacuation plan with your family in case of fire, as detailed above. If you live in a wooded area, developing and using a wildfire survival plan is critical.

This plan will help you take action and avoid making last-minute decisions that could prove deadly during a bushfire. The first thing you must decide is whether to leave for a safer place if a bushfire is approaching, or stay to actively defend your home.

Contact your local fire authority for advice, and make sure you write the plan down, give everybody in your household their own tasks, and have a list of actions to take if there is a wildfire.

Prepare your home to survive a wildfire, even if your plan is to leave. A well prepared and constructed house is more likely to survive a bushfire than an unprepared one. Firemen might not be able to defend a poorly prepared property, and their lives are at risk too.

Walk around your property and look for items likely to burn or places where embers could start a fire. For example, embers can enter through gaps in roofs, walls, evaporative air conditioners, and gutters. Cover them with stainless steel open weave mesh to keep sparks and embers out.

Clear vegetation and rubbish from around your property and create a 20-meter protection zone to reduce the risk that burning vegetation or debris will spark your house alight. In this zone:

- Cut long grass and dense scrub.
- Remove dead material.
- Remove all rubbish and rake up leaf litter, twigs, bark, and material that may catch fire.
- Maintain a minimum two-meter gap between your house and tree branches. Make sure that no trees overhang the house.
- Prune lower branches (up to two meters off the ground) to stop a fire on the ground spreading to the canopy of the trees.
- Do not clump shrubs. Ensure that there is a gap.
- Shrubs should be planted at a distance of at least three times their height at maturity from buildings.

Other actions you will need to take to reduce fuel loads are:

- Keep your gutters free of leaves and other combustible material.
- Create a mineral earth firebreak, with no vegetation along your boundary. ? Build your paths adjacent to the building and have your driveway placed so that it maximizes the protection of the house.
- If possible, plan your garden so that your vegetable garden, lawn, pool, or patio is on the side of the house, likely to face a fire (where the forest is).
- Store firewood away from the building.
- Ensure that your gas bottles are secured and positioned so that it will vent away from the building if it is subject to flame contact or radiant heat.

- Ensure fences are non-combustible so they can help to shield your home from a bushfire and radiant heat.

Storms, Hurricanes, Cyclones, Tornados

Thanks to climate change, extreme weather, including storms, hurricanes, cyclones, and tornados, are on the rise, causing major destruction all over the world. They not only cause damage to homes, property, and businesses, but they can also cause injury, loss of life, major structural damage to communities, disruption of utility and telecommunication services, and turn debris into dangerous missiles.

To prepare for these phenomena:

- Trim branches around your home to prevent them from falling on your roof or car and make sure trees on your street are cleared from power lines.
- Check your roof and gutters for damage or loose material. Replace any damaged or missing tiles.
- Clear gutters and downpipes of leaves and blockages so they don't overflow after heavy rain.
- Store or weigh down loose objects around your homes like outdoor furniture, playground equipment, and sheds.
- Park vehicles and boats under shelter.
- Charge your mobile phone to ensure you have reception.
- Unplug electrical appliances and avoid using landline telephones if there is lightning.
- Campers should find safe shelter away from trees, power lines, stormwater drains, and streams.

Earthquake

Earthquakes take place on a daily basis around the world because the Earth's tectonic plates are always moving and floating on molten rock.

They are the shaking and vibration at the surface of the Earth caused by underground movement along a fault plane or by volcanic activity. They can happen at any time and can last from a few seconds to a few minutes and may be followed by a series of aftershocks.

Earthquakes have the potential to cause major damage and loss of life, and as they are random events, they are difficult to prepare for.

To prepare for an earthquake:

- Learn about the safest area in your home if an earthquake strikes.
- Seek expert advice about the structural strength of your building.
- Make sure chairs and beds are clear of hanging items such as ceiling fans, pot plants, paintings, and mirrors.
- Brace freestanding furniture, such as bookshelves and water heaters.
- Store breakables, heavy items, and hazardous liquids, such as pesticides, cleaning fluids, and paint on the bottom shelves of cupboards.

Disease epidemic

SELCO ON INFECTIONS AND DISEASES DURING SHTF

Diseases will be there no matter how good you are prepared, simply because when the system goes down, too many things go down with it, and things fall apart, things that keep all kinds of diseases under the control.

Your main task here will be to keep those diseases out of your home with a lot of hygiene and some personal protection.

There were no men who had not to cope with hard cases of diarrhea and vomiting (including me) during the SHTF. Some died, others not, some were stronger from others. People coped from all kinds of rashes. It was a dirty word.

While you are preparing to prevent diseases (with proper hygiene and equipment), you also need to prepared for the fact that people in your home (maybe you too) will be sick, so learn at some level how to help and treat sick people.

Infectious diseases remain the number one killer of humans worldwide. If an influenza pandemic struck today, borders would close, the global economy would shut down, international vaccine supplies and healthcare systems would be overwhelmed, people would not be able to go to work, children would not be able to go to school, essential services, such as food, fuel, and police and fire services would quickly degrade, there would be electrical outages, and panic would reign.

Although we had a lucky escape from a global crisis with the recent containment of H5N1, or "bird flu," it remains a threat that looms over us, particularly because humans have no antibodies, meaning infection rates would be exceedingly high, and there is no cure or effective vaccine.

Flu pandemics are nothing new – there were three in the last century alone, killing over 100 million people. That puts the chances of a serious flu pandemic happening in your lifetime pretty high.

Stay informed. If you suspect a disease pandemic may be on the rise, monitor the World Health Organisation as well as mainstream media for information on the spread of the disease, updates on available vaccines, travel advisories, and tips for keeping yourself. ? Stay vaccinated and stay healthy. Although the current flu vaccine does not protect you from new strains of flu-like H5N1, it will help you to stay healthy, which in turn will help to prevent you from contracting the disease and help your body to fight it if you do catch it.

- If possible, also get vaccinated against pneumonia to protect yourself from secondary pneumonia infections.
- Stay clean. Hygiene is your number one defense against infectious disease. Minimize the contact that your hands make with your face (particularly your eyes, nose, and mouth) and with surfaces, and wash your hands frequently with an alcohol-based disinfectant. Wear gloves medical when possible.

- Minimize social contact while the threat of infection persists. Stay away from public events and public transport, work from home if possible, keep your children home from school, etc.
- Stock respirators and goggles and wear them if a pandemic is on the horizon. Ensure that there are no gaps between the respirator/goggles and the surface of your face.
- Have your doctor's number readily available and seek immediate medical attention upon the onset of symptoms.

Electromagnetic Pulse

An electromagnetic pulse (EMP) is a relatively short burst of electromagnetic energy that can have severe consequences. It may occur in a lightning strike or on a more devastating scale in a nuclear weapon attack.

EMP occurs with all nuclear explosions and becomes more pronounced and widespread as the size and altitude of a nuclear blast are increased. With extremism and terrorism reaching further and further across the globe, the need to become prepared for EMP technology getting into the wrong hands becomes more urgent.

Protecting Yourself

The main purpose of EMP weapons is to temporarily jam electronics systems, corrupt important computer data, or completely fry electric and electronic equipment.

While EMP weapons are generally considered non-lethal, they could easily kill people if they were directed towards particular targets. If an EMP knocked out a hospital's electricity, for example, any patient on life support would die immediately. An EMP weapon could also neutralize vehicles, including aircraft, causing catastrophic accidents.

Contrary to popular belief, in the levels created by a nuclear weapon, EMP would not pose a health hazard to plants or animals (including humans), as it is not concentrated.

It can, however, be concentrated if it is attracted by a stretch of metal, including metal girders, large stretches of wiring (such as telephone lines), long antennas, etc. In other words, if a nuclear war is on the horizon, get a safe distance (at least 10 feet) from concentrations of metal right away.

For the most part, nuclear blast kills people by an indirect means rather than by direct pressure. While a human body can withstand up to 30 psi of simple overpressure, the winds associated with as little as 2 to 3 psi could be expected to blow people out of typical modern office buildings. Most blast deaths result from the collapse of occupied buildings, from people being blown into objects, or from buildings or smaller objects being blown on to people. In other words, try to get away from buildings, walls, poles, etc. and into an open space.

Protecting Electrical Equipment

EMP does significant damage to electronic equipment, aircraft, and other objects. However, the good news is, it is possible to avoid much of the EMP damage that could be done to electrical equipment with a bit of preparation.

To protect your electrical equipment, first unplug it from AC outlets, phone systems, or long antennas. Use battery-operated equipment that has cords or antennas of only 30 inches or less in length until the threat has passed.

As long as the equipment isn't operated within 10 feet of another concentration of metal, it should be safe.

If you don't want to buy a tonne of batteries for every appliance you own or use a radio set up with longer than a 30-inch antenna, then you'll need to use equipment that is "hardened" against EMP.

Treat claims that products are hardened against EMP with a healthy dose of skepticism, and make sure you do your research.

A better option for sensitive electronic equipment is the Faraday box. A Faraday box is simply a metal box designed to divert and soak up the EMP.

If the object placed in the box is insulated from the inside surface of the box, it will not be affected by the EMP traveling around the outside metal surface of the box. The Faraday box simple and cheap and often provides more protection to electrical components than "hardening" through circuit designs that can't be adequately tested.

Many containers are suitable for make-shift Faraday boxes: cake boxes, ammunition containers, metal filing cabinets, etc. can all be used. The only two requirements for protection with a Faraday box are:

• The equipment inside the box does NOT touch the metal container (plastic, wadded paper, or cardboard can all be used to insulate it from the metal) and

• The metal shield is continuous without any gaps between pieces or extra-large holes in it.

You can make an effective Faraday box by simply using the cardboard packing box that equipment comes in and wrapping it in aluminum foil (ensuring it's securely taped). For extra protection, place the foil-wrapped box inside a larger cardboard box to ensure that the foil is not damaged.

By coating the door, walls, floor, and ceiling with it, the metal foil can create a shield to help you insulate a whole room from EMP. Ideally, the floor is then covered with a false floor of wood or with heavy carpeting to insulate everything and everyone inside.

Care must be taken not to allow electrical wiring connections to pierce the foil shield (i.e., no AC powered equipment or radio antennas can come into the room from outside). Care must also be taken that the door is covered with foil AND electrically connected to the shield with a wire and screws or some similar setup.

Many people think that cars are 100% EMP-proof as they sit on rubber tires. This is not the case – some cars will be affected, including those with a lot of IC circuits, fiberglass bodies, or located near large stretches of metal. To be on the safe side and optimize the chances of your vehicle surviving an EMP strike, you may wish to buy spare electronic ignition parts and keep them inside a Faraday box.

About the Authors

Selco Begovic

Selco survived the Balkan war of the 90's in a city under siege, without electricity, running water, or food distribution. He is a household name in preparedness circles, sharing the reality of SHTF in thousands of articles and online courses.

Find Selco's current work on TheOrganicPrepper.com

Toby Cowern

Toby Cowern has an extensive background in the military, emergency services, risk management, and business continuity, combined with applied wilderness and urban survival skills, specializing in extreme environments. Working alongside Selco he constructs, illustrates and teaches the application of effective preparedness/ survival models and frameworks grounded in context and correct application.

Find Toby's current work on TheOrganicPrepper.com

Selco's Amazon Best Sellers :

The Dark Secrets of SHTF Survival: The Brutal Truth About Violence, Death, & Mayhem You Must Know to Survive
SHTF Survival Stories: Memories from the Balkan War

An Amazing Offer

If you'd like to take the extensive online version of this course and listen to recordings from Selco, use the code BOOK50 to get an amazing $150 off the regular price.

You can find it at this link: https://learn.theorganicprepper.com/cartflows_step/what-you-must-know-when-the-shtf/

Be sure to use the code **BOOK50** to get your discount.

Printed in Great Britain
by Amazon